Emotions, Learning, and the Brain

The Norton Series on the Social Neuroscience of Education
Louis J. Cozolino, Mary Helen Immordino-Yang, Series Editors

The field of education is searching for new paradigms that incorporate our latest discoveries about the biological underpinnings of processes related to teaching and learning. Yet what is left out of these discussions is a focus on the social nature of human neurobiology, the interactive context of learning, and the quality of student-teacher relationships. The "interpersonal neurobiology of education" is a fresh perspective that will help teachers and administrators better understand how the relationships among educators, students, and the social environments they create within classrooms and schools promote brain development, support psychological health, and enhance emotional intelligence.

The Norton Series on the Social Neuroscience of Education publishes cutting-edge books that provide interdisciplinary explorations into the complex connections between brain and mind, social relationships and attachment, and meaningful learning. Drawing on evidence from research in education, affective and social neuroscience, complex systems, anthropology, and psychology, these books offer educators and administrators an accessible synthesis and application of scientific findings previously unavailable to those in the field. A seamless integration of up-to-date science with the art of teaching, the books in the series present theory and practical classroom application based in solid science, human compassion, cultural awareness, and respect for each student and teacher.

Emotions, Learning, and the Brain

*Exploring the Educational Implications
of Affective Neuroscience*

MARY HELEN IMMORDINO-YANG

Foreword by Howard Gardner
Afterword by Antonio Damasio

W.W. Norton & Company
New York • London

For Kurt Fischer,
my first mentor in this field

Copyright © 2016 by Mary Helen Immordino-Yang

For information about permission to reproduce selections from this book,
write to Permissions, W. W. Norton & Company, Inc.,
500 Fifth Avenue, New York, NY 10110

For information about special discounts for bulk purchases, please contact
W. W. Norton Special Sales at specialsales@wwnorton.com or 800-233-4830

Manufacturing by Maple Press
Production manager: Christine Critelli

ISBN 978-0-393-70981-0

W. W. Norton & Company, Inc.
500 Fifth Avenue, New York, N.Y. 10110
www.wwnorton.com

W. W. Norton & Company Ltd.
Castle House, 75/76 Wells Street, London W1T 3QT

1 2 3 4 5 6 7 8 9 0

Contents

Foreword

by Howard Gardner

In 1985, I published an introduction to the newly emerging interdisciplinary field called cognitive science. In *The Mind's New Science,* I documented the power as well as the limitations of the computer as a model for human cognition and showed how computational models and analyses were affecting fields such as psychology, linguistics, philosophy, and neuroscience. One limitation of the computational approach of the era was that it favored analyses that treated human cognition as being rational—a stance epitomized by the "general problem solving" computers of the era. Accordingly, while cognitive science provided insights into problem solving in mathematics, logic, and across the basic sciences, as well as in games like chess, certain aspects of the human psyche were ignored or minimized. Another limitation of cognitive science circa 1985 is that it assumed that all problems were akin to one another and that the approaches optimal in one domain (e.g. positing a possible solution and working backwards) were equally applicable in other domains.

Overall, in describing the lacuna of the cognitive approach of the nineteen eighties, I lamented the fact that the approach had little to say about the arts, creativity, the emotions, complex social interactions, or the importance of context in understanding human thought and behavior. One reason for these laments: these were areas of human life that I myself wanted to understand.

While reading Mary Helen Immordino-Yang's impressive collection of papers, I often thought back to the research panorama thirty years ago. As I write, in the second decade of the 21st century, we have a much broader and much deeper picture of the range of human thought and behavior. This progress is due to many scholars across several fields, among whom are Mary Helen's own teachers, such as Antonio Battro, Antonio Damasio, Hanna Damasio, Kurt Fischer, David Rose, and other important contributors, like George Lakoff. That said, Mary Helen stands out for the way in which she has drawn on the findings and perspectives of such scholars, initiated important lines of research in these areas, brought together her work with those of other innovative scholars into original powerful syntheses, and articulated the educational implications of cutting edge work in psychology, neurology, and other strands of the cognitive sciences.

Of the many significant findings and insights in this volume, let me mention ones that especially struck this chronicler of thirty years ago. At the time,

*We had no idea that one could study human emotions that emerge slowly over time—such as admiration or awe—and compare them psychologically and neurologically with emotions that emerge more quickly, such as surprise or fear. Nor did we suspect that such slow-emerging emotions drew on basic non-conscious forms of regulation of bodily processes.

*We were not cognizant of the importance and the neural substrate of unfilled time—time to step back, reflect, evaluate, even daydream.

*We assumed that surgery as drastic as the removal of an entire cerebral hemisphere would result in debilitating cognitive limitations; we could not envision individuals whose behavioral repertoire was normal or close to normal in many respects.

*We had little idea of similarities and contrasts in brain processing of individuals from different cultural groups, let alone of the advantages and disadvantages of various modes of processing.

*We had no idea that certain networks of neurons (now called mirror neurons) fire when others are carrying out actions, but only when the goals of those actions are understood.

Whether or not we are scientists ourselves, most literate individuals are intrigued to learn of new scientific findings. And findings involving the human brain seem to be especially riveting; I can well remember the excitement a half century ago when the different functions and capacities of the left cerebral hemisphere and the right cerebral hemisphere first became widely known. (The specializations of each hemisphere were actually first described in the latter half of the 19th century, but achieved notoriety only after it became possible, due to radical surgery that separates the two hemispheres, to study the capacities and functions of each hemisphere separately.) Indeed, so powerful are findings from neuroscience that individuals find the *same* results more compelling if they are simply accompanied by a photograph of a brain, even when the two accounts are otherwise identical!

Mary Helen Immordino-Yang is one of the pioneers in the interdisciplinary field of Mind-Brain-Education, launched around the turn of the millennium at the Harvard Graduate School of Education and at several other campuses around the world. Given the widespread fascination with brain findings and her path-breaking studies, there has been enormous interest in her work and its possible implications for the classroom. It would be all too easy to pander to this interest, over-interpreting findings, embracing seductive "neuro-myths," or using brain evidence simply to endorse practices that one would favor anyway. Indeed, such tendencies are widespread nowadays, even among researchers who should know better.

Just how to summarize often complex scientific findings and relate them to education is a tremendous challenge. Indeed, the challenge is sufficiently great that many scholars refuse to make the leap at all. While this caution is perhaps understandable, it leaves the field wide open to opportunists and even charlatans who say, "The Brain works like X; therefore, you should teach like Y, " or, "The brain works like A, and so students should learn in manner B."

In discussing the educational implications of her own research and that of other leading scholars, Mary Helen is admirably restrained. She acknowledges the considerable distance between a finding obtained in the laboratory and a practice executed in a classroom. She appreciates that education is suffused with values; one cannot simply stipulate that because the mind (or the brain) works in a certain way, that mode of functioning dictates how one *should* teach or how one *should* learn. Indeed, education is about choices, and many of those choices reflect one's values and/or the constraints of a given context—be it the youngsters in a given classroom, the predilections of a teacher or a parent, or the dictates of national policy.

Without wanting to put words into Mary Helen's artful vocabulary, I believe that she endorses the following perspective. A range of sciences (and other disciplines) provide suggestions about how best to educate. None of them is definitive, but it would be foolish to ignore any of them, and we are best off if we try to draw on the range of perspectives, paying particular attention when the various indices point in the same direction. Time and again, in her essays, she combines findings about psychological development, neural development, and cultural contexts in order to make suggestions about how educators might proceed. Sometimes, her recommendations are quite general: emotions are powerful motivators and teachers ignore them at their peril. At other times, the recommendations are more targeted: children can construe mathematical problems in quite specific ways, and the mode of pedagogy that will work best becomes clear when teachers understand the particular assumptions and predilections that students bring to the solution of a given math problem. Some of the recommendations apply generally across human beings—e.g., we work more effectively with digital devices when they are designed to give us a sense of agency. Others are targeted to teaching individuals with atypical brain organization: individuals with a given neurological profile tackle problems most effectively when they can re-construe the problems so that they can draw on spared cognitive capacities.

Science proceeds brick by brick, building gradually on earlier findings, making adjustments as necessary, always mindful of limitations in method and inference. Education, on the other hand, unfolds in real time, and parents, teachers, and learners have to make the best use of time, techniques, texts, and tools. As a teacher of science herself, both to middle school children and to university students, Mary Helen is keenly aware of the pressures and constraints under which educators work. At the same time, she knows that teachers are learners (that is a major reason that individuals choose to enter the profession) and that they are eager to pick up ideas and practices that can enhance their effectiveness. And so, throughout this collection, Mary Helen reports findings, weighs their significance, and makes useful suggestions without stating or implying an exalted status for any of them. Perhaps even more important, she provides a way of thinking about scientific discoveries that is at once exciting and prudent—precisely the frame of mind that we hope to inculcate in teachers and learners everywhere.

As I read through these essays, I had an uplifting feeling: readers of this book will be present at the birth and early stages of a new and vital field of knowledge. Building both on the initial vision of cognitive science, and on the important modifications and improvement introduced by her teachers, by other leading scholars, and as well by her own research, Mary Helen Immordino-Yang presents a panoply of important findings—fascinating in their own right and pregnant with implications for anyone who is interested in teaching and learning. And since we now know that these processes begin at birth—if not in utero!—and continue as long as one's mind is active, one can readily envision how a full-blown panorama of mind, brain, and education throughout the life cycle may emerge in the decades ahead. I can state with confidence that the work in these pages will be fundamental to this crucial field and I have every confidence that Mary Helen Immordino-Yang will continue her singular contributions to its vitality.

Acknowledgments

My mentors have taught me to view human behavior as dynamic and contextually embedded; psychological development as actively constructed; and emotions as biologically, evolutionarily, and developmentally adaptive. Each of these perspectives plays heavily into my thinking and I am deeply indebted especially to Antonio Damasio, Hanna Damasio, Kurt Fischer, Howard Gardner, and David Rose, whose revolutionary work provides the scaffold for my own. Each of these individuals has also provided me with their mentoring, their intellectual and emotional support, and their friendship. For that I am continually grateful.

Several of the chapters in this book originally appeared as co-authored articles with colleagues and students. The book therefore incorporates collaborative contributions from Antonio Damasio, Kurt Fischer, Joanna Christodoulou, Vanessa Singh, Matthias Faeth, and Lesley Sylvan.

Warm thanks go to my friend and colleague Margaret Lazzari for graciously allowing me to use her inspirational painting on the cover of this book. The painting depicts the white matter of a living person's brain, floating semi-translucent in a vibrant seascape. Red fish dart by, representing the creative energy of thoughts and ideas. To me, the painting is a reminder of the importance of understanding brain development ecologically. The brain image was acquired using 3 Tesla magnetic resonance imaging (MRI) at the Dornsife Cognitive Neuroscience Imaging Center (DNI), directed by Hanna Damasio at the University of Southern California.

Several institutions, individuals, and funders were instrumental to my progress. Most notably, the research presented in this book was completed at the Harvard University Graduate School of Education (HUGSE) and at the University of Southern California (USC). I thank especially my USC colleagues at the Brain and Creativity Institute (BCI), the Rossier School of Education, the Dornsife College of Arts and Sciences, and the Neuroscience Graduate Program. Robert Rueda, Karen Gallagher, Gale Sinatra, Pat Levitt,

Wendy Wood, Gayla Margolin, Ron Astor, Steve Lopez, and Bartlett Mel have been especially generous with their advocacy and mentoring. Catherine Snow, at HUGSE, has always willingly provided incisive and critical advice. The International Mind, Brain and Education Society (IMBES) has provided an important intellectual home. My work has been generously funded by the National Science Foundation, the Spencer Foundation, the American Association of University Women, the Annenberg Learner Foundation, the Brain and Creativity Institute Fund, the USC Rossier School of Education, and the USC Provost's Office, among other sources.

I remain grateful to Nico, Brooke, and their families for their willingness to participate in the research presented in Chapter 7 and for their patience with me through the years. I stand in admiration of their courage in overcoming incredible odds, as I suspect will many who learn here about their achievements after hemispherectomy.

This book has benefitted especially from the responses of master educators, especially Laura Jane Linck, Michelle Sullivan, Anne Carlin, Elizabeth Ross, Siri Fiske, and Lisa Tanita. Denny Blodget and David Daniel (a professor of psychology and education) have provided exceptionally helpful comments, criticism, and friendship. Though they have considerably different perspectives, both have read innumerable drafts and sat through innumerable phone conversations as I awkwardly waded into the sludge of my early ideas and writing. If ever I were stranded on a desert island, I shouldn't be surprised if one of them showed up to help me figure out how to build a rowboat.

Several additional colleagues have provided guidance and feedback along the way, including Lisa Feldman Barrett, Joe Blatt, Tom Carew, Maria Carreira, Ginger Clark, Jay Giedd, Shihui Han, Scott Barry Kaufman, Shinobu Kitayama, Maria Ott, Daphna Oyserman, Juliana Pare-Blagoev, Josef Parvizi, David Perkins, Larry Picus, Bill Tierney, Jeanne Tsai, Brendesha Tynes, Dan Willingham, and Ellen Winner, among others. The students in my courses at the USC Rossier School of Education and the many educators and schools who have attended and hosted my workshops and talks have shaped my thinking and research trajectory over time.

The members of the BCI are a constant source of enjoyment and instructive discussion. Among those with whom I have discussed the ideas in the book are Antoine Bechara, Jonas Kaplan, Lisa Azziz-Zadeh, Morteza Dehghani, John Monterosso, Jessica Wisnowski, Assal Habibi, and Glenn Fox. Xiaofei Yang has been a true collaborator in my neuroimaging and cross-cultural work. The current graduate students in my lab, Rebecca Gotlieb, Rodrigo Riveros, and Erik Jahner, make research fun and ever new. (Together with Fei and funding, they also make it possible.) The talented undergraduate and high school students who have interned in my lab over the years have contributed substantially to the work, though I regret that they are too numerous to list here.

Deborah Malmud and the editors at Norton have been patient, thoughtful, and wise, as has Lou Cozolino, my co-editor of this book series. I thank them for seeing me through this process so painlessly and skillfully.

Francis Crick once famously complained that he knew no laypeople to read his books for him and provide suggestions and criticisms. I, by contrast, am fortunate to have many extraordinarily insightful non-neuroscientists as friends and family, and they have provided an invaluable sounding board for many of the ideas I present in this book. My neighbors on 7th Street in Manhattan Beach are particularly notable in this regard, as are my mom and dad, Susan and Peter Immordino, my late aunt, Gail mally mack, and my siblings and their spouses, Nora and Chuck Feldpausch (Nora's knowledge of psychiatry has been particularly useful), Maggie and Brooke Borner, and Tim Immordino. Our conversations are usually way too loud but fantastically interesting (and accompanied by energetic children and delicious food). When my ideas are wrong, they tell me so.

And in the end, there is my precious family—my husband Kyle Yang and our children Nora and Theodore. From them I have learned more about human development and emotion, including my own, than from anyone else. My feelings are summed up by the South African concept of *Ubuntu*, which roughly translates as, "I am because you are." I thank Nora additionally for allowing me to use the poems included in Chapter 6. My unbounded love and gratitude go to my parents and to my husband's parents, Cynthia and Eugene Yang. It is partly because they love my children as much as I do that I am able to pursue this work. Without their help it would have been much more difficult, and maybe impossible.

Emotions, Learning,
and the Brain

Introduction:
Why Emotions Are Integral
to Learning

Teachers intuitively know that neither their nor their students' learning is steady and constant, the same day in and day out and moment to moment, consistent from topic to topic. Rather, we all have good and bad days; moments of excitement, engagement, and inspiration and moments of disappointment, disengagement, and frustration; afternoons just before vacation and mornings just after; some skills and topics that we find interesting and some that we don't. These differences influence how children learn and how teachers teach; they even affect what students know at a given time. In short, learning is dynamic, social, and context dependent because *emotions* are, and emotions form a critical piece of how, what, when, and why people think, remember, and learn.

The fundamental role of emotions in learning first became apparent to me during my first professional position after college, as a junior high school science teacher in a highly diverse, urban public school near Boston. The community I lived and worked in had many first-generation Americans, 81 languages total spoken in our school of 1,800, and many students living in underprivileged circumstances. Although I was teaching integrated science, a technical academic subject, I was intrigued that my students' questions and explanations seemed connected to their friendships, home situations, aesthetic tastes, and cultural values. I was fascinated but unprepared, for example, when the race relations among my seventh graders changed (and improved) dramatically after I taught a unit on hominid evolution that I designed with my former undergraduate professor. The students' new scientific understanding of natural selection for adaptive traits like dark or light skin seemed to powerfully influence their peer relationships and their own ethnic identities.

Why had the students interpreted the science in such a personal, emotional way? And why, after the classroom turbulence had settled, did so many of my students suddenly seem to take a new interest in science? I brought these questions with me to graduate school, and through my research I still seek satisfying and complete answers to them.

Scientific understanding of the influence of emotions on thinking and learning has undergone a major transformation in recent years. In particular, a revolution in neuroscience over the past two decades has overturned early notions that emotions interfere with learning, revealing instead that emotion and cognition are supported by interdependent neural processes. It is literally neurobiologically impossible to build memories, engage complex thoughts, or make meaningful decisions without emotion. And after all, this makes sense: the brain is highly metabolically expensive tissue, and evolution would not support wasting energy and oxygen thinking about things that don't matter to us. Put succinctly, we only think about things we care about. No wonder my seventh graders had taken that science lesson so personally and so seriously. They had found that science could help them make personally relevant meaning of the racial and ethnic diversity and identity issues they encountered in their daily lives.

This insight—that we only think deeply about things we care about—has important implications for education and pedagogy. It opens questions about how, when, and why students learn meaningfully (or just regurgitate facts and deploy procedures and algorithms, or possibly don't manage even those). It also raises issues about how technology, culture, and social relationships shape learning and how teachers can understand and leverage emotions more productively in the classroom. It suggests that, for school-based learning to have a hope of motivating students, of producing deep understanding, or of transferring into real-world skills—all hallmarks of meaningful learning, and all essential to producing informed, skilled, ethical, and reflective adults—we need to find ways to leverage the emotional aspects of learning in education.

To leverage emotions, it helps to understand what emotions are. Emotions, and the more biologically primitive drives that undergird them, such as hunger and sex, are action programs that have evolved as extensions of survival mechanisms. Put simply, emotions have evolved to keep us alive. Human beings have basic emotions, such as fear and disgust, to keep us off the edges of cliffs and to make us avoid spoiled food. We have social emotions such as love to make us affiliate, procreate, and care for our children. Thanks to our intelligent, plastic brain, we can also develop emotions that color and steer our intellectual and social endeavors, such as curiosity to make us explore and discover, admiration to make us emulate the virtue of others, and compassion, indignation, interest, and "flow" (Csíkszentmihályi, 1990).

These complex intellectual and social emotions are the subjective behavioral and mental reactions we have to situations and concepts of all sorts—reactions that play out in the body (e.g., through a racing heart) and in the mind through characteristic ways of thinking (e.g., searching for an escape route during fear, moving to help another person during compassion, or narrowing our attentional focus when we find something interesting). The feeling of these emotions organizes our sociality and morality, making us emulate role models, help those in need, or punish those who warrant it. It forms the basis for creativity and invention and for the decisions we make for now and for the future, even in academic contexts. For example, the act of dedicating one's professional life to teaching is possible only because of our ability to feel these emotions.

So, emotions evolved and are present in all complex creatures because they are essential to managing life. In humans, efficient life management means managing not just our physical survival but our social life and intellectual life. (These ideas derive from my work with Antonio Damasio; for seminal reading, see Damasio [1999] and Damasio and Carvalho [2013].) But where does the neurobiology come in? Among the most poignant and basic insights from affective neuroscience, the neuroscience of emotion, is that the emotions that regulate our sociocultural and intellectual lives appear to have co-opted the same neural systems that manage our survival in the basic biological sense. Just as poets and artists have suspected for millennia, we feel social relationships and appreciate intellectual achievements using the same brain systems that sense and regulate our guts and viscera, adjust our blood chemistry and hormones, and conjure our awareness and consciousness. No wonder our creations, reputations, cultural ideals, and personal relationships, including those in educational contexts, have such amazing psychological power.

But emotions have another dimension that is critically relevant to education. Complex emotional feelings, such as interest, inspiration, indignation, and compassion, are active mental constructions—they pertain not to the real physical context (the immediate context that we can see) but to abstract inferences, interpretations, and ideas. They pertain, in other words, to what we think we know about the world at the current time, interpreted in light of our past experiences and our imagined possible futures, using our available skills. When I say that many emotions are "complex," what I really mean is that they rely on subjective, cognitive interpretations of situations and their accompanying embodied reactions.

Even in academic subjects that are traditionally considered unemotional, such as physics, engineering, or math, deep understanding depends on making emotional connections between concepts. For example, one study using functional magnetic resonance imaging found that when mathematicians see equations that they judge to be "beautiful" and elegantly formulated instead of "ugly" and awkwardly formulated, they activate the same sensory, emotional brain region that activates during experiences of perceptual beauty, such as when admiring a painting (Zeki, Romaya, Benincasa, & Atiyah, 2014). In the Brain and Creativity Institute at the University of Southern California, we have found that this region also activates during experiences of moral beauty, such as those associated with feelings of admiration and compassion (Immordino-Yang, McColl, Damasio, & Damasio, 2009; see Chapter 9 for a description of this experiment). This and other evidence suggests that meaningful learning is actually about helping students to connect their isolated algorithmic skills to abstract, intrinsically emotional, subjective and meaningful experiences. Though supporting students in building these connections is a very hard job, it appears to be essential for the development of truly useful, transferable, intrinsically motivated learning.

In addition, emotions, like cognition, develop with maturity and experience. In this sense, emotions are skills—organized patterns of thoughts and behaviors that we actively construct in the moment and across our life spans to adaptively accommodate to various kinds of circumstances, including academic demands. (These ideas derive from my work with Kurt Fischer; for seminal reading, see Fischer and Bidell [2006].) The emotions of a preschooler are not the same as those of a fifth grader, a teenager, or a young or an older adult. The emotions of a brand new teacher are not the same as those of a veteran teacher. And even two people in the same developmental stage could construct different reactions to the same situation, sometimes substantially so. Why?

The reasons follow from emotion's survival-related roots and tie to emotion's centrality in learning. First, emotions involve automatic mental and bodily reactions to situations, and some people, cultural groups, and age groups are more reactive, or differently reactive, than others. For example, some individuals jump when startled, while others remain much calmer. These tendencies can also be influenced by culture; for instance, in many Asian cultures individuals strive to suppress their outward emotional displays, whereas in many Latino and Mediterranean cultures emotional expressiveness is valued. These differing ideals for emotion influence individuals' emotional behavior, including expression or suppression. In turn, our work suggests that by changing the magnitude of bodily reactions, cultural and individual differences in emotional expressiveness may affect what emotions "feel like"—how individuals know how they feel, or the subjective embodied quality of their feelings (Immordino-Yang, Yang, & Damasio, 2014).

Second, people learn through experience how to interpret situations, as well as how to make sense of their emotional reactions. Students' and teachers' emotion-laden interpretations and inferences, though often implicit or subconscious, form a central dimension of how they learn. The subjective inferences that individuals make, and their experiences of problem solving within an academic domain, imbue their memories and knowledge with emotional relevance. In the case described above, it was the mathematicians' subjective experience of thinking and solving problems within the mathematical domain that enabled them to appreciate certain equations as "beautiful." Their emotional reactions were possible only with an advanced level of technical expertise.

As we can see, understanding the role of emotions in learning goes far beyond recognizing the emotion a student is having *about* a situation in order to design learning environments that strategically manipulate students' reactions. For instance, giving candy to make children want to come to math class will not make students feel the joy of mathematical thinking. Instead, understanding emotions is also (and perhaps even more critically) about the *meaning* that students are making—that is, the ways in which students and teachers are *experiencing* or *feeling* their emotional reactions and how their feelings steer their thoughts and behavior, consciously or not. Emotions are not add-ons that are distinct from cognitive skills. Instead emotions, such as interest, anxiety, frustration, excitement, or a sense of awe in beholding beauty, become a dimension of the skill itself. This is one reason that anxiety can be so debilitating to students' performance, that interest can precipitate a lifetime commitment to studying a topic, that kids have such trouble applying themselves when they don't know why they would ever use a skill outside of class, and that offering kids candy will make them like coming to class but will not help them learn to appreciate mathematical thinking.

Given the central role of emotion in learning, this book is about the early stage of my intellectual journey to explore the educational implications of my and others' research in affective and social neuroscience. I begin the book with three chapters that together sketch an account of how people feel in educational and other learning contexts—that is, of how the brain constructs conscious experiences with emotional meaning. These experiences can be memories for past events or information, the subjective feeling of what is happening now, or plans and imaginings for the future. Educators have long known that personal relevance is important for learning and that the ability to hold goals and dreams is critical to motivation and persistence. Likewise, the ability to consolidate memories for facts, procedures, and events into conceptual wholes—in short, to understand what one has learned—is critical for long-term retention and application of the knowledge in new contexts. But why, and how does this happen? In Part I of the book, I attempt to give insights into these issues.

In Part II, I present a collection of chapters that move toward implications for learning and teaching, including the network-based, dynamic nature of skill development (Chapter 4) and pedagogical strategies to support the development of experience-based intuitions (Chapter 5). Chapter 6 is a short essay meant to demonstrate the interdependence of emotion and cognition in one girl's poetry writing development. Chapters 7 and 8 take us to the story of two high-functioning young men, each of whom suffered the removal of an entire brain hemisphere to control severe seizures. These remarkable students' learning affords interesting insights into the role of emotions in organizing the recruitment of neuropsychological compensatory strengths. Chapter 9 discusses the importance of considering nonconscious emotional processing and the hooking of the conscious mind into nonconscious biological regulatory systems. Chapter 10 offers insights into the design of digital learning technologies by proposing that designers conceptualize our digitized devices as social partners with whom we must empathize to learn effectively.

A MESSAGE FOR TEACHERS:
WHY I WROTE THIS BOOK, AND HOW TO READ IT

Though I was a teacher before I became a researcher, it is important to recognize that this book does not presume to provide answers to specific educational dilemmas—recipes for teaching or the proverbial "what to do on Monday morning." Instead, my hope is that you will let the ideas in the book inform and enrich your reflections and discussions about learning and teaching. As an affective neuroscientist, my aim is to start a conversation in which together we create new knowledge about what learning in the real-world actually entails and how curricula can be designed to better honor your and your students' subjective experiences of learning. To this end, I have tried to present the scientific evidence in the most straightforward, accurate, and complete way that I can and to usefully and creatively synthesize and interpret the findings.

However, I also recognize that I am taking a risk in publishing this volume. The practical applications that derive from the science will never be completely straightforward because the real world is highly complicated, with many moving parts and hidden complexities. Nonetheless, I am emboldened to publish this collection for one main reason: scientific discovery is a process, and your voice is needed to shape that process. Many practicing teachers have told me that they are hungry for scientific insight into the role of emotion in learning. These teachers seek the background knowledge to engage parents, colleagues, administrators, policy makers, and scientists in critical exchanges. Many feel intuitively that emotions and social contexts are central to learning and believe that the neuroscientific evidence could catalyze, clarify, validate, or possibly falsify their intuitions. Throughout the book, via framing comments and other means, I have tried to provide handles for you to grab hold of. In the end, I have aimed to contribute a new perspective to the conversations around your worktables, that of affective social neuroscience. I ask you to think critically not just about my work but about your own and, indeed, about any evidence or policies used to justify educational strategies and designs. I hope that through your debates we will collaboratively create new understanding and better practice in education.

Finally, though my research is in affective social neuroscience, I remain, at heart, a human development psychologist. This basically means that I come from a tradition of scholars who work to understand human behavior "in the midst of things," with all of the real-world messiness that this entails. The ultimate aim is to understand how human behavior and thinking result from a dynamic integration of component processes in context. Good scientific research isolates processes for study. But it is equally important to bring the pieces back together to understand how the isolated processes contribute to little skills, ideas, and interactions between people and, in turn, to understand how those sum to describe whole, thinking, and acting people in a social, cultural world. To do this means striving to understand how both neurobiological and psychological functioning dynamically change, or "develop," in organized, adaptive patterns that reflect features of the social, physical, and cognitive contexts and characteristics and preferences of the individual. Ecological validity and individual variability, that is, understanding what the scientific findings mean in the real world for real people, are of central interest. In essence, the work included in this book represents my attempt to bring ecological validity to the neuroscientific findings—to synthesize and interpret bodies of findings so that they may be useful in educational contexts.

REFERENCES

Csíkszentmihályi, M. (1990). *Flow: The psychology of optimal experience.* New York, NY: Harper & Row.

Damasio, A. R. (1999). *The feeling of what happens: Body and emotion in the making of consciousness.* New York, NY: Harcourt Brace.

Damasio, A., & Carvalho, G. B. (2013). The nature of feelings: Evolutionary and neurobiological origins. *Nature Reviews Neuroscience, 144,* 143–152.

Fischer, K. W., & Bidell, T. (2006). Dynamic development of action and thought. In

W. Damon & R. Lerner (Eds.), *Handbook of child psychology*, Vol. 1: *Theoretical models of human development* (6th ed., pp. 313–399). Hoboken, NJ: Wiley.

Immordino-Yang, M. H., McColl, A., Damasio, H., & Damasio, A. (2009). Neural correlates of admiration and compassion. *Proceedings of the National Academy of Sciences, USA, 106*(19), 8021–8026. Retrieved from http://www.pnas.org/content/106/19/8021

Immordino-Yang, M. H., Yang, X., & Damasio, H. (2014). Correlations between social-emotional feelings and anterior insula activity are independent from visceral states but influenced by culture. *Frontiers in Human Neuroscience, 8*, 728. doi:10.3389/fnhum.2014.00728

Zeki, S., Romaya, J. P., Benincasa, D. M. T., & Atiyah, M. F. (2014). The experience of mathematical beauty and its neural correlates. *Frontiers in Human Neuroscience, 8*, 68. doi:10.3389/fnhum.2014.00068

PART I

WHAT ARE EMOTIONAL
FEELINGS, AND HOW
ARE THEY SUPPORTED
BY THE BRAIN?

CHAPTER 1

We Feel, Therefore We Learn: The Relevance of Affective and Social Neuroscience to Education

Mary Helen Immordino-Yang & Antonio R. Damasio

Chapter description: This chapter is the first paper I published with Antonio Damasio and my first attempt to reconcile what was known about learning in educational contexts with what his laboratory had shown from twenty years of research with patients with stroke and other kinds of acquired brain damage. In essence, this research with patients had uncovered a very interesting and unexpected finding: patients with certain types of brain damage could have preserved cognitive abilities (intelligence in the traditional sense of IQ) but be utterly unable to manage their lives on a day-to-day basis. Why? Because they could not adequately incorporate emotion into their thinking. Instead of becoming more rational and logical when their decisions were free from emotion, these patients did not care what other people thought of their behavior, were unable to learn from their past mistakes, and did not stop and change course when it became clear that their current actions were leading them astray. Critically, these patients had intact knowledge but had no sense of risk or morality and so would plow ahead into decisions that any "rational" person would find, at best, short-sighted or a waste of time and, at worst, dangerous, stupid, or immoral. Building from these patients and from classical insights about the fundamental role of emotions in readying the body for survival-relevant actions like fight, flight, or reproduction, Antonio Damasio and his team led the field into a new view of intelligence in which emotion and feelings of emotion-related bodily reactions are critical to steering thinking and decision making. They conceptualized emotions as a repertoire of know-how and actions that allows people to respond appropriately in different situations. They argued that, without emotion, all decisions and outcomes are equal—people can have no preferences, no interests, no motivation, no morality, and no sense of creativity, beauty, or purpose.

Here, we laid out the consequences of this insight for education. The basic premise is that when learning and knowledge are relatively devoid of emotion, when people learn things by "rote" without internally driven motivation and without a sense of interest or real-world relevance, then it is likely that they won't be able to use what they learn efficiently in the real world. Patients with lesions teach us that it is the emotional dimensions of knowledge that allow people to call up memories and skills that are relevant to whatever task is at hand. Without the appropriate emotions, individuals may have knowledge but they likely won't be able to use it effectively when the situation requires. Emotions are, in essence, the rudder that steers thinking.

R ecent advances in the neuroscience of emotions are highlighting connections between cognitive and emotional functions that have the potential to revolutionize our understanding of learning in the context of schools. In particular, connections between decision making, social functioning, and moral reasoning hold new promise for breakthroughs in understanding the role of emotion in decision making, the relationship between learning and emotion, how culture shapes learning, and ultimately the development of morality and human ethics. These are all topics of eminent importance to educators as they work to prepare skilled, informed, and ethical students who can navigate the world's social, moral, and cognitive challenges as citizens. In this article, we sketch a biological and evolutionary account of the relationship between emotion and rational thought, with the purpose of highlighting new connections between emotional, cognitive, and social functioning and presenting a framework that we hope will inspire further work on the critical role of emotion in education.

Modern biology reveals humans to be fundamentally emotional and social creatures. And yet, those in the field of education often fail to consider that the high-level cognitive skills taught in schools, including reasoning, decision making, and processes related to language, reading, and mathematics, do not function as rational, disembodied systems, somehow influenced by but detached from emotion and the body. Instead, these crowning evolutionary achievements are grounded in a long history of emotional functions, themselves deeply grounded in humble homeostatic beginnings. Any competent teacher recognizes that emotions and feelings affect students' performance and learning, as does the state of the body, such as how well students have slept and eaten, or whether they are feeling sick or well. We contend, however, that the relationship between learning, emotion, and body state runs much deeper than many educators realize and is interwoven with the notion of learning itself. It is not that emotions rule our cognition, or that rational thought does not exist. It is, rather, that the original purpose for which our brains evolved was to manage our physiology, to optimize our survival, and to allow us to flourish. When one considers that this purpose inherently involves monitoring and altering the state of the body and mind in increasingly complex ways, one can appreciate that emotions, which play out in the body and mind, are profoundly intertwined with thought. And after all, this should not be surprising. Complex brains could not have evolved separately from the organisms they were meant to regulate.

But there is another layer to the problem of surviving and flourishing, which probably evolved as a specialized aspect of the relationship between emotion and learning. As brains and the minds they support became more complex, the problem became not only that of dealing with one's own self but also that of managing social interactions and relationships. The evolution of human societies has produced an amazingly complex social and cultural context, and flourishing within this context means that only our most trivial, routine decisions and actions, and perhaps not even these, occur outside of our socially and culturally constructed reality. Why does a high school student solve a math problem, for example? The reasons range from the intrinsic reward of having found the solution, to getting a good grade, to avoiding punishment, to helping tutor a friend, to getting into a good college, to pleasing her parents or the teacher. All of these reasons have a powerful emotional component and relate both to pleasurable sensations and to survival within our culture. Although the notion of surviving and flourishing is interpreted in a cultural and social framework at this late stage in evolution, our brains still bear evidence of their original purpose: to manage our bodies and minds in the service of living, and living happily, in the world with other people.

This realization has several important implications for research at the nexus of education and neuroscience. It points to new directions for understanding the interface of biology, learning, and culture, a critical topic in education that has proven difficult to investigate systematically (Davis, 2003; Rueda, 2006; Rueda, August, & Goldenberg, 2006). It promises to shed light on the elusive link between body and mind, for it describes how the health and sickness of the brain and body can influence each other. And, importantly, it underscores our fundamentally social nature, making clear that the very neurobiological systems that support our social interactions and relationships are recruited for the often covert and private decision making that underlies much of our thought. In brief, learning, in the complex sense in which it happens in schools or the real world, is not a rational or disembodied process; neither is it a lonely one.

REASONING, DECISION MAKING, AND EMOTION: EVIDENCE FROM PATIENTS WITH BRAIN DAMAGE

To understand why this is so, we begin with some history, and a problem. Well into the 1980s, the study of brain systems underlying behavior and cognition was heavily dominated by a top-down approach in which the processes of learning, language, and reasoning were understood as high-order systems that imposed themselves upon an obedient body. It is not that emotions were completely ignored, or that they were not viewed by some as having a brain basis. Rather, their critical role in governing behavior, and in particular rational thought, was overlooked (Damasio, 1994). Emotions were like a toddler in a china shop, interfering with the orderly rows of stemware on the shelves.

And then an interesting problem emerged. In a research atmosphere in which cognition ruled supreme, it became apparent that the irrational behavior of neurological patients who had sustained lesions to a particular sector of the frontal lobe could not be adequately accounted for by invoking cognitive mechanisms alone. After sustaining damage to the ventromedial prefrontal cortex (VMPF), these patients' social behavior was compromised, making them oblivious to the consequences of their actions, insensitive to others' emotions, and unable to learn from their mistakes. In some instances, these patients violated social convention and even ethical rules, failing to show embarrassment when it was due and failing to provide appropriate sympathetic support to those who expected it and had received it in the past.

These patients' ability to make advantageous decisions became compromised in ways that it had not been before. In fact, there was a complete separation between the period that anteceded the onset of the lesion, when these patients had been upstanding, reliable, and foresightful citizens, and the period thereafter, when they would make decisions that were often disadvantageous to themselves and their families. They would not perform adequately in their jobs, in spite of having the required skills; they would make poor business deals in spite of knowing the risks involved; they would lose their savings and choose the wrong partners in all sorts of relationships. Why would patients suffering from compromised social conduct also make poor decisions about apparently rational matters, such as business investments?

The traditional way to explain these patients' symptoms had been that something had gone wrong with their logical abilities or their knowledge base, such that they could no longer make decisions in a rational way. But, in fact, with further testing, it became apparent that these patients did not have a primary problem with knowledge, knowledge access, or logical reasoning, as had previously been assumed. To the contrary, they could explain cogently the conventional social and logical rules that ought to guide one's behavior and future planning. They had no loss of knowledge or lowering of IQ in the traditional sense. Instead, it gradually became clear that disturbances in the realm of emotion, which had been viewed as a secondary consequence of their brain damage, could provide a better account of their poor decision making. Those emotional aspects included a diminished resonance of emotional reactions generally, as well as a specific compromise of social emotions, such as compassion, embarrassment, and guilt. By compromising the possibility of evoking emotions associated with certain past situations, decision options, and outcomes, the patients became unable to select the most appropriate response based on their past experience. Their logic and knowledge could be intact, but they failed to use past emotional knowledge to guide the reasoning process. Furthermore, they could no longer learn from the emotional repercussions of their decisions or respond emotionally to the reactions of their social partners. Their reasoning was flawed because the emotions and social considerations that underlie good reasoning were compromised (Damasio, Grabowski, Frank, Galaburda, & Damasio, 1994; Damasio, Tranel, & Damasio, 1990, 1991).

In retrospect, these patients provided a first glimpse into the fundamental role of emotion in reasoning and decision making. They were missing a brain region that is now understood as needed to trigger a cascade of neurological and somatic events that together comprise a social emotion, such as embarrassment, compassion, envy, or admiration, and their social behavior suffered. This is significant in itself, but even more intriguing was the realization that without the ability to adequately access the guiding intuitions that accrue through emotional learning and social feedback, decision making and rational thought became compromised, as did learning from their mistakes and successes. While these patients can reason logically and ethically about standard cognitive and social problems in a laboratory setting (Saver & Damasio, 1991), out in the real world and in real time they cannot use emotional information to decide between alternative courses of action. They can no longer adequately consider previous rewards and punishments, successes and failures, nor do they notice others' praise or disapproval. These patients have lost their ability to analyze events for their emotional consequences and to tag memories of these events accordingly. Their emotions are dissociated from their rational thought, resulting in compromised reason, decision making, and learning.

What does this mean for our argument about relevance to education? In addition to data from these patients, further evidence from psychophysiological and other studies of brain-damaged and normal people has allowed us to propose specific neural mechanisms underlying the role and operation of emotional signaling in normal and abnormal decision making (Bechara, 2005; Bechara & Damasio, 1997; Damasio, 1996). While the details of these neural mechanisms and evidence are beyond the scope of this article, taken as a whole they show that emotions are not just messy toddlers in a china shop, running around breaking and obscuring delicate cognitive glassware. Instead, they are more like the shelves underlying the glassware; without them cognition has less support.

To recap, the patients with prefrontal lesions we have described have social deficits. We have argued that these are fundamentally problems of emotion and therefore manifest as well in the realm of decision making. The relationship between these symptoms is very informative, in that it suggests that hidden emotional processes underlie our apparently rational real-world decision making and learning. Furthermore, this relationship underscores the importance of the ability to perceive and incorporate social feedback in learning.

While the relevance of these insights to educational contexts has not yet been empirically tested, they lead us to formulate two important hypotheses. First, because these findings underscore the critical role of emotion in bringing previously acquired knowledge to inform real-world decision making in social contexts, they suggest the intriguing possibility that emotional processes are required for the skills and knowledge acquired in school to transfer to novel situations and to real life. That is, emotion may play a vital role in helping children decide when and how to apply what they have learned in school to the rest of their lives. Second, the close ties between these patients' decision making, emotion, and social functioning may provide a new take on the relationship between biology and culture. Specifically, it may be via an emotional route that the social influences of culture come to shape learning, thought, and behavior.

While more work on the educational and cultural implications of these findings is warranted, interestingly, and sadly, some further insights into the biological connections between learning, emotion, and social functioning, especially as they relate to our hypothesis about culture, can be gleaned from another group of patients that has been discovered over the past few years. In this group, patients sustained comparable prefrontal damage in early childhood, rather than as adults. As they developed, these children were cognitively normal in the traditional IQ sense, able to use logical reasoning and factual knowledge to solve the kinds of academic problems expected of students. However, while smart in the everyday sense of the word, these children slowly revealed themselves to have varying degrees of psychopathic and antisocial tendencies. They were insensitive to punishment and reward and did not seek approval or social acceptance as typical children do. As adults, they are unable to competently manage their lives, wasting time, squandering resources, and engaging in dangerous, antisocial, and aggressive behaviors. By outward appearances, these patients behave in most ways similarly to the patients described above, who sustained prefrontal damage as adults (Anderson, Bechara, Damasio, Tranel, & Damasio, 1999; H. Damasio, 2005).

Additional investigation of adult patients with childhood-onset brain damage, though, revealed an intriguing difference between childhood- and adult-onset prefrontal brain damage. While both groups can reason about traditional cognitive problems in the structure of the laboratory setting, and both have normal IQs in the traditional sense, unlike patients with adult-onset prefrontal damage, childhood-onset patients appear never to have learned the rules that govern social and moral behavior. While adult-onset patients know right from wrong in the lab but are unable to use this information to guide their behavior, childhood-onset patients have apparently not learned right from wrong or the proper rules of social conduct. They do not know the social and ethical rules that they are breaking.

What is happening with these patients, and how is it relevant to the argument at hand? Unlike the often remarkable compensation for linguistic and other capacities after early childhood brain damage, so far the system for social conduct and ethical behavior does not show this kind of compensation. It is not that access in an abstract sense to the rules of social conduct requires intact frontal cortices, as the adult-onset patients show, and it is not that a social or moral conduct center in the brain has been irreparably damaged, because this scenario would not explain changes in general decision-making. Instead, the situation is both simpler and more grave. These early-onset prefrontal patients may be suffering from the loss of what we might term the "emotional rudder." Without the ability to manipulate situations and to mark those situations as positive or negative from an affective point of view, these children fail to learn normal social behavior. In turn, they lose the commensurate decision-making abilities described earlier. Insensitive to others' responses to their actions, these children fail to respond to educators' and others' attempts to teach them normal behavior.

But there is another intriguing piece to be learned from these children regarding the relationship between cognition and emotion, and the role of the "emotional rudder" in learning. As in the adult-onset patients, it is still possible for these patients to have an operating cognitive system that allows them to be smart on certain measures and in certain contexts, solving standard cognitive tasks in a laboratory or structured educational setting without difficulty. In these contexts, their lack of knowledge is confined to the social and moral domains.

And yet, once outside of the structured school setting, their social deficits manifest as a much broader problem. They have the nonsocial knowledge they need, but without the guiding effects of the emotional rudder they cannot use this information to guide their everyday living, even in nonsocial contexts.

What these patients confirm is that the very neurobiological systems that support emotional functioning in social interactions also support decision making generally. Without adequate access to social and cultural knowledge, these children cannot use their knowledge efficaciously. As the psychologist Lev Vygotsky posited more than three quarters of a century ago, social and cultural functioning actually does underlie much of our nonsocial decision making and reasoning. Or, more precisely, social behavior turns out to be a special case of decision making, and morality to be a special case of social behavior (see A. R. Damasio, 2005, for a more complete treatment of this argument). The neurological systems that support decision making generally are the same systems that support social and moral behavior. Without adequate access to emotional, social, and moral feedback, in effect the important elements of culture, learning cannot inform real-world functioning as effectively.

A PHYSIOLOGICAL AND EVOLUTIONARY ACCOUNT OF EMOTION AND COGNITION: FROM AUTOMATIC RESPONSES TO MORALITY, CREATIVITY, HIGH REASON, AND CULTURE

In the perspective of the insights described earlier, and of much research in neurobiology and general biology in the two intervening decades, the connection between emotion and cognition is being seen in a very different light. To outline the current position, we shall present a simple scenario. Think of an ant crawling along a sidewalk, carrying a piece of food back to its nest. The ant scurries into a sidewalk crack to avoid being stepped on and then continues industriously on its way. What motivates this ant to preserve its own life? How did it decide, albeit nonconsciously and automatically, to carry the piece of food and to turn toward its nest? Clearly, the decisions to hide to avoid being crushed, to carry the food, and to continue in the direction of the nest are primitive instances of cognition, composed of complex packages of innate responses that enable the ant to react advantageously to particular classes of situations. But what is essential to understand is that these and myriads of other primitive examples of cognition, even in the lowly ant, act together in the service of an emotional goal: to maintain and promote homeostasis and thus fitness. In short, the ant behaves the way it does because those behaviors promote its survival and efficiency. (Humans, as conscious beings, perceive that efficiency as well-being and pleasure.) Every action the ant takes is inherently biased toward helping the ant, or its group, do well.

Taking an evolutionary perspective, even the simplest unicellular organism has within the nucleus of its cell a master controller that permits that living organism to maintain itself for a certain span of life and to seek during that period the conditions that will allow it to thrive. Emotions and the mechanisms that constitute them as behaviors, which humans experience as resulting in punishment or reward, pain or pleasure, are, in essence, nature's answer to one central problem, that of surviving and flourishing in an ambivalent world. Put simply, the brain has evolved under numerous pressures and oppressions precisely to cope with the problem of reading the body's condition and responding accordingly, and it begins doing so via the machinery of emotion. This coping shows up in simple ways in simple organisms and in remarkably rich ways as brains get more complex. In the brains of higher animals and in people, the richness is such that they can perceive the world through sensory processing and control their behavior in a way that includes what is traditionally called the mind. Out of the basic need to survive and flourish derives a way of dealing with thoughts, with ideas, and eventually with making plans, using imagination, and creating. At their core, all of these complex and artful human behaviors, the sorts of behaviors fostered in education, are carried out in the service of managing life within a culture and, as such, employ emotional strategies (Damasio, 1999).

Emotion, then, is a basic form of decision making, a repertoire of know-how and actions that allows people to respond appropriately in different situations. The more advanced cognition becomes, the more high-level reasoning supports the customization of these responses, both in thought and in action. With evolution and development, the specifications of conditions to which people respond, and the modes of response at their disposal, become increasingly nuanced. The more people develop and educate themselves, the more they refine their behavioral and cognitive options. In fact, one could argue that the chief purpose of education is to cultivate children's building repertoires of cognitive and behavioral strategies and options, helping them to recognize the complexity of situations and to respond in increasingly flexible, sophisticated, and creative ways. In our view, out of these processes of recognizing and responding, the very processes that form the interface between cognition and emotion, emerge the origins of creativity—the artistic, scientific, and technological innovations that are unique to our species. Further, out of these same kinds of processing emerges a special kind of human innovation: the social creativity that we call morality and ethical thought.

As the childhood-onset prefrontal patients show, morality and ethical decision making are special cases of social and emotional functioning. While the beginnings of altruism, compassion, and other notions of social equity exist in simpler forms in the nonhuman primates (Damasio, 2003; Hauser, 2006), human cognitive and emotional abilities far outpace those of the other animals. Our collective accomplishments range from the elevating and awe-inspiring to the evil and grotesque. Human ethics and morality are direct evidence that we are able to move beyond the opportunistic ambivalence of nature; indeed, the hallmark of ethical action is the inhibition of immediately advantageous or profitable solutions in the favor of what is good or right within our cultural frame of reference. In this way, ethical decision making represents a pinnacle cognitive and emotional achievement of humans. At its best, ethical decision making weaves together emotion, high reasoning, creativity, and social functioning, all in a cultural context (Gardner, Csikszentmihaly, & Damon, 2001).

Returning to the example of the ant: Our purpose in including this example was not to suggest that human emotions are equivalent to those of the ant, or that human behavior can be reduced to simple, nonspecific packages that unfold purely nonconsciously in response to particular situations. Although some aspects of human behavior and emotion could be characterized in this way, such reductionism would be grossly misplaced, especially in an essay about connections to education. Instead we aimed to illustrate that most, if not all, human decisions, behaviors, thoughts, and creations, no matter how far removed from survival in the homeostatic sense, bear the shadow of their emotive start.

In addition, as the prefrontal patients show, the processes of recognizing and responding to complex situations, which we suggest hold the origins of creativity, are fundamentally emotional and social. As such, they are shaped by and evaluated within a cultural context and, as we described in the previous section, are based upon emotional processing. No matter how complex and esoteric they become, our repertoire of behavioral and cognitive options continues to exist in the service of emotional goals. Neurobiologically and evolutionarily speaking, creativity is a means to survive and flourish in a social and cultural context, a statement that appears to apply from the relatively banal circumstances of daily living to the complex arena of ethical thought and behavior. In beginning to elucidate the neurobiological interdependencies between high reasoning, ethics, and creativity, all of which are fundamentally tied to emotion and critically relevant to education, we hope to provide a new vantage point from which to investigate the development and nurturance of these processes in schools.

EMOTIONAL THOUGHT: TOWARD AN EVIDENCE-BASED FRAMEWORK

In general, cognition and emotion are regarded as two interrelated aspects of human functioning. However, while it is perfectly reasonable and in fact necessary to distinguish between these two aspects in studying learning and development (Fischer & Bidell, 1998), the overly stringent preservation of this dichotomy may actually obscure the fact that emotions comprise cognitive as well as sensory processes. Furthermore, the aspects of cognition that are recruited most heavily in education, including learning, attention, memory, decision making, motivation, and social functioning, are both profoundly affected by emotion and in fact subsumed within the processes of emotion. Emotions entail the perception of an emotionally competent trigger, a situation either real or imagined that has the power to induce an emotion, as well as a chain of physiological events that will enable changes in both the body and mind (Damasio, 1994). These changes in the mind—involving focusing of attention, calling up of relevant memories, and learning the associations between events and their outcomes, among other things—are the processes with which education is most concerned. Yes, rational thought and logical reasoning do exist, although hardly ever truly devoid of emotion, but they cannot be recruited appropriately and usefully in the real world without emotion. Emotions help to direct our reasoning into the sector of knowledge that is relevant to the current situation or problem.

In Figure 1.1 we provide a graphical depiction of the neurological relationship between cognition and emotion. In the diagram, we have used the term *emotional thought* to refer to the large overlap between cognition and emotion. Emotional thought encompasses processes of learning, memory, and decision making, in both social and nonsocial contexts. It is within the domain of emotional thought that creativity plays out, through increasingly nuanced recognition of complex dilemmas and situations and through the invention of correspondingly flexible and innovative responses. Both the recognition and response aspects of creativity can be informed by rational thought and high reason. In our model, recognition and response processes are much like the concepts of assimilation and accommodation proposed by Piaget (1936/1952, 1937/1954). However, Piaget focused almost exclusively on cognition and the development of logic, and although he recognized a role for emotion in child development (Piaget, 1953–1954/1981), he did not fully appreciate the fundamentally emotional nature of the processes he described.

In the diagram, high reason and rational thought also contribute to high-level social and moral emotions, to form the specialized branch of decision making that is ethics. Motivated reasoning works in a similar manner and refers to the process by which emotional thoughts gain additional significance through the application of rational evidence and knowledge. In the other direction, rational evidence can be imposed upon certain kinds of emotional thought to produce the sort of automatic moral decision making that underlies intuitive notions of good and evil (Greene, Nystrom, Engell, Darley, & Cohen, 2004; Greene, Sommerville, Nystrom, Darley, & Cohen, 2001; Haidt, 2001). For example, in evaluating the morality of incest, experimental evidence suggests that people decide quickly at the subconscious and intui-

FIGURE 1.1. The evolutionary shadow cast by emotion over cognition influences the modern mind. In the diagram, the solid ellipse represents emotion; the dashed ellipse represents cognition. The extensive overlap between the two ellipses represents the domain of "emotional thought," in which emotion and cognition come together to produce the thought processes that educators care about, among them learning and memory. Emotional thought can be conscious or non-conscious, and is the means by which emotion-related bodily sensations come into our conscious awareness. High reason is a small section of the diagram, and requires consciousness. Reprinted with permission from Immordino-Yang and Damasio (2007).

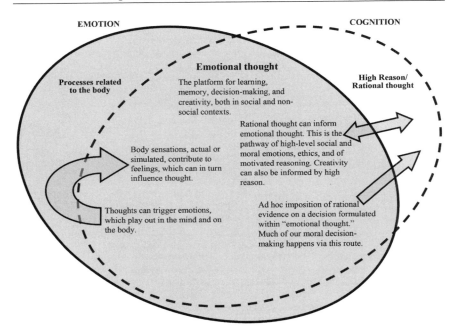

tive level and later impose ad hoc rational evidence on their decision (Haidt, 2001). Conversely, complex moral dilemmas such as whether to send a nation to war are (one hopes) informed by an abundance of rational evidence.

On the left side of the diagram, the bodily aspects of emotion are represented as a loop from emotional thought to the body and back. Here, emotional thoughts, either conscious or nonconscious, can alter the state of the body in characteristic ways, such as by tensing or relaxing the skeletal muscles or by changing the heart rate. In turn, the bodily sensations of these changes, either actual or simulated, contribute either consciously or nonconsciously to feelings, which can then influence thought. (*Simulated body sensation* refers to the fact that sometimes imagining bodily changes is sufficient; actually tensing the fists, for example, is not necessary.) This is the route by which rational deliberations over, say, a nation's wartime decisions can produce high-level social emotions such as indignation, as well as the bodily manifestations of these emotions, such as tensed fists, increased heart rate, or loss of appetite. The feeling of these bodily sensations, either consciously or not, can then bias cognitive processes such as attention and memory toward, in this case, aggression. The end result may be an unprovoked argument with one's friend over a topic totally unrelated to the war, the creation of a bleak and angry abstract painting, or a generally tense mood.

In addition to the evidence discussed above, support for these relationships between the body, emotion, and cognition comes mainly from neurobiological and psychophysiological research, in which the induction of emotion, either directly by a stimulus in the environment or indirectly via thoughts or memories, causes mental changes as well as physiological effects on the body. In turn, feelings of emotion rely on the somatosensory systems of the brain. That is, the brain areas associated with interoception (the sensing of body states) are particularly active as people feel emotions such as happiness, fear, anger, or sadness (Damasio et al., 2000).

To conclude, in presenting this model, our goal is not to devalue established notions of cognition and emotion but to provide a biologically based account of this relationship and to begin to specify the nature of the overlap between cognition and emotion in a way that highlights processes relevant to education. These processes include learning, memory, decision making, and creativity, as well as high reason and rational thinking. They also include the influence of the mind on the body and of the body on the mind.

EDUCATIONAL IMPLICATIONS:
A CALL FOR FURTHER RESEARCH

In teaching children, the focus is often on the logical reasoning skills and factual knowledge that are the most direct indicators of educational success. But there are two problems with this approach. First, neither learning nor recall happens in a purely rational domain, divorced from emotion, even though some of our knowledge will eventually distill into a moderately rational, unemotional form. Second, in teaching students to minimize the emotional aspects of their academic curriculum and function as much as possible in the rational domain, educators may be encouraging students to develop the sorts of knowledge that inherently do not transfer well to real-world situations. As both the early- and late-acquired prefrontal damage patients show, knowledge and reasoning divorced from emotional implications and learning lack meaning and motivation and are of little use in the real world. Simply having the knowledge does not imply that a student will be able to use it advantageously outside of school.

As recent advances in the neurobiology of emotions reveal, in the real world cognition functions in the service of life-regulating goals, implemented by emotional machinery. Moreover, people's thoughts and feelings are evaluated within a sociocultural context and serve to help them survive and flourish in a social, rather than simply opportunistic, world. While the idea that learning happens in a cultural context is far from new (Tomasello, Carpenter, Call, Behne, & Moll, 2005), we hope that these new insights from neurobiology, which shed light on the nested relationships between emotion, cognition, decision making, and social functioning, will provide a jumping off point for new thinking on the role of emotion in education. As educators have long known, it is simply not enough for students to master knowledge and logical reasoning skills in the traditional academic sense. They must be able to choose among and recruit these skills and knowledge usefully outside of the structured context of a school or laboratory. Because these choices are grounded in emotion and emotional thought, the physiology of emotion and its consequent process of feeling have enormous repercussions for the way we learn and for the way we consolidate and access knowledge. The better educators come to understand the nature of the relationship between emotion and cognition, the better they may be able to leverage this relationship in the design of learning environments.

In conclusion, new neurobiological evidence regarding the fundamental role of emotion in cognition holds the potential for important innovations in the science of learning and the practice of teaching. As researchers struggle with new directions and techniques for learning about these connections, a biological framework may help to constrain possibilities and generate new hypotheses and research directions. Just as neuroscience is coming to inform other education-related topics and problems (Goswami, 2006), the study of emotions, creativity, and culture is ripe for interdisciplinary collaborations among neuroscientists, psychologists, and educators. After all, we humans cannot divorce ourselves from our biology, nor can we ignore the high-level sociocultural and cognitive forces that make us special within the animal kingdom. When educators fail to appreciate the importance of students' emotions, they fail to appreciate a critical force in students' learning. One could argue, in fact, that they fail to appreciate the very reason that students learn at all.

ACKNOWLEDGMENTS

This work was supported by a grant from the Annenberg Center for Communication at the University of Southern California and by a grant from the Mathers Foundation.

REFERENCES

Anderson, S. W., Bechara, A., Damasio, H., Tranel, D., & Damasio, A. R. (1999). Impairment of social and moral behavior related to early damage in human prefrontal cortex. *Nature Neuroscience, 2*(11), 1032–1037.

Bechara, A. (2005). Decision making, impulse control and loss of willpower to resist drugs: A neurocognitive perspective. *Nature Neuroscience, 8*(11), 1458–1463.

Bechara, A., & Damasio, H. (1997). Deciding advantageously before knowing the advantageous strategy. *Science, 275*(5304), 1293–1295.

Damasio, A. R. (1994). *Descartes' error: Emotion, reason and the human brain.* New York, NY: Avon Books.

Damasio, A. R. (1996). The somatic marker hypothesis and the possible functions of the prefrontal cortex. *Philosophical Transactions of the Royal Society of London, Series B, Biological Sciences, 351,* 1413–1420.

Damasio, A. R. (1999). *The feeling of what happens.* New York, NY: Harcourt Brace.

Damasio, A. R. (2003). *Looking for Spinoza: Joy, sorrow and the feeling brain.* Orlando, FL: Harcourt.

Damasio, A. R. (2005). The neurobiological grounding of human values. In J. P. Changeux, A. R. Damasio, W. Singer, & Y. Christen (Eds.), *Neurobiology of human values.* London: Springer, 47–56.

Damasio, H. (2005). Disorders of social conduct following damage to prefrontal cortices. In *Neurobiology of human values.* London: Springer, 37–46.

Damasio, A. R., Grabowski, T. J., Bechara, A., Damasio, H., Ponto, L. L., Parvizi, J., & Hichwa, R. D. (2000). Subcortical and cortical brain activity during the feeling of self-generated emotions. *Nature Neuroscience, 3*(10), 1049–1056.

Damasio, A. R., Tranel, D., & Damasio, H. (1990). Individuals with sociopathic behavior caused by frontal damage fail to respond autonomically to social stimuli. *Behavioral Brain Research, 41,* 81–94.

Damasio, A. R., Tranel, D., & Damasio, H. (1991). Somatic markers and the guidance of behavior: Theory and preliminary testing. In H. S. Levin, H. M. Eisenberg, & A. L. Benton (Eds.), *Frontal lobe function and dysfunction* (pp. 217–229). New York, NY: Oxford University Press.

Damasio, H. (2005). Disorders of social conduct following damage to prefrontal cortices. In J. P. Changeux, A. R. Damasio, W. Singer, & Y. Christen (Eds.), *Neurobiology of human values.* London: Springer, 37–46.

Damasio, H., Grabowski, T., Frank, R., Galaburda, A. M., & Damasio, A. R. (1994). The return of Phineas Gage: Clues about the brain from the skull of a famous patient. *Science, 264*(5162), 1102–1105.

Davis, H. A. (2003). Conceptualizing the role and influence of student-teacher relationships on children's social and cognitive development. *Educational Psychologist, 38*(4), 207–234.

Fischer, K. W., & Bidell, T. R. (1998). Dynamic development of psychological structures in action and thought. In R. M. Lerner (Ed.), *Handbook of child psychology:*

Vol. 1. Theoretical models of human development (5th ed., pp. 467–561). New York, NY: Wiley.

Gardner, H., Csikszentmihaly, M., & Damon, W. (2001). *Good work: When excellence and ethics meet.* New York, NY: Basic Books.

Goswami, U. (2006). Neuroscience and education: From research to practice? *Nature Reviews Neuroscience, 7*(5), 406–411.

Greene, J. D., Nystrom, L. E., Engell, A. D., Darley, J. M., & Cohen, J. D. (2004). The neural bases of cognitive conflict and control in moral judgment. *Neuron, 44*(2), 389–400.

Greene, J. D., Sommerville, R. B., Nystrom, L. E., Darley, J. M., & Cohen, J. D. (2001). An fMRI investigation of emotional engagement in moral judgment. *Science, 293*(5537), 2105–2108.

Haidt, J. (2001). The emotional dog and its rational tail: A social intuitionist approach to moral judgment. *Psychological Review, 108*(4), 814–834.

Hauser, M. (2006). *Moral minds: How nature designed our universal sense of right and wrong.* New York, NY: Harper Collins.

Immordino-Yang, M. H., & Damasio, A. R. (2007). We feel, therefore we learn: The relevance of affective and social neuroscience to education. *Mind, Brain and Education, 1*(1), 3–10.

Piaget, J. (1952). *The origins of intelligence in children* (M. Cook, Trans.). New York, NY: International Universities Press. (Original work published 1936)

Piaget, J. (1954). *The construction of reality in the child* (M. Cook, Trans.). New York, NY: Basic Books. (Original work published 1937).

Piaget, J. (1981). *Intelligence and affectivity: Their relationship during child development* (T. A. Brown & C. E. Kaegi, Eds. & Trans.). Palo Alto, CA: Annual Reviews Monograph. (Originally presented as lectures, 1953–1954)

Rueda, R. (2006). Motivational and cognitive aspects of culturally accommodated instruction: The case of reading comprehension. In D. M. McInerney, M. Dowson, & S. V. Etten (Eds.), *Effective schools: Vol. 6. Research on sociocultural influences on motivation and learning* (pp. 135–158). Greenwich, CT: Information Age Publishing.

Rueda, R., August, D., & Goldenberg, C. (2006). The sociocultural context in which children acquire literacy. In D. August & T. Shanahan (Eds.), *Developing literacy in second-language learners: Report of the National Literacy Panel on Language-Minority Children and Youth* (pp. 319–340). Mahwah, NJ: Erlbaum.

Saver, J. L., & Damasio, A. R. (1991). Preserved access and processing of social knowledge in a patient with acquired sociopathy due to ventromedial frontal damage. *Neuropsychologia, 29*, 1241–1249.

Tomasello, M., Carpenter, M., Call, J., Behne, T., & Moll, H. (2005). Understanding and sharing of intentions: The origins of cultural cognition. *Behavioral and Brain Sciences, 28*, 675–735.

CHAPTER 2

"Rest Is Not Idleness": Implications of the Brain's Default Mode for Human Development and Education

Mary Helen Immordino-Yang, Joanna A. Christodoulou, and Vanessa Singh

Chapter description: This chapter had its origins in an intriguing finding published in our first report of the brain systems activated when individuals feel admiration and compassion, two cognitively complex, abstract emotions important for identity development and morality. The data from that study (Immordino-Yang, McColl, Damasio, & Damasio, 2009) revealed a novel functional subdivision in a part of the brain deep inside the back of the head (called the inferior/posterior posteromedial cortices). The network of brain regions involved suggested that these emotions relied on attention to the inner psychological self rather than to the outer world. Because the activity in this network is suppressed when people attend to the outer world or focus on accomplishing short-term, goal-directed tasks, this finding made us wonder whether consistently engaging children and adolescents in goal-directed and attention-grabbing activities without adequate opportunities to rest, daydream, and reflect might hinder healthy development—as suggested by the quote in the title, taken from John Lubbock's *The Use of Life* (1894). Specifically, we wondered whether it could undermine the development of complex moral emotions and skills for engaging abstract, personal and social-emotional thoughts, as well as the ability to interpret current decisions and actions in light of long-term future goals.

PAPER

Clinicians and teachers often discuss the benefits of "down time" and reflection for making sense of one's experiences and decisions about future behavior. For example, many experiential education programs emphasize the importance of time for introspection, and interventions and therapies that teach skills for quiet reflection and mindfulness produce benefits especially for social and emotional functioning (CASEL, 2007; Cohen, 2006; Semple, Lee, Rosa, & Miller, 2010), but also for academic achievement (Brackett, Rivers, Reyes, & Salovey, 2012). Why should this be, and how can developmental, clinical, and educational psychologists better conceptualize the role of off-line and reflective processing for human development? Conversely, how might researchers think in new ways about the impacts of high environmental attentional demands on learning and socioemotional development, including, for example, demands from entertainment media, from the challenges associated with urban settings, or in the classroom?

Emerging conceptions of brain functioning reveal that neural networks responsible for maintaining and focusing attention into the environment appear to toggle with a so-called default mode of brain function (DM) that is spontaneously induced during rest, daydreaming, and other nonattentive but awake mental states (Smallwood, Obonsawin, & Heim, 2003). Further evidence from social and affective neuroscience suggests the importance of brain systems implicated in the DM for active, internally focused psychosocial mental processing, for example, in tasks involving self-awareness and reflection, recalling personal memories, imagining the future, feeling emotions about the psychological impact of social situations on other people, and constructing moral judgments (Buckner, Andrews-Hanna & Schacter, 2008; Buckner & Carroll, 2007; Gilbert & Wilson, 2007; Spreng & Grady, 2010; Spreng, Mar, & Kim, 2009). Studies examining individual differences in the brain's DM connectivity, essentially measures of how coherently the areas of the network coordinate during rest and decouple during outward attention, find that people with stronger DM connectivity at rest score higher on measures of cognitive abilities, such as divergent thinking, reading comprehension, and memory (Li et al., 2009; Song et al., 2009; van den Heuvel, Stam, Kahn, & Hulshoff Pol, 2009; Wig et al., 2008). Taken together, these findings lead to a new neuroscientific conception of the brain's functioning "at rest"—namely, that neural processing during lapses in outward attention may be related to self and social processing and to thought that transcends concrete, semantic representations, and that the brain's efficient monitoring and control of task-directed and non-task-directed states (or of outwardly and inwardly directed attention) may underlie important dimensions of psychological functioning. These findings also suggest the possibility that inadequate opportunity for children to play and adolescents to quietly reflect and to daydream may have negative consequences—both for social-emotional well-being and for their ability to attend well to tasks.

Despite the potential implications, however, psychological scientists and educators are largely unaware of or have underappreciated the relevance of this actively growing body of neural findings, and cognitive neuroscientists interested in development and education have largely focused on the immediate, negative effects of attention lapses on task-directed performance (e.g., Kane et al., 2007; McVay & Kane, 2010; Smallwood, Beach, Schooler, & Handy, 2008; Smallwood, Fishman, & Schooler, 2007). Therefore, our goals in this article are (a) to introduce psychological scientists to recent advances in understanding the functioning of the brain and mind during lapses in outward attention; (b) to generate an early hypothesis from the neuroscience findings concerning the effects of consistently high external attention demands in schools and leisure environments on socioemotional development in children and adolescents; (c) to propose preliminary examples of productive connections between this hypothesis and current educational and developmental psychological research findings, in order to demonstrate the utility of the neural findings for psychologists; and (d) to advocate educational practices that promote more effective balance between children's needs for external attention and internal reflection. The overarching premise of the article is that although daydreaming and other lapses in outward attention lead to poor performance on concentration-requiring tasks in the moment, skills for reflecting during lapses in outward attention, and time for safely indulging mind wandering, may be critical for healthy development and learning in the longer term.

LOOKING OUT AND LOOKING IN: THE DISCOVERY OF COMPLEMENTARY BRAIN NETWORKS

Neuroscience studies over the past several decades have revealed that contrary to early theories, attention is not a general property of the whole brain but the product of specific networks that contribute to various aspects of processing. Decades of study have differentiated three systems responsible for monitoring and responding to the environment around us and for focusing our mental processing on incoming stimuli: alerting, orienting, and executive control (see Corbetta & Shulman, 2002; Fan, McCandliss, Sommer, Raz, & Posner, 2002; Posner & Petersen, 1990). These functions, which rely heavily on lateral frontal and parietal regions, are important for cognitive development, and interventions that support children in strengthening skills related to these aspects of attention improve cognitive and academic performance in a variety of domains (Posner & Rothbart, 2005; Smallwood et al., 2007; Stevens, Lauinger, & Neville, 2009).

But, what does the brain do when not engaged in a focused, goal-directed task? Newly emerging theories of the brain's functional architecture reveal that the attention networks described above are part of a broader complement of brain networks that can roughly be conceptualized as supporting two alternating systems. One of these networks is "task positive": its recruitment is associated with active engagement in goal-directed tasks involving attention into the world and evaluating the salience of external stimuli (Seeley et al., 2007). This network supports what we will call the "looking out" system. Another network, known variously as the "task-negative" or "resting" network, has been associated with the brain's "default mode" of operation (Buckner & Vincent, 2007; Raichle et al., 2001). This network comprises mainly regions along the midline of the brain, in both the parietal and the frontal lobes, along with more lateral regions in the inferior part of the parietal lobe and the medial part of the temporal lobe (see Figure 2.1). During neuroimaging experiments, the activity in these regions is heightened most reliably during passive rest (Greicius, Krasnow, Reiss, & Menon, 2003), induced by paradigms such as asking participants to stare for several minutes at a plus sign shown in the center of their field of vision, or to relax with eyes open or closed. We will call this the "looking in" system. (Note on nomenclature: we use the term *network* to describe sets of brain regions whose activity is functionally coordinated. We use the term *system* to describe the psychologically relevant capacities that are supported by the brain "network.")

The past decade of neuroscience research has revealed that as one network is increasingly engaged, the other is decreasingly engaged (Esposito et al., 2006; Fox et al., 2005). It is thought that the toggling of these networks reflects a shift from a state of external monitoring and focus on goal-directed activity (looking out) into a more free-form, internally directed, stimulus-independent mental state (looking in; see Smallwood, Brown, Baird, & Schooler, 2011, for a related argument). Recent research suggests that these networks' efficiency and coregulation improve as the brain matures through childhood (Fair et al., 2008) but that the rudiments of this functional organization are present in childhood (Supekar et al., 2010; Thomason et al., 2008), infancy, and possibly even prenatally (Doria et al., 2010; Fransson et al., 2007; but see Fransson, Åden, Blennow, & Lagercrantz, 2011).

In addition, it is likely that the networks that support systems for "look-

FIGURE 2.1.   Overview of the main brain regions comprising the "default mode" (DM) network, with brief descriptions of associated socioemotional functions. The DM regions listed are relatively more active and show coordinated activity during wakeful "rest." The regions depicted are also involved in many other functions, including various cognitive association functions and aspects of homeostatic regulation and somatosensation, especially for the milieu of the internal body (i.e., the "guts"). The left side of the image is the front of the brain; the right and left hemispheres are split apart to show the medial surface. Note that these brain areas cannot be said to "do" the functions listed. Instead, they are especially "associated" with these functions and, as such, are thought to play important roles within the complex networks of regions underlying the functions.

1. **Ventromedial prefrontal cortex (vmPFC):** induction of social emotions; nonconscious induction of somatic responses such as skin sweating associated with a sense of risk; modulation of the parasympathetic branch of the autonomic nervous system (important for calming of heart rate)

2. **Dorsomedial prefrontal cortex (dmPFC):** representation of self in relation to others; predicting emotional outcomes of social interactions for self and close others; judging psychological and emotional qualities and traits; feeling emotions about others' mental situations

3. **Anterior middle cingulate cortex (ACC):** a centrally connected "hub" of the cortex, also heavily interconnected with somatosensory regions that feel the guts and viscera; error monitoring, emotion and empathy, feeling physical and social pain, modulation of the sympathetic branch of the autonomic nervous system (important for activation of heart rate, arousal)

4. **Posteromedial cortices (PMC):** the most centrally connected "hub" of the cortex; high-level integrative representation of the physiological condition of the visceral "gut" body; construction of a subjective sense of self-awareness; activated in social emotions, moral decision making, episodic memory retrieval; contains dorsal posterior cingulate cortex (dPCC), involved in attention monitoring/switching and integration of information

5. **Inferior parietal lobule (IPL):** Involved in successful episodic memory retrieval; empathically simulating others' perspectives and the goals of others' actions

6. **Hippocampus** (a seahorse-shaped structure that curls underneath the temporal lobe; not visible in these views): formation and recall of long-term memories; information consolidation

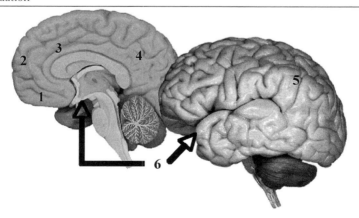

ing in" and "looking out" are codependent and coregulate one another—the functioning of one, both in the moment and over the longer term, has been found to predict the functioning of the other. A growing body of neuroscience studies show that the quality of DM brain activity during rest is related to the quality of subsequent neural and behavioral responses to environmental stimuli and that momentary and longer-lasting complementary fluctuations in these networks are important for perception, attention, and goal-directed cognition (see Northoff, Duncan, & Hayes, 2010, for a review; see also Spreng, Stevens, Chamberlain, Gilmore, & Schacter, 2010). For example, in a neuroimaging experiment in which participants alternated blocks of resting with looking at images and listening to sounds, the more effectively the DM regions were activated during rest and deactivated while attending to the images and sounds, the more brain activation there was in sensory cortices during the image and sound presentations (Greicius & Menon, 2004). Longitudinal studies also suggest that there is considerable variability in the strength of DM connectivity among adults and that, although patterns of activity during rest are relatively stable in adulthood (Beason-Held, Kraut, & Resnick, 2009), training introspection (e.g., through meditation) can alter the functioning of DM networks as well as improve skills for sustained attention on a task (e.g., Brefczynski-Lewis, Lutz, Schaefer, Levinson, & Davidson, 2007; Brewer et al., 2012; Chiesa, Calati, & Serretti, 2010; Hölzel et al., 2007; Jha, Krompinger, & Baime, 2007; Tang et al., 2007).

Relations to Individual Differences in Socioemotional Functioning

The efficiency with which a brain toggles between activity associated with DM and outward attention, as well as the strength of functional connectivity between DM regions during "rest," seem also to be associated with neural and psychological health, especially around social and emotional functioning. Atypicalities in DM functioning have been related to social-emotional symptoms in schizophrenia (Whitfield-Gabrieli et al., 2009), autism (Cherkassky, Kana, Keller, & Just, 2006; Kennedy, Redcay, & Courchesne, 2006), attention deficit disorder (Castellanos et al., 2008; Tomasi & Volkow, 2012; Uddin et al., 2008), anxiety disorders (Etkin, Prater, Schatzberg, Menon, & Greicius, 2009; Zhao et al., 2007), depression (Greicius et al., 2007), and other conditions. The differences in DM functioning among these populations seem to relate consistently to the hallmark symptoms of the disorder. For instance, autism is associated with atypically low levels of functional connectivity between DM regions during rest; these findings are thought to reflect a paucity of social and psychological thought and emotion (Kennedy &

Courchesne, 2008). People with schizophrenia, by contrast, show heightened activation and hyperconnectivity in the DM network that are insufficiently attenuated during outward attention (Bluhm et al., 2007; Garrity et al., 2007; Zhou et al., 2007); this pattern is thought to produce a heightened propensity toward mentalizing and a blurring of boundaries between one's own and others' minds that contribute to disordered thought when coupled with schizophrenics' excessive alertness to the external environment (Whitfield-Gabrieli et al., 2009).

Relations to Individual Differences in Cognitive Functioning

Tantalizing new evidence suggests that certain aspects of DM functioning during "rest" and during tasks are related to intelligence in adults as indexed by standardized IQ scores, to reading and memory abilities, and to performance ability on attention-demanding cognitive tasks. For example, studies have found that when people with higher IQ scores "rest" in the functional magnetic resonance imaging (fMRI) scanner, the DM connectivity in their brains, especially for long-range connections, is stronger than that measured in the brains of people with average IQs (Li et al., 2009; Song et al., 2009). The main finding concerns not the *amount* of activation in DM regions but the functional coordination or extent of "cross talk" between DM regions. In participants with higher IQs, there is more efficient communication and coordination between frontal and parietal DM regions during "rest," which is thought to underlie better cognitive abilities for making connections between disparate pieces of information (van den Heuvel et al., 2009).

With regard to reading and memory ability, findings are related to efficient toggling between the complementary networks. In reading studies, clearer functional segregation during "rest" between DM regions and a key brain region specialized for reading (the left fusiform gyrus, not part of the DM) is associated with reading skill among adults; this clear segregation is not yet mature in children 8–14 years of age (Koyama et al., 2011). In memory studies, better long-term recall is associated with greater deactivation of DM regions involved in encoding and recall, specifically the hippocampus and its neighboring parahippocampal gyrus, during simple cognitive tasks compared to during "rest" (Wig et al., 2008). Failure to adequately deactivate another DM region, the posteromedial cortices, during a task requiring outwardly focused attention is also associated with memory declines in older adults (Miller et al., 2008).

Finally, measures of efficient downregulation of DM network activity during external attention-demanding tasks have been found to predict cognitive performance on these tasks in real time. For example, in an experiment using deep-brain electrode recording during simpler and more complex visual search tasks, magnitude of moment-to-moment suppression in DM networks increased with the complexity of processing required and predicted subjects' performance (Ossandon et al., 2011).

To summarize, although the main focus in attention research relevant to development and education to date has been on "looking out" into the environment, for example, the facility with which a child filters out distractions and maintains focus on a task (Posner & Rothbart, 2005; Rueda, Rothbart, McCandliss, Saccomanno, & Posner, 2005), the neuroscience findings reviewed here suggest that (a) the quality of neural processing that supports the system for "looking out" is tied to the quality of neural processing that supports the system for "looking in" and to individuals' abilities to move between these two modes efficiently; and (b) the quality of neural processing during "looking in" is related to socioemotional functioning, as well as to other dimensions of thought that transcend the here and now. Yet, the implications of these neural findings for psychological development in naturalistic environments, such as schools, have not been studied. The next section provides an overview of the psychological operations that have been related to activity in DM brain regions in adults, in order to begin a conversation among psychological scientists about the dimensions of thought associated with lapses in outward attention and developmental implications. We focus on socioemotional functioning to highlight the interdependence of the neural networks that support attentive mental states and states that may promote meaning making and socioemotional well-being.

WHAT DOES THE MIND DO WHEN THE BRAIN IS "AT REST"? MEMORIES, PROSPECTIONS, EMOTIONS, AND THE MENTAL "SELF"

As any normal human being can attest, when a person disengages from externally oriented goal-directed behavior, her mind is not idle—instead, she can become absorbed in a dynamic stream of free-form thought that is associated with mind wandering, spontaneous recollection of previous memories, production of hypothetical scenarios and future plans, and other personal and social thoughts and imaginings (Andreasen et al., 1995; Smallwood & Schooler, 2006). When considered this way, it is no wonder that some sectors of the brain are highly active during neuroimaging paradigms meant to induce "rest." The mind is not idle in the absence of externally focused, goal-directed tasks—instead, the relative lapse in perceptual vigilance provides an opportunity to mentally wander far from the current physical context, maintaining just enough attention to engage automatic behaviors and to monitor the environment for interruptions, while indulging thoughts, fantasies, and memories about the social world and the psychological self.

Interestingly, in addition to studies reporting signature DM activations during non-goal-directed activities like "rest" in the fMRI scanner, there is now a growing list of neuroimaging studies that report activations in DM regions during goal-directed tasks involving introspective, socioemotional and self-referential processing or simulation. For instance, activation in DM regions has been found for activities like feeling compassionate for a young mother with cancer or inspired by her determination (Immordino-Yang, McColl, Damasio, & Damasio, 2009), imagining how your own opinions would change if you awoke one day as the opposite sex (Tamir & Mitchell, 2011), evaluating moral scenarios such as depicting treatment of wartime prisoners (Harrison et al., 2008), and recalling memories for personal experiences (see Wagner, Shannon, Kahn, & Buckner, 2005, for a review).

Notably, processing related to cognitive perspective taking or traditional theory-of-mind functions, or that related to evaluating the more concrete and immediate physical and cognitive aspects of social situations, is *not* especially associated with DM regions (see Waytz & Mitchell, 2011, for a related argument). Instead, DM regions seem to be recruited for processing that pertains less to factual knowledge from one's memory or deduction about another's knowledge state and more to simulation and evaluation of abstract social, emotional, and moral implications of one's own or others' knowledge states. For example, several studies have implicated the dorsomedial prefrontal cortex in judgments about psychological traits and emotional qualities of the self and close others (Blakemore & Frith, 2004; Jenkins & Mitchell, 2011; Kelley et al., 2002; Kitayama & Park, 2010; Mitchell, Banaji, & Macrae, 2005; Northoff et al., 2006), an effect that can be modulated by in-group/out-group racial comparisons (Mathur, Harada, & Chiao, 2012) and by cultural conceptions of interdependent versus independent self (Markus & Kitayama, 1991; Harada, Li, & Chiao, 2010). Involvement of the inferior/posterior sector of the posteromedial cortices, the most centrally connected "hub" of the DM network (Hagmann et al., 2008), has been related to self-awareness (Buckner et al., 2008) and autobiographical self (Damasio & Meyer, 2009) and has been consistently implicated in episodic and personal memory retrieval (Wagner et al., 2005; Immordino-Yang & Singh, 2013), daydreaming (Christoff, Gordon, Smallwood, Smith, & Schooler, 2009), moral judgment tasks (Greene, Sommerville, Nystrom, Darley, & Cohen, 2001), and social emotions about others' mental qualities and circumstances, such as admiring another's virtuous commitment to those less fortunate or feeling compassion for someone who has lost a loved one (Immordino-Yang et al., 2009). By contrast, tasks that require simply recognizing and labeling an emotional facial expression from a picture, or emotionally reacting to a person's skillful performance or physical injury, do not recruit this network (and in fact may suppress its activation since they require outward attention; Immordino-Yang et al., 2009; Sreenivas, Boehm, & Linden, 2012).

Taking this evidence together, we find that brain regions involved in the DM appear to be specifically recruited and specialized for processing abstract information relevant to the psychological, affective, and subjective aspects of the self and other people, both in everyday contexts and for more complex moral, socioemotional, prospective, and retrospective functions. This description is necessarily broad—after all, DM activation could be said to underlie half of what the mind does. Our aim in providing this description is to give psychological scientists a sense of the dimensions of thought associated with lapses in outward attention, for comparison with those associated with heightened outward attention (e.g., sensory perception and vigilance to the physical context, cognitive processing of situationally relevant tasks, motor control and coordination of actions, perception of social and emotional stimuli [but not deep reflection on their meaning], or recalling semantic or factual information). This comparison is important because, judging from what is being learned of brain functioning, activating the neural platform that supports mental processes associated with DM regions may be relatively incompatible with externally focused attention or vigilance into the environment, especially while control systems for monitoring and alternately engaging inward focus and outward attention are immature. Our hope is that in distilling the neural findings we have provided a starting point for appreciating the breadth of their applicability. The next section grounds these ideas with a naturalistic example, in order to narrow the focus onto a new hypothesis for development.

AN EXAMPLE OF SPONTANEOUS "LOOKING IN" DURING SOCIAL LEARNING

Consider the reaction of one college-age participant, "John," during a one-on-one social emotion-induction interview in which he was told a true story meant to induce compassion. The story is about a young boy who grew up in a small industrial city in China during an economic depression that often left him hungry. The boy's father had died just after his son's birth, leaving his mother to work long hours as a laborer. John is shown a video clip in which the boy's mother describes how, one winter afternoon, she found a coin on the ground and used it to buy warm cakes for her son, who had been all day at school with nothing to eat. The mother recounts how her son had been so hungry, yet he had offered her the last cake, which she declined by lying that she had eaten already. After the video, the experimenter asks John how this situation makes him feel, to which John responds:

> This is the one [true story from the experiment] that's hit me the most, I suppose. And I'm not very good at verbalizing emotions. But . . . um . . . I can almost feel the physical sensations. It's like there's a balloon or something just under my sternum, inflating and moving up and out. Which, I don't know, is my sign of something really touching . . . [pause] And, so, the selflessness of the mother . . . and then also of the little boy. You know, having these wonderful cakes that he never gets to have, and still offering them to her . . . and then her turning them down, is . . . uh . . . [long pause] It makes me think about my parents, because they provide me with so much and I don't thank them enough, I don't think . . . I *know* I don't. So, I should do that. (adapted from Immordino-Yang, 2011)

In answering the straightforward question of how this story makes him feel, John reveals a common pattern in which deliberations leading to a complex reaction to a social situation begin with a general report of feeling emotionally touched or moved ("hit"), sometimes accompanied by visceral sensations ("a balloon . . . under my sternum"). Even though John does not seem to really know yet what emotion he is having ("I'm not very good at verbalizing"), he notices the emotional power of the story based on feeling physiological "signs." But he does not stop there. Instead, after briefly reviewing the relevant actions from the story (who gave whom what to eat), and their meaning based on what he knows about the situation (there is a shortage of food, so sharing food implies "selflessness"), John pauses. He appears to briefly withdraw from the interaction with the experimenter and blankly gaze into his lap. Then, he emerges with a report of having spontaneously evaluated his own relationship with his parents. It appears that by evaluating the emotional implications of another boy's situation, John seems to have learned to better appreciate his own.

How does this example pertain to the argument at hand? John's reaction to the compassion-inducing story nicely demonstrates how new insights and understandings are actively, dynamically constructed (Fischer & Bidell, 2006; Fischer & Immordino-Yang, 2002)—learners build from prior knowledge and work to actively accommodate new information to make sense of the current situation. It also demonstrates the value of a reflective pause in moving from considering the concrete, action-oriented, context-specific details of *this* situation (knowing what happened and why) to constructing an understanding of the broader and longer-term emotional implications for one's own or *any* situation (in John's case, what the actions mean for the protagonists' psychological qualities, and how recognizing these qualities leads him to express greater appreciation of his own parents' sacrifices for him). Interestingly, our neural data support the interpretation that John's pauses are a behavioral manifestation of DM neural activity. Our current analyses reveal that the more participants reflectively pause in the social emotions interview, the more cognitively abstract and complex their answers (i.e., the higher the construal level;, the more DM activity they will later show when feeling emotions with moral connotations in the fMRI scanner, and the stronger the participants' DM connectivity during rest (Immordino-Yang, M.H., Yang, X., Pavarini, G., & Schnall, 2013).

In the next section, we focus on two developmental implications of the findings. First, we suggest that time and skills for constructive internal reflection are beneficial for emotional learning and well-being. Second, we suggest that inordinately biasing children's and adolescents' attention into the external world may undermine the development of abilities to think about the abstract, moral and social-emotional aspects of situations, information, memories, and self. Put another way, we hypothesize that consistently imposing high attention demands on children, either in school, through entertainment, or through living conditions, may rob them of opportunities to advance from thinking about "what happened" or "how to do this" to constructing knowledge about "what this means for the world and for the way I live my life." For instance, it could lead teenagers to admire a skillful sports player but not the mental fortitude of, say, a courageous civil rights leader.

WHAT THIS MEANS FOR CHILDREN: TOWARD THE HYPOTHESIS THAT HEALTHY PSYCHOLOGICAL DEVELOPMENT REQUIRES OPPORTUNITIES AND SKILLS FOR "LOOKING IN"

One implication of the DM findings is that the brain seems to honor a distinction between the processing of information about concrete, physical, and immediate circumstances, facts, and procedures and abstract information about mental, hypothetical, and longer-term circumstances and implications. Given that deliberating on abstract social-emotional and hypothetical circumstances seems to be associated with the "looking in" system, we hypothesize that these kinds of thinking may be particularly vulnerable to disruption by external distraction, especially while attentional monitoring and control are immature. Had the experimenter above interrupted John during his reflective pause, would he have made the conceptual leap from considering the story to evaluating his own relationship with his parents? If John had grown up under conditions that did not support time for safe internal reflection, would he have failed to fully develop this skill? We do not know the answers to these questions. But, given the accumulating neural evidence, it seems reasonable to conjecture that important skills for reflection and for building personal meaning may depend heavily upon psychological functions associated with activity in DM brain networks and may therefore be curtailed if environmental attention demands and distractions are consistently overly high.

Preliminary Connections to Education

Although education research on learning and achievement has not been framed to highlight transitions to internally focused attention, there are hints that teaching skills for productive internal, self-directed processing in schools may be beneficial both for socioemotional well-being and for academic skills (see also Yeager & Walton, 2011; Immordino-Yang & Sylvan, 2010). For example, high school students encouraged before a test to write in a journal about their beliefs about the implications of their test performance for their life more broadly overcame anxiety and performed better (Ramirez & Beilock, 2011). Similarly, envisioning advantageous possibilities for one's future identity and connecting these possibilities to current behavioral choices have been found to powerfully improve school performance and motivation (Oyserman, Terry, & Bybee, 2002), but the efficacy of these activities is heavily dependent on students' subjective interpretation of their experiences (Hatcher & Bringle, 1997; Oyserman & Destin, 2010). In elementary-school-age children, emotional well-being, self-confidence, and academic achievement are bolstered for students taught to take a "meta-moment" in which they remove themselves from distracting circumstances, reflectively evaluate their memories and feelings, envision an ideal "self," and then make an appropriate plan (Brackett et al., 2012).

Together, these interventions may improve academic performance, compared to various control interventions without a socioemotional focus, in part because they set up neuropsychological circumstances optimally conducive to extracting the emotional meaning of situations, to connecting this meaning to personal memories, and to imagining a better future course of action. Of course, students should not be encouraged to waste time or to dwell on inconsequential or irrelevant private musings during work time; doing so clearly decreases productivity (Smallwood et al., 2007). Still, the DM research reviewed here suggests that for students to optimally engage attentively to tasks, they may also require skills and opportunities for high-quality knowledge consolidation. Considering the neural and psychological evidence together suggests that adequate developmental opportunity for appropriate lapses in outwardly directed attention, and potentially even for high-quality introspective states, may be important for well-being and for optimal performance on focused tasks, as the quality of thought during "looking in" and "looking out" may be interdependent. Because of this, it may be that educational experiences and settings crafted to promote balance between "looking out" and "looking in," in which children are guided to navigate between and leverage the brain's complementary networks skillfully and in which teachers work to distinguish between loss of attentive focus and engaging a mindful, reflective focus, will prove optimal for development. Put another way, leaving room for self-relevant processing in school may help students *own* their learning, both the process and the outcomes.

Emerging Evidence on the Effects of Heavy Social Media Use

The prevalence of digitally mediated communication and entertainment among youths has dramatically increased in recent years, and texting is reputedly superseding all other forms of friendship interaction among teens in developed nations (Pew Research Center, 2010; Smith 2011). This shift in technology use has caused widespread concern about how heavy reliance on digitally mediated communication may affect development. Are children losing skills for face-to-face social interaction, and how would this loss of skill manifest psychologically?

Although very little published research to date addresses these questions, cumulative evidence on DM functioning would suggest a relatively straightforward implication. If youths overuse social media, if they spend very little waking time free from the possibility that a text will interrupt them, we would expect that these conditions might predispose youths toward focusing on the concrete, physical, and immediate aspects of situations and self, with less inclination toward considering the abstract, longer-term, moral and emotional implications of their and others' actions. One recent study of more than 2,300 young adults (Canadian college students 18–22 years of age) tested related hypotheses and found results that accord remarkably with these predictions (Trapnell & Sinclair, 2012). The study found that higher levels of social texting among research participants were weakly but consistently positively associated with out-group prejudice and materialism, for example, with reporting lower positivity toward indigenous Canadians and with believing that physical attractiveness is an important personal value. Conversely, higher levels of texting were consistently negatively associated with measures of moral reflectiveness, for example, with motivation to promote social equality or justice in the community, and with perceived importance of living with integrity.

Although it is not clear in this study whether texting caused the moral changes or whether youths with particular social dispositions gravitate toward heavy use of texting, there are hints that the effects might be causal. Trapnell and Sinclair (2012) also found that an increase in texting over the five years of the study (2007–2011) paralleled a decrease in reported reflectivity. A separate experimental manipulation study by Abraham, Pocheptsova, and Ferraro (2012) found that after being asked to draw and describe their cell phone, participants showed temporary decreases in prosocial behavior (as measured by willingness to donate time or resources to a charity for the homeless) but increases in perceived social connectedness. Another small-scale study reported that, among youths, higher texting frequency was associated with finding friendships less "fulfilling" (Angstermichael & Lester, 2010). The somewhat alarming implication, still not directly tested, is that if youths are habitually pulled into the outside world by distracting media snippets, or if their primary mode of socially interacting is via brief, digitally transmitted communications, they may be systematically undermining opportunities to reflect on the moral, social, emotional, and longer-term implications of social situations and personal values. This situation could potentially alter the perceived quality of their social relationships and over time might bias identity development toward focusing on concrete or physical abilities, traits, and accomplishments.

Of note, in our opinion the preliminary findings described here should not be taken as de facto evidence that access to technology is necessarily bad for development or weakens morality. After all, texting is another (digital) tool that is only as good as the user's purposes or goals. If texting is used to change momentary, context-specific behavior, for example, to remind individuals with health problems to engage in particular health-related behaviors, evidence suggests that it can be remarkably effective (Cole-Lewis & Kershaw, 2010). Instead, these data should be taken as an early warning of the possibility that overusing technologies that reduce social communication to short snippets that continually interrupt the receiver, and that restrict communication to less reflective content, could be harmful. "High texting" youths in the Trapnell and Sinclair (2012) study sometimes reported receiving or sending upward of three hundred non-work-related texts per day, which is more than twice the average reported by the Pew Research Center (2011).

Of course, the flip side of the coin might also be true: access to these same technologies, if used well, could promote social reflectiveness and moral responsibility by facilitating communication between people who are far from each other, and who would not otherwise have opportunities to interact, in order to foster empathic understanding of world situations and cross-cultural perspectives. For example, in the Iranian election protests of 2009–2010, rapid-fire social media is thought to have been instrumental both for the organization of the political movement and for garnering international empathy for protesters (Kamalipour, 2010). For another example, primary schools with a global curricular focus by necessity employ digital media to connect classrooms oceans apart, so that students can share experiences and beliefs with students from different cultural backgrounds (Süssmuth, 2007; see also http://www.iearn.org). In the end, the question will not be as much about what the technology does to people as about how best to use the technology in a responsible, beneficial way that promotes rather than hinders social development.

MEANING MAKING AND THE BRAIN: FORGING AN INTERDISCIPLINARY RESEARCH FOCUS ON CONSTRUCTIVE INTERNAL REFLECTION

Taken together, the neurobiological research suggests a need to conceptualize and study processes of knowledge building that may be supported during internally focused thought and vulnerable to disruption by external input. The findings suggest that these processes may span from relaxed mind wandering and daydreaming to intense and effortful internal focus. Relaxed daydreaming is potentially important for deriving and sifting through the social and emotional implications of everyday situations and relationships and connecting them to personal experiences and future goals (see also Baird, Smallwood, & Schooler, 2011); effortful internal focus is potentially important for making meaning of new information and for distilling creative, emotionally relevant connections between complex ideas. We use the term *constructive internal reflection* to describe this range of skills and behaviors in the hope that future research will flesh out and validate the dimensions of internally focused thought and their relation to psychological constructs such as attention, memory, abstract concepts, identity formation, critical thinking, and socioemotional development.

Future research could also address the possibility of individual differences in thinking during "rest" in the scanner, to explore the naturalistic thought patterns that individuals call up as they daydream idly or reflect purposefully, and relations to social behavior and other developmental outcomes. For a classic example, work by Mischel and others on self-control in children demonstrates the beneficial effects of strategic abstraction on the ability to delay immediate gratification (Mischel, Ebbesen, & Zeiss, 1972; Mischel, Shoda, & Rodriguez, 1989). Famously, four-year-olds who were able to distract themselves from eating a marshmallow when left alone with it, in order to successfully wait fifteen minutes to obtain a promised additional marshmallow (or other treat), later grew into more academically and socioemotionally competent adolescents and more successful adults than children who were unable to delay their gratification for a later reward (Mischel, Shoda, & Peake, 1988; Moffitt et al., 2011). Interestingly, though, differences in the thought strategies preschool children used to avoid eating the treat were associated with how long they were able to wait: children who distracted themselves and avoided looking at the marshmallow did relatively well. But children who instead imagined future and hypothetical possibilities, for example, focusing on how delicious the second marshmallow would taste, or imagining that the marshmallow in front of them was a cloud, delayed the longest (for reviews, see Mischel et al., 1989, 2011).

Building from these findings, in launching a research focus on constructive internal reflection our recommendation is that the new research build from work on the primacy of meaning making for human development—beginning with classic work by Frankl (1946/2006), Bruner (1990), Kegan (1982), Mezirow (2000), and others and continuing with more modern work (see Park, 2010, for a review). This work collectively recognizes the importance of revisiting and reorganizing one's memories to reconcile them with current experiences, in order to purposefully move forward with a productive, fulfilling life. These researchers' theories also universally recognize the role of internal reflection in this reconciliation process. But we would contend that neuroscientific studies hold the potential to offer a new view of this psychological landscape, as well as new tools to probe it—suggesting explanations and mechanisms for *why* meaning making requires reflection, as well as an early hypothesis about how development may be reshaped under conditions of systematically high environmental attention demands.

In conclusion, a new research focus is needed to formulate and explore the implications of the brain's DM functioning for psychological development. This research would more deeply probe the conditions under which internally and externally focused attention become active, as well as how the development of mechanisms for monitoring and shifting between these modes is shaped by experience, context, and biological predispositions. As therapists, teachers, and parents who discuss the benefits of "down time" well know, as does anyone who has had a creative insight in the shower: rest is indeed not idleness, nor is it a wasted opportunity for productivity. Rather, constructive internal reflection is potentially critical for learning from one's past experiences and appreciating their value for future choices, and for understanding and managing ourselves in the social world.

ACKNOWLEDGMENTS

We thank Denny Blodget, Ginger Clark, Antonio Damasio, David Daniel, Kaspar Meyer, Robert Rueda, Gale Sinatra, Jonathan Smallwood, Xiaofei Yang, and anonymous reviewers for their comments on an earlier version of the manuscript. M.H.I.-Y. was supported by the Brain and Creativity Institute Fund, by the Rossier School of Education, and by a grant from the Office of the Provost at the University of Southern California. V.S. was supported in part by a Valentine Award for graduate studies at the Psychology Department of USC. M.H.I.-Y. and V.S. were also supported by NIH grant P01 NS19632 to A. Damasio and H. Damasio.

REFERENCES

Abraham, A., Pocheptsova, A., & Ferraro, R. (2012). *The effect of mobile phone use on prosocial behavior* (Working paper). Available from: aabraham1@rhsmith.umd .edu

Andreasen, N. C., O'Leary, D. S., Cizadlo, T., Arndt, S., Rezai, K., Watkins, G. L., . . . Hichwa, R. D. (1995). Remembering the past: Two facets of episodic memory explored with positron emission tomography. *American Journal of Psychiatry*, *152*(11), 1576–1585.

Angstermichael, A., & Lester, F. (2010). An exploratory study of students' use of cell phones, texting and social networking sites. *Psychological Reports*, *107*(2), 402–404.

Baird, B., Smallwood, J., & Schooler, J. W. (2011). Back to the future: Autobiographical planning and the functionality of mind-wandering. *Consciousness and Cognition*, *20*(4), 1604–1611.

Beason-Held, L., Kraut, M., & Resnick, S. (2009). Stability of default-mode network activity in the aging brain. *Brain Imaging and Behavior*, *3*(2), 123–131.

Blakemore, S. J., & Frith, U. (2004). How does the brain deal with the social world? *Neuroreport*, *15*(1), 119–128.

Bluhm, R. L., Miller, J., Lanius, R. A., Osuch, E. A., Boksman, K., Neufeld, R. W., . . . Williamson, P. (2007). Spontaneous low-frequency fluctuations in the BOLD signal in schizophrenic patients: Anomalies in the default network. *Schizophrenia Bulletin*, *33*(4), 1004–1012.

Brackett, M. A., Rivers, S. E., Reyes, M. R., & Salovey, P. (2012). Enhancing academic performance and social and emotional competence with the RULER feeling words curriculum. *Learning and Individual Differences, 22*(2), 218–224. doi:10.1016/j.lindif.2010.10.002

Brefczynski-Lewis, J. A., Lutz, A., Schaefer, H. S., Levinson, D. B., & Davidson, R. J. (2007). Neural correlates of attentional expertise in long-term meditation practitioners. *Proceedings of the National Academy of Sciences, USA, 104*(27), 11483–11488.

Brewer, J. A., Worhunsky, P. D., Gray, J. R., Tang, Y.-Y., Weber, J., & Kober, H. (2012). Meditation experience is associated with differences in default mode network activity and connectivity. *Proceedings of the National Academy of Sciences, USA, 108*(50), 20254–20259.

Bruner, J. (1990). *Acts of meaning (four lectures on mind and culture—Jerusalem-Harvard Lectures)*. Cambridge, MA: Harvard University Press.

Buckner, R. L., Andrews-Hanna, J. R., & Schacter, D. L. (2008). The brain's default network: Anatomy, function, and relevance to disease. *Annals of the New York Academy of Sciences, 1124,* 1–38.

Buckner, R. L., & Carroll, D. C. (2007). Self-projection and the brain. *Trends in Cognitive Sciences, 11*(2), 49–57.

Buckner, R. L., Vincent, J. L. (2007). Unrest at rest: Default activity and spontaneous network correlations. *NeuroImage 37*(4), 1091–1096.

CASEL (Collaborative for Academic, Social, and Emotional Learning). (2007). *Background on social and emotional learning (SEL)*. CASEL Briefs. Retrieved from http://www.casel.org.

Castellanos, F. X., Margulies, D. S., Kelly, C., Uddin, L. Q., Ghaffari, M., Kirsch, A., . . . Milham, M. P. (2008). Cingulate-precuneus interactions: A new locus of dysfunction in adult attention-deficit/hyperactivity disorder. *Biological Psychiatry, 63*(3), 332–337.

Cherkassky, V. L., Kana, R. K., Keller, T. A., & Just, M. A. (2006). Functional connectivity in a baseline resting-state network in autism. *Neuroreport, 17*(16), 1687–1690.

Chiesa, A., Calati, R., & Serretti, A. (2010). Does mindfulness training improve cognitive abilities? A systematic review of neuropsychological findings. *Clinical Psychology Review, 31*(3), 449–464.

Christoff, K., Gordon, A. M., Smallwood, J., Smith, R., & Schooler, J. W. (2009). Experience sampling during fMRI reveals default network and executive system contributions to mind wandering. *Proceedings of the National Academy of Sciences, USA, 106*(21), 8719–8724.

Cohen, J. (2006). Social, emotional, ethical, and academic education: Creating a climate for learning, participation in democracy, and well-being. *Harvard Educational Review, 76*(2), 201–237.

Cole-Lewis, H., & Kershaw, T. (2010). Text messaging as a tool for behavior change in disease prevention and management. *Epidemiologic Reviews, 32*(1), 56–69.

Corbetta, M., & Shulman, G. L. (2002). Control of goal-directed and stimulus-driven attention in the brain. *Nature Reviews Neuroscience, 3*(3), 201–215.

Damasio, A., & Meyer, K. (2009). Consciousness: An overview of the phenomenon and of its possible neural basis. In S. Laureys and G. Tononi (Eds.), *The neurology of consciousness* (pp. 3–14). London: Elsevier.

Doria, V., Beckmann, C. F., Arichi, T., Merchant, N., Groppo, M., Turkheimer, F. E., . . . Edwards, A. D. (2010). Emergence of resting state networks in the preterm human brain. *Proceedings of the National Academy of Sciences, USA, 107*(46), 20015–20020.

Esposito, F., Bertolino, A., Scarabino, T., Latoffe, V., Blasi, G., Popolizio, T., . . . Di Salle, F. (2006). Independent component model of the default-mode brain function: Assessing the impact of active thinking. *Brain Research Bulletin, 70*(4–6), 263–269.

Etkin, A., Prater, K. E., Schatzberg, A. F., Menon, V., & Greicius, M. D. (2009). Disrupted amygdalar subregion functional connectivity and evidence of a compensatory network in generalized anxiety disorder. *Archives of General Psychiatry, 66*(12), 1361–1372.

Fair, D. A., Cohen, A. L., Dosenbach, N. U., Church, J. A., Miezin, F. M., Barch, D. M., . . . Schlaggar, B. L. (2008). The maturing architecture of the brain's default network. *Proceedings of the National Academy of Sciences, USA, 105*(10), 4028–4032.

Fan, J., McCandliss, B., Sommer, T., Raz, A., & Posner, M. (2002). Testing the efficiency and independence of attentional networks. *Journal of Cognitive Neuroscience, 14*(3), 340–347.

Fischer, K. W., & Bidell, T. (2006). Dynamic development of action and thought. In W. Damon & R. Lerner (Eds.), *Handbook of child psychology: Vol. 1. Theoretical models of human development* (6th ed., pp. 313–399). Hoboken, NJ: Wiley.

Fischer, K. W., & Immordino-Yang, M. H. (2002). Cognitive development and education: From dynamic general structure to specific learning and teaching. In E. Lagemann (Ed.), *Traditions of scholarship in education*. Chicago: Spencer Foundation.

Fox, M. D., Snyder, A. Z., Vincent, J. L., Corbetta, M., Van Essen, D. C., & Raichle, M. E. (2005). The human brain is intrinsically organized into dynamic, anti-correlated functional networks. *Proceedings of the National Academy of Sciences, USA, 102*(27), 9673–9678.

Frankl, V. E. (2006). *Man's search for meaning*. Boston, MA: Beacon Press. (Original work published 1946)

Fransson, P., Åden, U., Blennow, M., & Lagercrantz, H. (2011). The functional architecture of the infant brain as revealed by resting-state fMRI. *Cerebral Cortex, 21*(1), 145–154.

Fransson, P., Skiold, B., Horsch, S., Nordell, A., Blennow, M., Lagercrantz, H., & Aden, U. (2007). Resting-state networks in the infant brain. *Proceedings of the National Academy of Sciences, USA, 104*(39), 15531–15536.

Garrity, A. G., Pearlson, G. D., McKiernan, K., Lloyd, D., Kiehl, K. A., & Calhoun, V. D. (2007). Aberrant "default mode" functional connectivity in schizophrenia. *American Journal of Psychiatry, 164*(3), 450–457.

Gilbert, D. T., & Wilson, T. D. (2007). Prospection: Experiencing the future. *Science, 317*(5843), 1351–1354.

Greene, J. D., Sommerville, R. B., Nystrom, L. E., Darley, J. M., & Cohen, J. D. (2001). An fMRI investigation of emotional engagement in moral judgment. *Science, 293*(5537), 2105–2108.

Greicius, M. D., Flores, B. H., Menon, V., Glover, G. H., Solvason, H. B., Kenna, H., . . . Schatzberg, A. F. (2007). Resting-state functional connectivity in major depression: Abnormally increased contributions from subgenual cingulate cortex and thalamus. *Biological Psychiatry, 62*(5), 429–437.

Greicius, M. D., Krasnow, B., Reiss, A. L., & Menon, V. (2003). Functional connectivity in the resting brain: A network analysis of the default mode hypothesis. *Proceedings of the National Academy of Sciences, USA, 100*(1), 253–258.

Greicius, M. D., & Menon, V. (2004). Default-mode activity during a passive sensory task: Uncoupled from deactivation but impacting activation. *Journal of Cognitive Neuroscience, 16*(9), 1484–1492.

Hagmann, P., Cammoun, L., Gigandet, X., Meuli, R., Honey, C. J., Wedeen, V. J., & Sporns, O. (2008). Mapping the structural core of human cerebral cortex. *PLoS Biology, 6*(7), e159.

Harada, T., Li, Z., & Chiao, J. Y. (2010). Differential dorsal and ventral medial prefrontal representations of the implicit self modulated by individualism and collectivism: An fMRI study. *Social Neuroscience, 5*(3), 257–271.

Harrison, B. J., Pujol, J., López-Solà, M., Hernández-Ribas, R., Deus, J., Ortiz, H., . . . Cardoner, N. (2008). Consistency and functional specialization in the default mode brain network. *Proceedings of the National Academy of Sciences, USA, 105*(28), 9781–9786.

Hatcher, J. A., & Bringle, R. G. (1997). Reflection: Bridging the gap between service and learning. *College teaching, 45*(4), 153–158.

Hölzel, B. K., Ott, U., Hempel, H., Hackl, A., Wolf, K., Stark, R., & Vaitl, D. (2007). Differential engagement of anterior cingulate and adjacent medial frontal cortex in adept meditators and non-meditators. *Neuroscience Letters, 421*(1), 16–21.

Immordino-Yang, M. H. (2011). Me, myself and *you*: Neuropsychological relations between social emotion, self awareness, and morality. *Emotion Review, 3*(3), 313–315.

Immordino-Yang, M., McColl, A., Damasio, H., & Damasio, A. (2009). Neural correlates of admiration and compassion. *Proceedings of the National Academy of Sciences, USA, 106*(19), 8021–8026.

Immordino-Yang, M.H., Yang, X., Pavarini, G., & Schnall, S. (2013, November). *Spontaneous gaze aversion during interview-induced moral elevation predicts subsequent default-network activation.* Poster presented at the annual meeting of the Society for Neuroscience, San Diego, CA.

Immordino-Yang, M. H., & Singh, V. (2013). Hippocampal contributions to the processing of social emotions. *Human Brain Mapping, 34*(4), 945–955. doi:10.1002/hbm.21485

Immordino-Yang, M. H., & Sylvan, L. (2010). Admiration for virtue: Neuroscientific perspectives on a motivating emotion. *Contemporary Educational Psychology, 35*(2), 110–115.

Jenkins, A. C., & Mitchell, J. P. (2011). Medial prefrontal cortex subserves diverse forms of self-reflection. *Social Neuroscience, 6*(3), 211–218.

Jha, A. P., Krompinger, J., & Baime, M. J. (2007). Mindfulness training modifies subsystems of attention. *Cognitive Affective and Behavioral Neuroscience, 7*(2), 109–119.

Kamalipour, Y. (2010). *Media, power and politics in the digital age: The 2009 presidential election uprising in Iran.* Plymouth, UK: Rowman & Littlefield.

Kane, M. J., Brown, L. H., McVay, J. C., Silvia, P. J., Myin-Germeys, I., & Kwapil, T. R. (2007). For whom the mind wanders, and when: An experience-sampling study of working memory and executive control in daily life. *Psychological Science, 18*(7), 614–621.

Kegan, R. (1982). *The evolving self.* Cambridge, MA: Harvard University Press.

Kelley, W. M., Macrae, C. N., Wyland, C. L., Caglar, S., Inati, S., & Heatherton, T. F. (2002). Finding the self? An event-related fMRI study. *Journal of Cognitive Neuroscience, 14*(5), 785–794.

Kennedy, D. P., & Courchesne, E. (2008). Functional abnormalities of the default network during self- and other-reflection in autism. *Social Cognitive Affect Neuroscience, 3*(2), 177–190.

Kennedy, D. P., Redcay, E., & Courchesne, E. (2006). Failing to deactivate: Resting functional abnormalities in autism. *Proceedings of the National Academy of Sciences, USA, 103*(21), 8275–8280.

Kitayama, S., & Park, J. (2010). Cultural neuroscience of the self: Understanding the social grounding of the brain. *Social Cognitive and Affective Neuroscience, 5*(2–3), 111–129.

Koyama, M. S., Di Martino, A., Zuo, X.-N., Kelly, C., Mennes, M., Jutagir, D. R., . . . Milham, M. P. (2011). Resting-state functional connectivity indexes reading competence in children and adults. *Journal of Neuroscience, 31*(23), 8617–8624.

Li, Y., Liu, Y., Li, J., Qin, W., Li, K., Yu, C., & Jiang, T. (2009). Brain anatomical network and intelligence. *PLoS Computational Biology, 5*(5), e1000395.

Markus, H., & Kitayama, S. (1991). Culture and the self: Implications for cognition, emotion, and motivation. *Psychological Review, 98*(2), 224–253.

Mathur, V., Harada, T., & Chiao, J. Y. (2012). Racial identification modulates default network activity for same and other races. *Human Brain Mapping, 33*(8), 1883–1893. doi:10.1002/hbm.21330

McVay, J. C., & Kane, M. J. (2010). Does mind wandering reflect executive function or executive failure? Comment on Smallwood and Schooler (2006) and Watkins (2008). *Psychological Bulletin, 136*(2), 188–207.

Mezirow, J. (2000). *Learning as transformation: Critical perspectives on a theory in progress.* San Francisco, CA: Jossey-Bass.

Miller, S. L., Celone, K., DePeau, K., Diamond, E., Dickerson, B. C., Rentz, D., . . . Sperling, R. A. (2008). Age-related memory impairment associated with loss of parietal deactivation but preserved hippocampal activation. *Proceedings of the National Academy of Sciences, USA, 105*(6), 2181–2186.

Mischel, W., Ayduk, O., Berman, M. G., Casey, B. J., Gotlib, I. H., Jonides, J., . . . Shoda, Y. (2011). "Willpower" over the life span: Decomposing self-regulation. *Social Cognitive Affective Neuroscience, 6*(2), 252–256.

Mischel, W., Ebbesen, E. B., & Zeiss, A. R. (1972). Cognitive and attentional mechanisms in delay of gratification. *Journal of Personality and Social Psychology, 21*(2), 204–218.

Mischel, W., Shoda, Y., & Peake, P. K. (1988). The nature of adolescent competencies predicted by preschool delay of gratification. *Journal of Personality and Social Psychology, 54*(4), 687–696.

Mischel, W., Shoda, Y., & Rodriguez, M. (1989). Delay of gratification in children. *Science, 244,* 933–938.

Mitchell, J. P., Banaji, M. R., & Macrae, C. N. (2005). The link between social cognition and self-referential thought in the medial prefrontal cortex. *Journal of Cognitive Neuroscience, 17*(8), 1306–1315.

Moffitt, T. E., Arseneault, L., Belsky, D., Dickson, N., Hancox, R. J., Harrington, H., . . . Caspi, A. (2011). A gradient of childhood self-control predicts health, wealth, and public safety. *Proceedings of the National Academy of Sciences, USA, 108*(7), 2693–2698.

Northoff, G., Duncan, N. W., & Hayes, D. J. (2010). The brain and its resting state activity—experimental and methodological implications. *Progress in Neurobiology, 92*(4), 593–600.

Northoff, G., Heinzel, A., de Greck, M., Bermpohl, F., Dobrowolny, H., & Panksepp, J. (2006). Self-referential processing in our brain—a meta-analysis of imaging studies on the self. *NeuroImage, 31*(1), 440–457.

Ossandon, T., Jerbi, K., Vidal, J. R., Bayle, D. J., Henaff, M. A., Jung, J., . . . Lachaux, J. P. (2011). Transient suppression of broadband gamma power in the default-mode network is correlated with task complexity and subject performance. *Journal of Neuroscience, 31*(41), 14521–14530.

Oyserman, D., & Destin, M. (2010). Identity-based motivation: Implications for intervention. *The Counseling Psychologist, 38*(7), 1001–1043.

Oyserman, D., Terry, K., & Bybee, D. (2002). A possible selves intervention to enhance school involvement. *Journal of adolescence, 25*(3), 313–326.

Park, C. L. (2010). Making sense of the meaning literature: An integrative review of meaning making and its effects on adjustment to stressful life events. *Psychological Bulletin, 136,* 257–301.

Pew Research Center. (2010, December 20). *Global digital communication: Texting, social networking popular worldwide.* Retrieved February 22, 2012, from http://

www.pewglobal.org/2011/12/20/global-digital-communication-texting-social-net
working-popular-worldwide/

Posner, M. I., & Petersen, S. E. (1990). The attention system of the human brain. *Annual Review of Neuroscience, 13*, 25–42.

Posner, M. I., & Rothbart, M. K. (2005). Influencing brain networks: Implications for education. *Trends in Cognitive Sciences, 9*(3), 99–103.

Raichle, M. E., MacLeod, A. M., Snyder, A. Z., Powers, W. J., Gusnard, D. A., & Shulman, G. L. (2001). A default mode of brain function. *Proceedings of the National Academy of Sciences, USA, 98*(2), 676–682.

Ramirez, G., & Beilock, S. L. (2011). Writing about testing worries boosts exam performance in the classroom. *Science, 331*(6014), 211–213.

Rueda, M. R., Rothbart, M. K., McCandliss, B. D., Saccomanno, L., & Posner, M. I. (2005). Training, maturation, and genetic influences on the development of executive attention. *Proceedings of the National Academy of Sciences, USA, 102*(41), 14931–14936.

Seeley, W. W., Menon, V., Schatzberg, A. F., Keller, J., Glover, G. H., Kenna, H., . . . Greicius, M. D. (2007). Dissociable intrinsic connectivity networks for salience processing and executive control. *Journal of Neuroscience, 27*(9), 2349–2356.

Semple, R., Lee, J., Rosa, D., & Miller, L. (2010). A randomized trial of mindfulness-based cognitive therapy for children: Promoting mindful attention to enhance social-emotional resiliency in children. *Journal of Child and Family Studies, 19*(2), 218–229.

Smallwood, J., Beach, E., Schooler, J. W., & Handy, T. C. (2008). Going AWOL in the brain: Mind wandering reduces cortical analysis of external events. *Journal of Cognitive Neuroscience, 20*(3), 458–469.

Smallwood, J., Brown, K., Baird, B., & Schooler, J. W. (2011). Cooperation between the default mode network and the frontal-parietal network in the production of an internal train of thought. *Brain Research, 1428*, 60–70.

Smallwood, J., Fishman, D. J., & Schooler, J. W. (2007). Counting the cost of an absent mind: Mind wandering as an underrecognized influence on educational performance. *Psychonomic Bulletin and Review, 14*(2), 230–236.

Smallwood, J., Obonsawin, M., & Heim, D. (2003). Task unrelated thought: The role of distributed processing. *Consciousness and Cognition, 12*(2), 169–189.

Smallwood, J., & Schooler, J. W. (2006). The restless mind. *Psychological Bulletin, 132*(6), 946–958.

Smith, A. (2011, September 19). *Americans and text messaging.* Pew Research Center. Retrieved February 22, 2012, from http://pewinternet.org/Reports/2011/Cell-Phone-Texting-2011/Summary-of-Findings.aspx

Song, M., Liu, Y., Zhou, Y., Wang, K., Yu, C., & Jiang, T. (2009). Default network and intelligence difference. *Conference Proceedings IEEE Engineering in Medicine and Biology Society, 2009*, 2212–2215.

Spreng, R. N., & Grady, C. L. (2010). Patterns of brain activity supporting autobiographical memory, prospection, and theory of mind, and their relationship to the default mode network. *Journal of Cognitive Neuroscience, 22*(6), 1112–1123.

Spreng, R. N., Mar, R. A., & Kim, A. S. N. (2009). The common neural basis of auto-biographical memory, prospection, navigation, theory of mind, and the default mode: A quantitative meta-analysis. *Journal of Cognitive Neuroscience, 21*(3), 489–510.

Spreng, R. N., Stevens, W. D., Chamberlain, J. P., Gilmore, A. W., & Schacter, D. L. (2010). Default network activity, coupled with the frontoparietal control network, supports goal-directed cognition. *Neuroimage, 53*(1), 303–317.

Sreenivas, S., Boehm, S. G., & Linden, D. E. (2012). Emotional faces and the default mode network. *Neuroscience Letters, 506*(2), 229–234.

Stevens, C., Lauinger, B., & Neville, H. (2009). Differences in the neural mech-anisms of selective attention in children from different socioeconomic back-grounds: An event-related brain potential study. *Developmental Science, 12*(4), 634–646.

Supekar, K., Uddin, L. Q., Prater, K., Amin, H., Greicius, M. D., & Menon, V. (2010). Development of functional and structural connectivity within the default mode network in young children. *NeuroImage, 52*(1), 290–301.

Süssmuth, R. (2007). On the need for teaching intercultural skills. In M. Suárez-Orozco (Ed.), *Learning in the global era: International perspectives on globaliza-tion and education.* Berkeley, CA: University of California Press.

Tamir, D. I., & Mitchell, J. P. (2011). The default network distinguishes constru-als of proximal versus distal events. *Journal of Cognitive Neuroscience, 23*(10), 2945–2955.

Tang, Y. Y., Ma, Y. H., Wang, J., Fan, Y. X., Feng, S. G., Lu, Q. L., . . . Posner, M. I. (2007). Short-term meditation training improves attention and self-regulation. *Proceedings of the National Academy of Sciences, USA, 104*(43), 17152–17156.

Thomason, M. E., Chang, C. E., Glover, G. H., Gabrieli, J. D. E., Greicius, M. D., & Gotlib, I. H. (2008). Default-mode function and task-induced deactivation have overlapping brain substrates in children. *NeuroImage, 41*(4), 1493–1503.

Tomasi, D., & Volkow, N. (2012). Abnormal functional connectivity in children with attention-deficit/hyperactivity disorder. *Biological Psychiatry, 71*(5), 443–450.

Trapnell, P., & Sinclair, L. (2012, January). *Texting frequency and the moral shallow-ing hypothesis.* Poster session presented at the annual meeting of the Society for Personality and Social Psychology, San Diego, CA.

Uddin, L. Q., Kelly, A. M., Biswal, B. B., Margulies, D. S., Shehzad, Z., Shaw, D., . . . Milham, M. P. (2008). Network homogeneity reveals decreased integrity of default-mode network in ADHD. *Journal of Neuroscience Methods, 169*(1), 249–254.

van den Heuvel, M. P., Stam, C. J., Kahn, R. S., & Hulshoff Pol, H. E., 2009. Effi-ciency of functional brain networks and intellectual performance. *Journal of Neuroscience 29*(23), 7619–7624.

Wagner, A. D., Shannon, B. J., Kahn, I., & Buckner, R. L. (2005). Parietal lobe contributions to episodic memory retrieval. *Trends in Cognitive Sciences*, 9(9), 445–453.

Waytz, A., & Mitchell, J. P. (2011). Two mechanisms for simulating other minds. *Current Directions in Psychological Science*, 20(3), 197–200.

Whitfield-Gabrieli, S., Thermenos, H. W., Milanovic, S., Tsuang, M. T., Faraone, S. V., McCarley, R. W., . . . Seidman, L. J. (2009). Hyperactivity and hyperconnectivity of the default network in schizophrenia and in first-degree relatives of persons with schizophrenia. *Proceedings of the National Academy of Sciences, USA*, 106(4), 1279–1284.

Wig, G. S., Grafton, S. T., Demos, K. E., Wolford, G. L., Petersen, S. E., & Kelley, W. M. (2008). Medial temporal lobe BOLD activity at rest predicts individual differences in memory ability in healthy young adults. *Proceedings of the National Academy of Sciences, USA*, 105(47), 18555–18560.

Yeager, D. S., & Walton, G. M. (2011). Social-psychological interventions in education: They're not magic. *Review of Educational Research*, 81(2), 267–301.

Zhao, X. H., Wang, P. J., Li, C. B., Hu, Z. H., Xi, Q., Wu, W. Y., & Tang, X. W. (2007). Altered default mode network activity in patients with anxiety disorders: An fMRI study. *European Journal of Radiology*, 63(3), 373–378.

Zhou, Y., Liang, M., Tian, L., Wang, K., Hao, Y., Liu, H., . . . Jiang, T. (2007). Functional disintegration in paranoid schizophrenia using resting-state fMRI. *Schizophrenia Research*, 97(1–3), 194–205.

CHAPTER 3

Implications of Affective and Social Neuroscience for Educational Theory

Mary Helen Immordino-Yang

Chapter description: This chapter establishes links between educational theories of social learning and neurobiological research on how emotions evolved to promote survival. I wanted to propose to educators a neurobiological explanation for why we care so much about our social reputations and for why our social relationships and beliefs have such power to make us act. No animal but humans will act to defend the righteousness of its beliefs. Our social survival and our biological survival have been evolutionarily and developmentally intertwined in this late stage of our evolution. In effect, the legacy of our intelligent brain is our social and emotional mind.

ADVANCES IN SOCIAL AND AFFECTIVE NEUROSCIENCE: BRINGING NEUROSCIENTIFIC EVIDENCE TO INFORM EDUCATIONAL THEORY

Anyone involved in raising and educating children, from parents to teachers to coaches, mentors, and beyond, knows that social learning is a major force in children's development. That is, typical children watch and engage with other people, imitate other people's actions (including mental actions and beliefs), and look to trusted adults and peers for emotional and other feedback on their behavior. They imagine how other people feel and think, and those thoughts in turn influence how they feel and think.

Interestingly, evidence from social and affective neuroscience is shedding new light on the neural underpinnings of such social processing, affective responses, and their relation to learning. These new discoveries link body and mind, self and other, in ways that only poets have described in the past (Casebeer & Churchland, 2003). They dissolve traditional boundaries between nature and nurture in development (Immordino-Yang & Fischer, 2009) and underscore the importance of emotion in "rational" learning and decision making (Damasio, 2005; Haidt, 2001; Immordino-Yang & Damasio, 2007). The challenge now for educators is to reconcile the new neuroscientific findings with established educational theories, to discover how this new information can be used to improve teaching and learning.

Our Bodies, Our Minds; Our Cultures, Our Selves

Traditional Western views of the mind and body, such as that of Descartes, divorced high-level, rational thought from what were thought of as the basal, emotional, instinctual processes of the body (Damasio, 1994/2005). By contrast, recent work in affective and social neuroscience has revealed a new view of the mind. Far from divorcing emotions from thinking, this research collectively suggests that emotions, such as anger, fear, happiness and sadness, are cognitive and physiological processes that involve both the body and mind (Damasio et al., 2000). As such, they utilize brain systems for body regulation (e.g., for blood pressure, heart rate, respiration, digestion) and sensation (e.g., for physical pain or pleasure, for stomach ache). They also influence brain systems for cognition, changing thought in characteristic ways—from the desire to seek revenge in anger, to the search for escape in fear, to the receptive openness to others in happiness, to the ruminating on lost people or objects in sadness. In each case, the emotion is played out on the face and body, a process that is felt via neural systems for sensing and regulating the body. And in each case, these feelings interact with other thoughts to change the mind in characteristic ways and to help people learn from their experiences. Put simply, affective neuroscience is revealing that the mind is influenced by an interdependency of the body and brain; both the body and brain are involved, therefore, in learning (Immordino-Yang & Damasio, 2007).

Further, educators have long known that thinking and learning, as simultaneously cognitive and emotional processes, are carried out not in a vacuum but in social and cultural contexts (Fischer & Bidell, 2006). A major part of how people make decisions has to do with their past social experiences, reputation, and cultural history. Now, social neuroscience is revealing some of the basic biological mechanisms by which social learning takes place (Frith & Frith, 2007; Mitchell, 2008). According to current evidence, social processing and learning generally involve internalizing one's own subjective interpretations of other people's feelings and actions (Uddin, Iacoboni, Lange, & Keenan, 2007). We perceive and understand other people's feelings and actions in relation to our own beliefs and goals, and we vicariously experience these feelings and actions as if they were our own (Immordino-Yang, 2008). Just as affective neuroscientific evidence links our bodies and minds in processes of emotion, social neuroscientific evidence links our own selves to the understanding of other people.

For example, how do we know that the atrocities committed on 9/11/2001 are wrong? And why do most Americans have such a difficult time understanding how the terrorists were able to carry out these actions? We automatically, albeit many times nonconsciously, imagine how the passengers on those planes must have felt, empathically experiencing both what they were thinking about and their emotions around these thoughts. For many, just thinking of the images of planes hitting buildings induces a fearful mindset with all its physiological manifestations, like a racing heart and anxious thoughts. Similarly, we have difficulty empathizing with the terrorists who brought down the planes, because the values, morals, and emotions that motivated these men are so different from our own.

Human Nature, Human Nurture

From the perspective of affective neuroscience, the social emotions that motivated the terrorists, as well as those we experience when empathizing with the passengers, represent a uniquely human achievement, and one that is relevant to education: the ability to feel emotions and engage in actions about the vicariously experienced beliefs of another person. Social emotions and their associated thoughts and actions are biologically built but culturally shaped; they reflect our neuropsychological propensity to internalize the actions of others but are interpreted in light of our own social, emotional, and cognitive experiences. Put another way, human nature is to nurture and be nurtured. We act on our own accord but interpret and understand our choices by comparing them against the norms of our culture, learned through social, emotional, and cognitive experiences.

As is the case for basic emotions, the neural processes for experiencing and interpreting these various choices are not independent from our bodies. Instead, social emotions, though arguably a pinnacle human achievement, remain biologically grounded in our most basic physiological life-regulatory processing. The feeling of these emotions appears to modulate the neural systems that sense stomachache and regulate blood chemistry, for example.

Especially intriguing, these emotions also involve systems associated with visceral self-awareness that are related to consciousness. Quite literally, it appears that the ability to treat others as we would be treated relies on feeling the empathic welling in our throat or "punch" in our gut—feeling these on the substrate of our own psychological and bodily selves and interpreting them in light of personal experience and cultural knowledge, including that provided by education.

For example, let us take an educationally relevant problem—why does a student solve a physics problem? The reasons are fundamentally emotional and range from pleasing his parents, to the intrinsic reward of finding the solution, to avoiding punishment or the teacher's disapproval, to the desire to attend a good college. Each of these reasons involves an implicit or explicit social or emotional value judgment, as the student imagines how others would react to his behavior or how it would feel to solve the problem. And how does the student solve the problem? To apply problem-solving skills usefully in physics, the student must first motivate and engage himself sufficiently, must recognize the type of problem that is before him, and must call up information and strategies that will steer him toward a correct solution. Emotion plays a critical role in all of these stages of problem solving, helping the student to evaluate, either consciously or nonconsciously, which knowledge and skills are likely relevant and which will lead to a correct solution, based on his past learning. As he begins thinking through the solution, he is emotionally evaluating whether each cognitive step is likely to bring him closer to a useful solution or whether it seems to be leading him astray. From a neuropsychological perspective, the brain systems for emotion form the "rudder" that steers his thinking toward the development and recruitment of an effective skill (Immordino-Yang & Damasio, 2007), in this case for the solving of physics problems. Through regulating and inciting attention (Posner & Rothbart, 2005), motivation, and evaluation of possible social and cognitive outcomes, emotion serves to facilitate the student's recruitment of brain networks that support the skills he is developing. Here we use the example of solving a hypothetical physics problem, but the same mechanisms would be at play in the solving of other sorts of problems, too, such as deciding how to help one's friend or how to vote in a presidential election.

EMOTION (BODY AND MIND)
IN EDUCATIONAL CONTEXT

Schools are social contexts. Each school is a community that functions inside a broader culture, and the social and emotional experiences that children have as members of a school's culture will shape their cognitive learning (Rueda, 2006). Children's bodies, brains, and minds are meaningful partners in learning. Each child builds on his or her biological predispositions, his or her "nature," grappling with his or her own biological and psychological "self" as a platform on which to understand the thoughts and actions of other people, both peers and teachers.

When understood in this way, we can appreciate that even the driest, most logical academic learning cannot be processed in a purely rational way. Instead, the student's body, brain, and mind come together to produce cognition and emotion, which are subjectively intertwined as the student constructs culturally relevant knowledge and makes decisions about how to act and think.

Taken together, the neuroscientific evidence linking emotion, social processing, and self suggests a new approach to understanding how children engage in academic skills, such as reading and math. While such skills certainly have cognitive aspects, the reason that we engage in them, the importance we assign to them, the anxiety we feel around them, and the learning that we do about them are driven by the neurological systems for emotion, social processing, and self. Neuroscientific evidence suggests that we can no longer justify learning theories that dissociate the mind from the body, the self from social context. To learn, students empathically recognize the teacher's actions, thoughts, and goals, a process that reflects each student's own social and cognitive experiences and preferences. For example, to learn how to do a math problem, the students in the class must understand the goal of the exercise and be able to relate that goal to the teachers' actions and thoughts, as well as to their own skills and memories. Using their own experience as a platform, the students struggle to discern and reconstruct the teacher's often-times invisible mental actions in their own mind. This process is subjective, emotional, and grounded in each student's personal history.

AFFECTIVE AND SOCIAL NEUROSCIENCE AND EDUCATIONAL THEORY: A PLAN FOR THE FUTURE

Despite their obvious relevance to educational environments, for the findings described above to have their full impact, educators and neuroscientists need to debate the general principles that the findings reveal, in order to derive testable hypotheses for education. In bringing neuroscience to inform education, this updating of educational theory is often neglected. Many times, educators and neuroscientists alike, caught up in their zeal for new and exciting information and seeing the desperate need to improve education, overlook the importance of theory building. Take, for example, the Mozart effect—this sound scientific finding relating spatial ability to music listening was vastly misrepresented and misapplied as a learning tool. Attempting to move directly from brain research to educational innovation without passing through a theory-building stage limits the generalizability of the new tool and is sometimes even dangerous for children (Hirsh-Pasek & Bruer, 2007).

For education to truly benefit from these neuroscientific findings in a durable, deep way, for the full implications to become apparent, educators must examine closely the theory on which good practice is built, to reconcile the new and exciting evidence with established educational models and philosophies. For example, affective and social aspects of development are generally considered in examining curricula intended for young children. Affective and social neuroscience findings suggest, however, that emotion and cognition, body and mind, work together in students of all ages. Future research and theory in education should attempt to understand how best to characterize and capitalize on the emotional and social dimensions of learning in older students, including adults, keeping in mind what is known of the biological underpinnings of these processes.

In conclusion, there is a revolution imminent in education. The past decade has seen unprecedented advances in scientists' understanding of the brain and mind, and new information about the brain is expanding the influence of cognitive neuroscience into the classroom. The neuroscientific findings from affective and social neuroscience in particular could have profound implications for education, eventually leading to innovations in practice and policy. To discover these, we must lay the findings on the table for theoretical and philosophical debate. Irrespective of their scientific value, the individual brain findings are powerful for education only insofar as they suggest changes to our general knowledge of how learning and development happen. This is the next frontier for educational neuroscience. Neuroscientists and educators must work together to produce the Holy Grail: new ways of understanding development that have practical implications for the design of learning environments.

REFERENCES

Casebeer, W. D., & Churchland, P. S. (2003). The neural mechanisms of moral cognition: A multiple-aspect approach to moral judgment and decision-making. *Biology and Philosophy, 18*(1), 169–194.

Damasio, A. R. (2005). *Descartes' error: Emotion, reason and the human brain.* London: Penguin. (Original work published 1994)

Damasio, A. R. (2005). The neurobiological grounding of human values. In J. P. Changeux, A. R. Damasio, W. Singer, & Y. Christen (Eds.), *Neurobiology of human values* (pp. 47–56). London: Springer.

Damasio, A. R., Grabowski, T. J., Bechara, A., Damasio, H., Ponto, L. L., Parvizi, J., & Hichwa, R. D. (2000). Subcortical and cortical brain activity during the feeling of self-generated emotions. *Nature Neuroscience*, 3(10), 1049–1056.

Fischer, K. W., & Bidell, T. (2006). Dynamic development of action and thought. In W. Damon & R. Lerner (Eds.), *Handbook of child psychology*, Vol. 1: *Theoretical models of human development* (6th ed., pp. 313–399). Hoboken, NJ: Wiley.

Frith, C. D., & Frith, U. (2007). Social cognition in humans. *Current Biology*, 17(16), R724–R732.

Haidt, J. (2001). The emotional dog and its rational tail: A social intuitionist approach to moral judgment. *Psychological Review*, 108(4), 814–834.

Hirsh-Pasek, K., & Bruer, J (2007). The brain/education barrier. *Science*, 317, 1293.

Immordino-Yang, M. H. (2008). The smoke around mirror neurons: Goals as sociocultural and emotional organizers of perception and action in learning. *Mind, Brain, and Education*, 2(2), 67–73.

Immordino-Yang, M. H., & Damasio, A. R. (2007). We feel, therefore we learn: The relevance of affective and social neuroscience to education. *Mind, Brain and Education*, 1(1), 3–10.

Immordino-Yang, M. H., & Fischer, K. W. (2009). Neuroscience bases of learning. In V. G. Aukrust (Ed.), *International encyclopedia of education* (3rd ed.). Oxford, UK: Elsevier.

Mitchell, J. P. (2008). Contributions of functional neuroimaging to the study of social cognition. *Current Directions in Psychological Science*, 17(2), 142–146.

Posner, M. I., & Rothbart, M. K. (2005). Influencing brain networks: Implications for education. *Trends in Cognitive Sciences*, 9(3), 99–103.

Rueda, R. (2006). Motivational and cognitive aspects of culturally accommodated instruction: The case of reading comprehension. In D. M. McInerney, M. Dowson, & S. V. Etten (Eds.), *Effective schools*, Vol. 6: *Research on sociocultural influences on motivation and learning* (pp. 135–158). Greenwich, CT: Information Age Publishing.

Uddin, L. Q., Iacoboni, M., Lange, C., & Keenan, J. P. (2007). The self and social cognition: The role of cortical midline structures and mirror neurons. *Trends in Cognitive Sciences*, 11(4), 153–157.

PART II

WHAT INSIGHTS CAN AFFECTIVE NEUROSCIENCE OFFER ABOUT LEARNING AND TEACHING?

CHAPTER 4

Neuroscience Bases of Learning

Mary Helen Immordino-Yang and Kurt W. Fischer

Chapter description: This chapter was written as a general introduction to the process of relating studies of the brain to studies of learning. It argues for a conversation between neuroscientists and educators and makes clear that informed educators could be instrumental in shaping new questions for neuroscientists to pursue. The chapter also provides a conceptual overview of studies relating neuroscience to education in reading, math, memory, attention, and emotion. It takes a cautionary tone, laying out some of the potential dangers and pitfalls, as well as the educators' and scientists' responsibilities. Following Kurt Fischer's theoretical contributions, the chapter also emphasizes the dynamic nature of learning and the importance of considering individual and cultural variability in paths to skill acquisition. Children use whatever capacities they have to learn the most important skills they need, and although there is often a modal way of learning a specific skill, people can adapt their capacities to learn skills in diverse ways.

BEYOND "NEUROMYTHS": MIND, BRAIN, AND EDUCATION AS A CROSS-DISCIPLINARY FIELD

All human behavior and learning, including feeling, thinking, creating, remembering, and deciding, originate in the brain. Rather than a hardwired biological system, the brain develops through an active, dynamic process in which a child's social, emotional, and cognitive experiences organize his or her brain over time, in accordance with biological constraints and principles (Immordino-Yang, 2007; National Research Council, 1999). In the other direction, a child's particular neuropsychological strengths and weaknesses shape the way he or she perceives and interacts with the world. Like the weaving of an intricate and delicate web (Fischer & Bidell, 2006), physiological and cultural processes interact to produce learning and behavior in highly nuanced and complex patterns of human development.

People in the field of education often begin with a preconception that biology refers to traits that children are born with, that are fixed and unfold independent of experience, while children's social and cultural experiences, including schooling, are at the mercy of these biological predispositions, somehow riding on top of, but not influencing, biology. However, current research in neuroscience reinforces the notion that children's experiences shape their biology as much as biology shapes children's development. The fields of neuroscience and more broadly biology are leading education toward analyzing the dynamic relationship between nurture and nature in development and schooling. A more nuanced understanding of how biology and experience interact is critically relevant to education. As neuroscientists learn about which aspects of experience are most likely to influence biology and vice versa, educators can develop increasingly tailored educational experiences, interventions, and assessments.

Because of this bidirectional relationship between a child's biological predispositions and social and cognitive experiences, the fields of neuroscience and education are coming increasingly into a research partnership. This relationship can be studied at many levels of analysis, from the workings of genes inside cells to the workings of communities inside cultures (Shonkoff & Phillips, 2000). However, in order for new information about the brain and learning to influence the design of learning environments, teachers and others involved in educational policy and design need to know about the newest principles about the brain and learning. Likewise, neuroscientists need to investigate phenomena that are relevant to real-world learning and development. To these ends, a new field has gradually taken shape over the last few years: Mind, Brain, and Education. As a field, Mind, Brain, and Education encompasses educational neuroscience (a branch of neuroscience that deals with educationally relevant capacities in the brain), philosophy, linguistics, pedagogy, developmental psychology, and others.

In this interdisciplinary and applied climate, educators are in a particularly good position to help generate new questions and topics for research on learning and the brain, as they deal on a daily basis with the developmental issues and situations that affect real children and adults in their learning. For this reason, educators, including teachers, should have some familiarity with neuroscience and brain functioning, in order to become more informed "consumers" of educationally relevant findings, as well as, ideally, contributors who help identify and shape new questions for neuroscience to pursue. For example, teachers can use information on the development of networks for numeric processing to design more effective curricula to teach math concepts, and educational assessments of students' math learning can help to shape new scientific questions about the development of math networks.

However, this does not mean that neuroscience is capable of contributing insights into all educational problems. One of the challenges for the new field of Mind, Brain, and Education is for educators to learn about the applicability, implications, and limits of neuroscience research methods to various sorts of educational questions, and for neuroscientists at the same time to learn about the problems, issues, and processes of education, so that the two fields can collaborate as profitably as possible. For this to happen, educators and educational researchers need to know something about the tools, techniques, assumptions, and approaches that guide neuroscience research on learning and need to develop a critical ability to consume and digest neuroscience findings and evaluate them for their potential applicability in the classroom. Toward this goal, teacher-training programs are beginning to incorporate information about the science of learning into their course offerings, and several new graduate programs in Mind, Brain, and Education have launched at major universities in several countries in the last few years.

Before proceeding further, we felt the need to insert a strong cautionary note. As is typical during periods of rapid discovery, technological innovation, and theoretical advance, the field of Mind, Brain, and Education, as well as other related fields seeking to apply brain science to mainstream societal issues, are experiencing a lag between new technologies and findings, on the one hand, and the ability to interpret these findings on the other. In recent years, multiple examples of brain research misapplied have gone forward, including, for example, the overt labeling of elementary students as different categories of learners, from kinesthetic to auditory and beyond. Indeed, the scientific community agrees that much of what has been called "brain-based education" rests on very shaky ground. There is a proliferation of books written by nonscientists about the applications of neuroscience to learning, and while some of these books might present useful interpretations of neuroscience for educators, many of them suffer from a lack of basic understanding about the meaning and limitations of neuroscience research on learning and related processes. These books should be read with skepticism, as they often present models that are so oversimplified as to be misleading or even harmful or dangerous to children.

Overall, major changes in neuroscience research methods and theory are allowing better applicability of brain findings to educational issues and questions and new insights into the processes that happen in schools. Here we focus on the prominent contribution of neuroimaging to the current view of learning as the construction of distributed neural networks that support skills, and how the development and recruitment of these neural networks are modulated and facilitated by domain-general processes in the brain, including emotion, attention, and mechanisms of social learning. We conclude with a call for further research that evaluates neuroscientific principles as they play out in classroom contexts.

NEW NEUROSCIENCE METHODS BRING
NEW INFORMATION AND NEW CHALLENGES
FOR INTERPRETATION

Educators' views of brain research have shifted in the past few years. While many educators continue to cling to so-called neuromyths (Goswami, 2006), neuroscientists in the Mind, Brain, and Education field have been working to dispel these myths. In particular, the last decade has seen huge advances in in vivo neuroimaging technologies. Scientists are now able to study the workings of the human mind in healthy participants as they solve problems and perform other sorts of cognitive and emotional tasks in real time. Availability of these new research technologies is pushing the field forward at an unprecedented pace; hardly a week goes by, it seems, without a picture of the brain appearing on the cover of a major magazine or in a major newspaper article.

To make sense of the new findings, it is critical that educators understand the logic and constraints in the neuroscience research underlying these articles. While neuroimaging techniques differ in their specifics, there are three main approaches. The first approach involves measuring and localizing changes in the flow of blood in the brain as subjects think in different ways, under the assumption that changes in regional blood flow are indicative of changes in neural activity. The second approach involves measuring the electrical activity of the brain, generated by the firing of networks of neurons (brain cells). The third approach involves measuring changes in the anatomy and structure of the brain. In conjunction or separately, these techniques can be used to study the neurological correlates of a wide variety of tasks, such as reading, math, or social processing, as well as developmental changes (for reviews, see Katzir & Pare-Blagoev, 2006; Thatcher, North, & Biver, 2008).

While these recent advances in neuroimaging have had a profound effect on the field of neuroscience and its potential relevance to education, it is important to remember that new technological capabilities inevitably come with limitations. For example, in functional magnetic resonance imaging (fMRI), the changes in regional blood flow in the brain associated with a particular task of interest are not absolute but either implicitly or explicitly calculated from comparisons between a target and a control task. The design of the two tasks and the differences between them are critical to the findings and interpretation. When one brain area is reported to "light up" (i.e., to become more active) for a particular task, this does not mean that the "lighted" brain area is the only area actively processing. Instead, this means that this particular area was relatively more active for this task than for the control task. Many other areas are certainly actively involved but are equivalently active in the two conditions. In reality, a network of neural areas always supports the skill being tested. Because educators are concerned with supporting the development of coherent functional skills rather than isolated brain areas, it is essential that neuroimaging findings be correctly interpreted before any attempt can be made to apply them in the classroom.

EDUCATIONAL SKILLS ARE SUPPORTED BY SPECIALIZED NEURAL NETWORKS

Nonetheless, the advent of neuroimaging has precipitated major advances in neuroscientists' understanding of how the brain works. In the past, the neuroscientific localization tradition prevailed; that is, cognitive functions were mapped onto specific locations in the brain, as much as possible in one-to-one correspondence. However, neuroscientists now understand that learning involves the development of connections between networks of brain areas, spread across many regions of the brain. This means that while specific brain areas do carry out characteristic kinds of processing, skills for real-world and academic tasks are embodied in the networks they recruit, rather than in any one area of the brain. For example, there is no "music," "reading," or "math" area of the brain that is not also involved in processing many other skills and domains (culturally constructed areas of knowledge).

Instead of one brain area, learning involves actively constructing neural networks that functionally connect many brain areas. Because of the constructive nature of this process, different learners' networks may differ, in accordance with the person's neuropsychological strengths and predispositions and with the cultural, physical, and social context in which the skills are built (Immordino-Yang, 2008). There are various routes to effective skill development, for example, in reading (Fischer, Bernstein, & Immordino-Yang, 2007) or math (Singer, 2007). The job of education is to provide support for children with different neuropsychological profiles to develop effective yet flexible skills (Immordino-Yang, 2007; Rose & Meyer, 2006). Children use whatever capacities they have to learn the most important skills in their lives, and although there is often a modal way of learning a specific skill, people can adapt their capacities to learn skills in diverse ways. For example, Knight and Fischer (1992) found that young children followed one of three pathways in learning to read words. In a related vein, in studying two high-functioning adolescent boys who had recovered from the surgical removal of half of their brain, Immordino-Yang (2007 [see Chapter 7]) found that each boy had compensated for weaknesses by transforming important neuropsychological skills into new ones that suited his remaining strengths.

Neural Networks for Mathematics

One area that has seen much advance in the past few years is the study of neurological networks underlying processing for mathematics and number representation. Overall, the findings suggest that networks for processing in math are built from networks for the representation of quantity that start in infancy—one for the approximate representation of numerosity (numeric quantity), and one for exact calculation using numbers (Izard, Dehaene-Lambertz, & Dehaene, 2008). These networks are further organized and differentiated with development and training in math concepts (Singer, 2007). For example, preschoolers go beyond innate number systems to build a mental number line, gradually adding one digit at a time (Le Corre, Van de Walle, Brannon, & Carey, 2006).

Interestingly, this math network shares many processing areas and features with language processing, including reading. Current research is exploring how math processing relates to other domains, such as spatial representation (Hubbard, Piazza, Pinel, & Dehaene, 2005), as well as the development of math networks in atypically developing populations, such as children with learning disabilities.

Neural Networks for Reading

Another area of concentrated research interest is the study of reading development, both in typically developing and in dyslexic children. Acquiring literacy skills impacts the functional organization of the brain (Petersson, Silva, Castro-Caldas, & Reis, 2007), differentially recruiting networks for language, visual, and sound representation in both hemispheres, as well as increasing the amount of white matter tissue connecting brain areas. Work on individual differences in the cognitive paths to reading has enriched the interpretation of the neurological research (e.g., Knight & Fischer, 1992) and helped to bridge the gap between the neuroscience findings and classroom practice (Katzir & Pare-Blagoev, 2006; Wolf & O'Brien, 2006). In dyslexic readers, progress is being made toward better understanding of the contributions of rapid phonological processing (Gaab, Gabrieli, Deutsch, Tallal, & Temple, 2007; Simos et al., 2000), orthographic processing (Bitan et al., 2007), and visual processing to reading behaviors, as well as to thinking in other domains (Boets, Wouters, van Wieringen, Smedt, & Ghesquière, 2008). For example, the visual field of dyslexics may show more sensitivity in the periphery and less in the fovea compared to nondyslexics, leading to special talents in some dyslexics for diffuse pattern recognition (Schneps, Rose, & Fischer, 2007). Most recently, research looking at developmental differences in neurological networks for reading across cultures has begun to appear (e.g., Cao et al., 2009), which ultimately may contribute to knowledge about how different kinds of reading experiences shape the brain.

The neural networks for learning reading and math have important impli-cations for education, as the most effective lessons implicitly scaffold the development of brain systems responsible for the various component skills. For example, successful math curricula help students to connect skills for calculation with those for the representation of quantity, through scaffolding the development of such mental structures as the number line (Carey & Sar-necka, 2006; Griffin, 2004; Le Corre et al., 2006). While different students will show different propensities for the component skills, all students will ultimately need to functionally connect the brain systems for quantity and calculation to be successful in math.

DOMAIN-GENERAL AND EMOTION-RELATED PROCESSES ENABLE LEARNING

The brain is a dynamic, plastic, experience-dependent, social, and affective organ. Because of this, the centuries-long debate over nature versus nurture is an unproductive and overly dichotomous approach to understanding the complexities of the dynamic interdependencies between biology and culture in development. New evidence highlights how humans are fundamentally social and symbolic beings (Herrmann, Call, Hernandez-Lloreda, Hare, & Tomasello, 2007), and just as certain aspects of our biology, including our genetics and our brains, shape our social, emotional, and cognitive propensi-ties, many aspects of our biology, including processes as fundamental as body growth, depend on adequate social, emotional, and cognitive nurturance. Learning is social, emotional, and shaped by culture!

For a stark example of this interdependence between biology, social inter-action, and cognitive stimulation, in their work with Romanian orphans Nelson et al. (2007) found that cognitive, social, and physical growth were delayed in institutionalized children relative to their peers raised in foster or biological families. Although the institutionalized children's basic physical needs were met, the lack of high-quality social interaction and cognitive stim-ulation led these children not to thrive.

Overall, while educators often focus on neural networks for domain-specific skills like reading and math, domain-general and emotion-related networks function as modulators and facilitators of memory and domain-specific learn-ing. These networks include emotion, social processing, and attention.

Emotion and Social Processing

One cutting-edge area of research in neuroscience is the study of affective and social processing. All good teachers know that the way students feel, includ-ing their emotional states (e.g., stressed vs. relaxed, depressed vs. enthusias-tic) and the state of their bodies (e.g., whether they are sick or well, whether they have slept enough, whether they have eaten), are critical factors affecting learning. In addition, it is now becoming increasingly evident that emotion plays a fundamental role not only in background processes like motivation for learning but also in moment-to-moment problem solving and decision making. That is, emotion forms the rudder that steers learners' thinking, in effect helping them to call up information and memories that are relevant to the topic or problem at hand (Immordino-Yang & Damasio, 2007 [see Chap-ter 1]). For example, as a student solves a math problem, she is emotionally evaluating whether each cognitive step is likely to bring her closer to a useful solution or whether it seems to be leading her astray.

From a neurobiological perspective, emotional processing in the brain depends on somatosensory systems—the systems in the brain responsible for sensing the state of the viscera and body (Adolphs, Damasio, Tranel, Cooper, & Damasio, 2000; Damasio et al., 2000). These systems can reflect actual changes to the state of the body during emotions (i.e., increased heart rate during fearful states, or a feeling of having been "kicked in the stomach" when hearing bad news), or they can reflect simulated body states, conjuring how the viscera and body *would* feel, without actually imposing those phys-iological changes onto the body (Damasio, 1994/2005). Through regulating and inciting attention, motivation, and evaluation of simulated or actual out-comes, emotion serves to modulate the recruitment of neural networks for domain-specific skills, for example, for math or reading. In this way, cognition and emotion in the brain are "two sides of the same coin," and most of the thought processes that educators care about, including memory, learning, and creativity, among others, critically involve both cognitive and emotional aspects (Fischer & Bidell, 2006; Immordino-Yang & Damasio, 2007 [see Chapter 1]).

In addition, social processing in the brain is strongly interrelated with the processing of emotion. People's behavior is organized and influenced by cultural factors and the social context, which in turn reflect experience and learning. For example, many of the reasons the student above solves her math problem relate to the emotional aspects of her social relationships and cultural goals—the way her parents will feel about her behavior, or her desire to go to college. In turn, she feels the influences of these cultural constructs as emotional reactions that play out in her body and mind and predispose her to think in particular ways (for more, see also Chapter 2).

But how does this student internalize or predict the emotional reactions of her parents? Interestingly, research over the past decade has revealed glimmers of the workings of a basic biological system for internalizing the actions, emotions, and goals of others, in order to learn from, empathize with, and influence others in social contexts (Immordino-Yang, 2008; Oberman, Pineda, & Ramachandran, 2007). Specifically, it appears that watching other people's actions and inferring their emotions and implicit goals recruit some of the same neural systems involved in planning and carrying out those actions in one's own self. This discovery was dubbed "mirroring" by its discoverers (di Pellegrino, Fadiga, Fogassi, Gallese, & Rizzolatti, 1992; Gallese, Fadiga, Fogassi, & Rizzolatti, 1996; Umiltà et al., 2001), and while neural systems for "mirroring" do not tell the whole story of the neurological system for social learning, current research suggests that they afford an important low-level mechanism on which social and cultural learning can build. (For more on mirroring and mirror neurons in learning and implications for education, see Chapter 8.)

Memory and Attention: Conjuring One's Own Reality

To understand the current state of research on memory and attention, it is helpful to first discuss current views on how reality is constructed in the mind and brain, and the relationship of this process to perception. Work in various areas of neuroscience, for example, in vision or somatosensory perception and location of the body in space, has shown that, unlike the often predominant intuitive view, we humans do not construct reality directly from our perception of the environment, as if we were equipped with some sort of internal video camera (for an interesting discussion, see Ramachandran, 1998). Instead, our prior learning, our neuropsychological predispositions, and the current context heavily influence the reality that we construct and experience. That is, "reality" is never perceived directly from the environment. Instead, we construct "reality" based on our own best guesses, interpretations, and expectations. For a trite but illustrative example, imagine why visual illusions work: our visual system uses context and prior experience with the world to construct images that incorporate our "best guesses" about the color, form, movement, and identity of what is actually in front of our eyes.

Related to this, our memories do not reflect the "objective" replaying of an actual occurrence but, rather, our iterative mental reconstruction of an event, fact, or procedure, for example, the skills to solve a math problem, or a student's conversation with her teacher about her test grade. This means that the iterative reconstruction or mental conjuring of a remembered event will be very similar to the neural processes for imagining an event that never happened or for simulating possible outcomes of future events. Notably, each of these processes is organized by our emotions and reflects the subjective meaningfulness and relevance of the remembered, imagined, or simulated thought, as well as the social, physical, biological, and developmental contexts in which the person is operating. Given all these factors, it is no wonder that different teachers and learners perceive, experience, and remember lessons and educational contexts in different ways!

Another process that is related to the study of memory and emotion, and that is an important prerequisite for the recruitment of neural networks, is attention. The last decade marks theoretical and methodological advances in the study of attention and its relationship to the development of academic skills (Corbetta & Shulman, 2002). In particular, Posner and his colleagues have distinguished three different attentional networks important for learning: networks for alerting, orienting, and executive attention (for a review, see Posner & Rothbart, 2007). Posner and colleagues have also shown that individual differences in attention networks can be related to genetic and environmental factors and that training in these aspects of outwardly directed attention, that is, the ability to regulate one's focus on different aspects of the environmental context, can improve preschoolers' academic abilities in various areas, such as reading skills and social interaction at school (Berger, Kofman, Livneh, & Flenik, 2007). Future work should investigate how attention monitoring can be taught in schools, as a way to increase the efficiency with which neural networks are built and recruited.

BACK TO THE BIG PICTURE:
MIND, BRAIN, AND EDUCATION ARE
BECOMING USEFULLY CONNECTED

Over a decade ago, John Bruer cautioned educators that, given the current state of knowledge, directly connecting brain science and education was premature—a "bridge too far" (Bruer, 1997). But, much has happened since then to narrow the chasm between these two sources of knowledge about development and learning. A new field has been established whose aim is to further knowledge about children's learning by bringing together methods and evidence from various fields, among them neuroscience, psychology, cognitive science, and education.

In this stimulating climate, it is important that new neuroscience advances be carefully examined in light of psychological, developmental, and pedagogical theory and research, to ensure that the field proceeds with caution as well as optimism toward educational innovation. In the past, techniques and ideas from so-called brain-based education have led to the formation of neuromyths—oversimplified, misunderstood, or misapplied notions whose integration into educational contexts is unjustified and, in some cases, detrimental or even dangerous (Goswami, 2006). Instead, findings from neuroscience must be carefully implemented and evaluated, starting in educational microcosms such as research schools, where students and faculty partner with cognitive neuroscientists in the design and assessment of research.

In conclusion, it is an exciting time for the field of Mind, Brain, and Education and for studying the neuroscientific bases of learning. In the end, learning happens primarily in the brain; studying the neuroscientific bases of learning can therefore provide educationally relevant insights that, with careful implementation and evaluation, may improve schools and other learning environments for the generations to come.

GLOSSARY

Domain: A culturally constructed area of knowledge, such as language, math, music, or social interaction.

Neural network: A set of neurons that are structurally and functionally interconnected so that they activate in coherent patterns associated with mental functions.

Neuroimaging: A variety of research techniques, some invasive and some not, concerned with measuring and mapping the physiology and structure of the brain.

Neuromyth: A misguided, oversimplified, or incorrect tenet in education that concerns the brain or neuroscience.

Skill: An ability to behave or think in an organized way in a particular context.

REFERENCES

Adolphs, R., Damasio, H., Tranel, D., Cooper, G., & Damasio, A. R. (2000). A role for somatosensory cortices in the visual recognition of emotion as revealed by three-dimensional lesion mapping. *Journal of Neuroscience, 20*(7), 2683–2690.

Berger, A., Kofman, O., Livneh, U., & Flenik, A. (2007). Multidisciplinary perspectives on attention and the development of self-regulation. *Progress in Neurobiology, 82*(5), 256–286.

Bitan, T., Burman, D. D., Chou, T. L., Lu, D., Cone, N. E., Cao, F., . . . Booth, J. R. (2007). The interaction between orthographic and phonological information in children: An fMRI study. *Human Brain Mapping, 28*(9), 880–891.

Boets, B., Wouters, J., van Wieringen, A., Smedt, B. D., & Ghesquière, P. (2008). Modelling relations between sensory processing, speech perception, orthographic and phonological ability, and literacy achievement. *Brain and Language, 106*(1), 29–40.

Bruer, J. (1997). Education and the brain: A bridge too far. *Educational Researcher, 26*(8), 4–16.

Cao, F., Peng, D., Liu, L., Jin, Z., Fan, N., Deng, Y., & Booth, J. R. (2009). Developmental differences of neurocognitive networks for phonological and semantic processing in Chinese word reading. *Human Brain Mapping, 30*(3), 797–809.

Carey, S., & Sarnecka, B. W. (2006). The development of human conceptual representations: A case study. In Y. Munakata & M. H. Johnson (Eds.), *Processes of change in brain and cognitive development*. Oxford, UK: Oxford University Press.

Corbetta, M., & Shulman, G. L. (2002). Control of goal-directed and stimulus-driven attention in the brain. *Nature Neuroscience Reviews, 3*, 210–215.

Damasio, A. R. (2005). *Descartes' error: Emotion, reason and the human brain*. London: Penguin. (Original work published 1994)

Damasio, A. R., Grabowski, T. J., Bechara, A., Damasio, H., Ponto, L. L., Parvizi, J., & Hichwa, R. D. (2000). Subcortical and cortical brain activity during the feeling of self-generated emotions. *Nature Neuroscience, 3*(10), 1049–1056.

di Pellegrino, G., Fadiga, L., Fogassi, L., Gallese, V., & Rizzolatti, G. (1992). Understanding motor events: A neurophysiological study. *Experimental Brain Research, 91*(1), 176–180.

Fischer, K. W., Bernstein, J. H., & Immordino-Yang, M. H. (Eds.). (2007). *Mind, brain and education in reading disorders*. Cambridge, UK: Cambridge University Press.

Fischer, K. W., & Bidell, T. (2006). Dynamic development of action and thought. In

W. Damon & R. Lerner (Eds.), *Handbook of child psychology*, Vol. 1: *Theoretical models of human development* (6th ed., pp. 313–399). Hoboken, NJ: Wiley.

Gaab, N., Gabrieli, J. D. E., Deutsch, G. K., Tallal, P., & Temple, E. (2007). Neural correlates of rapid auditory processing are disrupted in children with developmental dyslexia and ameliorated with training: An fMRI study. *Restorative Neurology and Neuroscience*, 25(3–4), 295–310.

Gallese, V., Fadiga, L., Fogassi, L., & Rizzolatti, G. (1996). Action recognition in the premotor cortex. *Brain*, 119, 593–609.

Goswami, U. (2006). Neuroscience and education: From research to practice? *Nature Reviews Neuroscience*, 7(5), 406–411.

Griffin, S. (2004). Building number sense with Number Worlds: A mathematics program for young children. *Early Childhood Research Quarterly*, 19(1), 173–180.

Herrmann, E., Call, J., Hernandez-Lloreda, M. V., Hare, B., & Tomasello, M. (2007). Humans have evolved specialized skills of social cognition: The cultural intelligence hypothesis. *Science*, 317(5843), 1360–1366.

Hubbard, E. M., Piazza, M., Pinel, P., & Dehaene, S. (2005). Interactions between number and space in parietal cortex. *Nature Reviews Neuroscience*, 6(6), 435–448.

Immordino-Yang, M. H. (2007). A tale of two cases: Lessons for education from the study of two boys living with half their brains. *Mind, Brain and Education*, 1(2), 66–83.

Immordino-Yang, M. H. (2008). The smoke around mirror neurons: Goals as sociocultural and emotional organizers of perception and action in learning. *Mind, Brain, and Education*, 2(2), 67–73.

Immordino-Yang, M. H., & Damasio, A. R. (2007). We feel, therefore we learn: The relevance of affective and social neuroscience to education. *Mind, Brain and Education*, 1(1), 3–10.

Izard, V., Dehaene-Lambertz, G., & Dehaene, S. (2008). Distinct cerebral pathways for object identity and number in human infants. *PLoS Biology*, 16(2), e11. doi:10.1371/journal.pbio.0060011

Katzir, T., & Pare-Blagoev, J. (2006). Applying cognitive neuroscience research to education: The case of literacy. *Educational Psychologist*, 41(1), 53–74.

Knight, C., & Fischer, K. W. (1992). Learning to read words: Individual differences in developmental sequences. *Journal of Applied Developmental Psychology*, 13, 377–404.

Le Corre, M., Van de Walle, G., Brannon, E. M., & Carey, S. (2006). Re-visiting the competence/performance debate in the acquisition of counting as a representation of the positive integers. *Cognitive Psychology* (52), 130–169.

National Research Council. (1999). *How people learn: Brain, mind, experience, and school*. Washington, DC: National Academy Press.

Nelson, C. A., Zeanah, C. H., Fox, N. A., Marshall, P. J., Smyke, A. T., & Guthrie, D. (2007). Cognitive recovery in socially deprived young children: The Bucharest early intervention project. *Science*, 318, 1937–1940.

Oberman, L. M., Pineda, J. A., & Ramachandran, V. S. (2007). The human mirror neuron system: A link between action observation and social skills. *Social, Cognitive and Affective Neuroscience, 2*(1), 62–66.

Petersson, K. M., Silva, C., Castro-Caldas, A., & Reis, A. (2007). Literacy: A cultural influence on functional left-right differences in the inferior parietal cortex. *European Journal of Neuroscience, 26*(3), 791–799.

Posner, M. I., & Rothbart, M. K. (2007). Research on attention networks as a model for the integration of psychological science. *Annual Review of Psychology, 58,* 1–23.

Ramachandran, V. (1998). *Phantoms of the brain: Probing the mysteries of the human mind.* New York, NY: William Morrow.

Rose, D. H., & Meyer, A. (Eds.). (2006). *A Practical Reader in Universal Design for Learning.* Cambridge, MA: Harvard Education Press.

Schneps, M. H., Rose, T. L., & Fischer, K. W. (2007). Visual learning and the brain: Implications for dyslexia. *Mind, Brain, and Education, 1*(3), 128–139.

Shonkoff, J. P., & Phillips, D. A. (Eds.). (2000). *From neurons to neighborhoods: The science of early childhood development.* Washington, DC: National Academy Press.

Simos, P. G., Breier, J. I., Fletcher, J. M., Foorman, B. R., Bergman, E., Fishbeck, K., & Papanicolaoua, A. C. (2000). Brain activation profiles in dyslexic children during non-word reading: A magnetic source imaging study. *Neuroscience Letters, 290*(1), 61–65.

Singer, F. M. (2007). Beyond conceptual change: Using representations to integrate domain-specific structural models in learning mathematics. *Mind, Brain, and Education, 1*(2), 84–97.

Thatcher, R. W., North, D. M., & Biver, C. J. (2008). Development of cortical connections as measured by EEG coherence and phase delays. *Human Brain Mapping, 29*(12), 1400–1415.

Umiltà, M. A., Kohler, E., Gallese, V., Fogassi, L., Fadiga, L., Keysers, C., & Rizzolatti, G. (2001). I know what you are doing: A neurophysiological study. *Neuron, 31*(1), 155–165.

Wolf, M., & O'Brien, B. (2006). From the Sumerians to images of the reading brain: Insights for reading theory and intervention. In G. Rosen (Ed.), *The dyslexic brain.* Timonium, MD: York Press.

CHAPTER 5

The Role of Emotion and Skilled Intuition in Learning

Mary Helen Immordino-Yang and Matthias Faeth

Chapter description: This chapter examines a long tradition of research using a clever game originally invented to study patients whose brain damage prevents them from adequately utilizing emotion to learn, and to investigate via these patients' performance Antonio Damasio's somatic marker hypothesis. The task, called the Iowa Gambling Task, has been used by Antoine Bechara and his collaborators to demonstrate that as people learn about a new task, they accrue subtle emotional markers of success and failure—in effect, embodied implicit memories or "somatic markers." These memories come to steer subsequent behavior, making individuals avoid situations and choices that previously resulted in failure. Subconscious "hunches" at first, over time people can become explicitly aware of the rules governing the game. Though both patients and healthy participants eventually infer the rules and learn to predict which moves will be risky and which will be safer, only the healthy participants can use these predictions to advantageously steer their subsequent choices.

Here, we reexamine the findings about how emotional hunches accrue with experience into "skilled intuitions" that form the basis for implementing procedural knowledge. We then forge connections to school-based learning and pedagogical practice. We argue that, although its influence during learning may not be openly visible, emotion stabilizes the direction of a learner's decisions and behaviors over time, helping the learner to steer toward strategies that have worked well in similar situations in the past. In this way, implicit emotional memories are an integral part of learning and thinking.

WHAT DO EDUCATORS NEED TO KNOW
ABOUT THE EMOTIONAL BRAIN?

Advances in neuroscience have been increasingly used to inform educational theory and practice. However, while the most successful strides forward have been made in the areas of academic disciplinary skills such as reading and mathematical processing, a great deal of new evidence from social and affective neuroscience is prime for application to education (Immordino-Yang & Damasio, 2007; Immordino-Yang & Fischer, 2009). In particular, social and affective neuroscience are revealing more clearly than ever before the interdependence between cognition and emotion in the brain, the importance of emotion in guiding successful learning, and the critical role of teachers in managing the social environment of the classroom so that optimal emotional and cognitive learning can take place (vanGeert & Steenbeek, 2008). The message from social and affective neuroscience is clear: no longer can we think of learning as separate from or disrupted by emotion, and no longer can we focus only at the level of the individual student in analyzing good strategies for classroom instruction. Students and teachers are socially interacting and learning from one another in ways that cannot be done justice by examining only the "cold" cognitive aspects of academic skills. Like other forms of learning and interacting, building academic knowledge involves integrating emotion and cognition in social context. Academic skills are "hot," not "cold"!

BEYOND NEUROMYTHS

In this chapter, we aim to help educators move beyond the oversimplified and oftentimes misleading "neuromyths" that have abounded in education (Goswami, 2004, 2006), replacing these with a set of strategies for fostering the sound development of academic emotions (Pekrun, Goetz, Titz, & Perry, 2002) through the use of emotionally relevant and socially contextualized educational practices (Brackett, Rivers, Shiffman, Lerner, & Salovey, 2006). These strategies are not taken directly from the details of neuroscience findings, as drawing such a direct connection would be inappropriate and premature. Instead, we interpret these findings to present a neuroscientific view of the functionality of emotions in learning new information, and we build from this discussion a set of socially embedded educational practices that teachers can use to improve the emotional and cognitive aspects of classroom learning.

Before we proceed, we would like to insert a strong cautionary note. While the emerging field of Mind, Brain, and Education is making strong strides toward informing educational practice with neuroscientific findings, it is important to maintain a cautious stance (Fischer et al., 2007). Too often in education, out of the sincere desire to understand and help students, educators have grabbed onto various "brain-based" teaching strategies that are based either in misunderstandings or in misapplications of neuroscientific information to education. The teaching and popular press literatures are rife with examples, from the overt labeling of elementary school students as different categories of learners, such as kinesthetic or auditory, to the notion that young babies should listen to Mozart to develop better spatial cognition. At best, these neuromyths have wasted monetary or other educational resources; at worst, they may even have been harmful or dangerous to children.

Here, we take a different approach. Rather than presenting details about brain systems and findings that are not directly relevant to the question of how best to educate children, we instead aim to interpret findings from a body of neuroscience research that has made use of a very productive paradigm for studying the emotional and body-related signals underlying learning. This paradigm, known as the Iowa Gambling Task (IGT), was designed by Antoine Bechara and others some years ago (Bechara, Damasio, Tranel, & Damasio, 2005), and it has taught neuroscientists a great deal about the formative role of emotions in cognition and learning. In this chapter, we aim to distill what neuroscientists have learned into a series of neuroscience-based recommendations about emotion and learning in social context that can inform teachers' practice. These recommendations are likely to be reliable and usable, because they reflect not one experiment or brain area but a consensus on the principles of brain functioning that has accumulated from several years of neuroscientific experimentation and debate.

To do this, we first describe the IGT and the important insights it has revealed into the role of nonconscious emotional "intuition" in successful, efficient learning. We present a typical participant's performance in this paradigm to illustrate the reliable patterns that have been revealed through the many emotion and learning experiments that have made use of this paradigm, and we interpret this typical pattern in light of various researchers' findings with normal and brain-damaged patients. We then go on to describe how interference with emotional processing during learning, due either to the intrusion of other emotions irrelevant to the task at hand or, in extreme cases, to damage of relevant brain regions, can interfere with the building of sound emotional intuitions that guide skilled, rational behavior. In the second half of the chapter, we explicitly address strategies that teachers can use to help students manage and skillfully recruit their emotions in the service of meaningful learning, building from what the neuroscience experiments have taught us. The overall aim of the first part of the chapter is to describe five contributions from neuroscience research that have taught neuroscientists about the relationship between emotion and cognition in learning and that we feel have important implications for teaching in social settings such as schools. The overall aim of the second half of the chapter is to distill the implications of these contributions into a series of three strategies that could be used to improve teaching and learning in schools. We hope this chapter, taken together, will guide teachers in beginning to incorporate meaningful emotional experiences into their students' learning.

The Brain and Learning: Why Does Emotion Matter?

Consider the following intriguing scenario from the Iowa Gambling Task (IGT): A participant in a study is seated at a table with a card game before her. Her task is to choose cards from four decks. With each card she draws she has the chance to win some amount of money. Unbeknownst to her, some decks contain cards with larger wins than other decks, but these decks also result in occasional enormous losses that make these decks a bad choice in the long run. How does a typical person learn to play this game and deduce the "cognitive" rules for calculating and weighing the relative long-term outcomes of the different decks? The answer to this question relies on five reasons why emotions matter for learning.

Reason 1: Emotion Guides Cognitive Learning

In examining our IGT player's performance, we will see that the process of learning how to play this game involves both emotional and cognitive processing and begins with the development of (generally) nonconscious emotional "intuitions" that eventually become conscious "rules" that she can describe in words or formulas. The development and feeling of these intuitions are critical for successful, usable knowledge to be constructed. As she begins the game, she at first randomly selects cards from one deck or another, noting wins and losses as they come. But soon, before she is even consciously aware that the decks are biased, she begins to show an anticipatory emotional response in the moment before choosing a card from a high-risk deck (her palms begin to sweat in microscopic amounts, measured as galvanic skin response). Nonconsciously, she is accumulating emotional information about the relative riskiness of some decks. As she proceeds, this emotional information steers her toward the "safe" decks and away from those with high gains but the possibility of large losses. After playing for a while longer she accumulates enough information about the decks that she is able to describe the rule about which decks to play and which to avoid, and we would say that she has "learned."

The IGT and other experiments have taught neuroscientists about the importance of emotion in the learning process, an importance that probably applies not just here but to math learning, social learning, and learning in various other arenas in which a person must accumulate information from his or her experiences and use this information to act advantageously in future situations (Bechara & Damasio, 1997). Emotion is guiding the learning of our participant much like a rudder is guiding a vessel or airplane (Immordino-Yang & Damasio, 2007). Though it and its influence may not be openly visible, emotion is providing a force that is stabilizing the direction of a learner's decisions and behaviors over time and helping the learner to recognize and call up relevant knowledge—for example, knowledge about which deck to pick from or which math formula to apply.

Reason 2: Emotional Contributions to Learning Can Be Conscious or Nonconscious

In the example of the IGT, the anticipatory emotional response guiding the participant's choice is not present from the very beginning but must be slowly learned with experience playing the game. Although she understands that she is engaging in a game of chance with uncertain outcomes, our participant at first has no information—intuitive or factual—that might help her to distinguish between the decks. As she draws, she will at first surely be attracted to the large-gain/large-loss decks—as long as she is experiencing the delivery of higher rewards. At this stage, she will already be developing a nonconscious emotional reaction to these decks: one of excitement and attraction. It is only after her first encounter with an enormous loss that her reaction will change, rapidly shifting from excitement to disappointment. Was this an isolated event? Or should she learn from it and adjust her future choices accordingly? From now on, she will not draw from these decks in the same way as before. She will likely continue to draw from the high-risk deck occasionally, feeling tempted by the higher rewards, but she will do so while at the same time fearing to be punished again for her risk taking. As we can see, her emotional rudder is steering her behavior and teaching her about the decks, making her reluctant to reach for the risky decks, helping her to overcome the temptation of higher rewards, and giving her the energy and impetus to think twice. And as the neuroscience experiments show, all this can be happening underneath the level of her conscious awareness; she may still report that she does not know yet how to play the game or what to expect from the different decks. Only her nonconscious palm sweating gives away the hidden force of her emotional learning at this early point in the learning process.

Reason 3: Emotional Learning Shapes Future Behavior

Having an emotional rudder is helpful when playing the IGT, but it is just as helpful in many other situations we encounter—both inside schools and out. Consider the third-grade student who incorrectly solves a math problem and receives a red X on his paper or, alternatively, correctly solves the problem and gets a good grade. Consider the community college student whose essay draft misses the mark or who raises his hand in class and gets an encouraging nod from the instructor. Just as we saw for the IGT player, the learners' emotional reactions to the outcomes of their behavioral choices become implicitly attached to the cognitive knowledge about the domain—here, either class or math or essay writing. These academic activities are no longer neutral to the learner; they become "risky" and uncomfortable or else exciting and challenging, depending in part on the learner's emotional interpretation of the outcome. In each of these examples, the learner's emotional reaction to the outcome of his efforts consciously or nonconsciously shapes his future behavior, inciting him either to behave in the same way the next time or to be wary of situations that are similar.

Reason 4: Emotion Is Most Effective at Facilitating the Development of Knowledge When It Is Relevant to the Task at Hand

In the context of schools, emotion is often considered ancillary or secondary to learning, rather than an integral part of the knowledge being learned. We expect children, for example, to "get their feelings out of the way" so that they can focus on their studies. In this view, emotions are seen as a disruptive force, antagonistic to good cognition, and in need of regulation and suppression in the interest of mature judgment—be it with respect to social dilemmas such as how to treat your friends, moral dilemmas such as dealing with an instance of cheating (Haidt, 2001), or cognitive dilemmas such as deciding which equation to apply to a problem in math class (Immordino-Yang & Fischer, 2009). However, as the IGT task demonstrates, neuroscience is revealing that rather than working to eliminate or "move beyond" emotion, the most efficient and effective learning incorporates emotion into the cognitive knowledge being built. In effect, efficient learners build useful and relevant "intuitions" that guide their thinking and decision making

(Damasio, 1994/2005; Immordino-Yang & Damasio, 2007). These intuitions integrate their emotional reactions with their cognitive processing and incorporate what has been learned from experience. These intuitions are not randomly generated nonconscious whims—critically, because they are shaped and organized by experience with a task or domain, they are specific and relevant to the particular contexts in which they are learned.

But how can we distinguish between relevant and irrelevant emotions, and how does this distinction play out in academic learning? To understand how the development of the emotional rudder can go wrong, let's return again to the example above. How effectively would the gambler described above learn the game if she were so anxious that she could not "feel" the subtle emotional changes telling her about the valence of the decks? Alternatively, what if she were so excited about an upcoming football game that she could not concentrate on the task at hand? In both cases, she would clearly have an emotional reaction, but with respect to the task it would be a static and invariable one. She would be anxious or excited independent of the particular deck she had drawn from—and independent of the particular outcome obtained. In both of these examples, she would quite possibly not learn to effectively distinguish the different decks based on her emotional intuition because all decks would be experienced with the same type of undifferentiated emotionality. Her learning of the game would fail. Taken together, these examples show that effective learning does not involve *removing* emotion; rather, it involves skillfully cultivating an emotion state that is relevant and informative to the task at hand.

Reason 5: Without Emotion, Learning Is Impaired

To bring home the importance of emotion in the learning process, consider now an alternate scenario: a different person is gambling in the task and trying to win the money. However, this person is a neurological patient with damage to an area of the brain that lies just above the eyes (the ventromedial prefrontal cortex) and intermediates between the feeling of the body during emotion and the learning of cognitive strategies. How would this person's performance differ? This patient has perfectly intact cognitive abilities; she solves logic problems and does fine on standardized IQ tests. Will she be able to learn how to play the game successfully, though, given that her choice of cognitive strategy cannot be subtly informed by her nonconscious emotional reactions to risky decks? Maybe getting emotion out of the way will clear the way for a more direct assessment of the game's rules?

Sadly, this is not the case. The patient would start out just like the typical person, randomly selecting cards from one deck or another. However, instead of developing the anticipatory emotional response that would tell her about the differential riskiness of the decks, her emotional reaction to choosing the cards would not inform her future choices. While normal participants gradually shift to picking from the "safe" decks, the ventromedial prefrontal cortex patient would remain attracted to the large-gain/large-loss decks, picking from them at least as often as from the "safe" decks. Although she would notice that some decks produce high losses, and although she would feel disappointed when these losses occurred, she would not use this information to guide her future game-playing strategy. Most normal participants are able to identify a conscious rule about which decks to play and which ones to avoid by the time they have picked a total of eighty cards. And even the normal participants who fail to fully and correctly state the rule have developed an advantageous pattern of choosing from the decks by then. But among the group of ventromedial prefrontal cortex patients things look very different: they continue to choose disadvantageously *even if* they succeed in identifying a conscious rule about which decks to play and which ones to avoid. Put another way, they never successfully learn to play the game. Their conscious knowledge, emotional reactions, and cognitive strategies are not integrated or aligned. The result is that these patients are unable learn from their experiences, and unable to use what they may consciously appear to "know." (Notably, this deficit extends into the decisions these patients make in their daily lives; these patients are unable to effectively manage their lives as they did prior to sustaining brain injury and must be constantly supervised.)

How does this apply to the argument at hand? What this means for the interaction of emotion and cognition is that factual knowledge alone is useless without a guiding emotional intuition. Some ventromedial prefrontal patients know very well which decks are good and which are bad, but this information has no relevance for them when it comes to making decisions. And students in the classroom struggle with very much the same problem: if they feel no connection to the knowledge they learn in school, the academic content will seem emotionally meaningless to them; even if they manage to regurgitate the factual information, it will lay barren and without any influence on their decisions and behavior. Sure, unlike the ventromedial prefrontal patients they have the capacity to develop emotional reactions to the material they learn. But if the design of the curriculum does not allow the teacher to support the development of emotional reactions, if emotions are not taken seriously when they occur and are not given appropriate room to influence decisions and thinking in the classroom, then the effective integration of emotion and cognition in learning will be compromised just as it is for the group of patients. For good cognition to manifest in the classroom and beyond, emotions need to be an honored part of the learning experience all along.

STRATEGIES TO BRING EMOTIONS
BACK INTO CLASSROOM LEARNING

Here we offer three strategies that teachers might apply in the classroom to help facilitate students' development of emotional thought in academic contexts.

Strategy 1: Foster Emotional Connection to the Material

The first and possibly most important strategy that teachers can use to foster meaningful learning through emotion is to design educational experiences that encourage relevant emotional connection to the material being learned. This fostering of emotional connection can start with the selection of the topic to be explored itself. Sometimes teachers may have some leeway in deciding which specific topics to present and how to engage the students in these topics. Why not, in a serious and responsible manner, involve students in these selection processes? For example, if the topic to be covered involves learning about ancient Rome, why not allow the students some choice as to whether to write and perform a play about key events, to write research reports about these events, or to design a model senate that mimics that of the early Romans? When the students are involved in designing the lesson, they become clearer on the goal of the lesson and more emotionally invested in and attached to the learning outcomes. This participatory approach has the power to instill in them a sense of ownership that can go a long way toward making the later learning meaningful and the emotions they experience relevant.

In addition, teachers can make room to relate the material to the life of the students and to students' interests. This relating can take the form of showing how what will be learned can affect their everyday experiences, or it can again rely on the students themselves to identify and probe possible connections. As much as possible, students can be encouraged to follow their interests and passions, with the teacher helping them to see the relevance and usefulness of the academic material to these choices. How, for example, did Julius Caesar feel and think about issues like wars that are as relevant today as they were then? When students are encouraged to engage in and identify with the academic material in a meaningful way, the emotional intuitions they develop will be more relevant to the decision making that faces them in their everyday lives.

Another effective tool from the viewpoint of emotional engagement is teaching students to solve open-ended problems, because these problems allow the students to wrestle with the definition of the task itself, recruiting their intuitive knowledge regarding relevance, familiarity, creativity, and interest in the process (Ablin, 2008). Portfolio, project, and group work, although usually more closely guided, can also turn out to be effective in enabling these emotional aspects of thought. In general, teachers should strive to design activities that create space—space for emotional reactions to appear, along with space to safely make mistakes and learn from them. This likely means breaking away from a highly prescriptive approach that aims to move students along the fastest and most direct way toward mastering specific content, because this fast and direct way will often be emotionally impoverished. It is in the detours and missteps, as well as in refinding the path, that rich emotionality is played out, that valuable emotional memories are accumulated, and that a powerful and versatile emotional rudder is developed. In times of standardized testing and curricula packed to the brim it might sound like sacrilege, but from an affective neuroscientific perspective, the direct and seemingly most efficient path turns out to be inefficient, leading too often to heaps of factual knowledge poorly integrated into and therefore ineffective for students' real lives.

Strategy 2: Encourage Students to Develop Smart Academic Intuitions

Once a topic is chosen, teachers should encourage their students to use their own intuitions when engaging in learning and problem solving activities in the classroom. From a neuroscientific perspective, intuition can be understood as the incorporation of the nonconscious emotional signal into the knowledge being acquired. Thinking back to the IGT, normal participants playing the game begin to show signals of emotional unease before choosing from risky decks; only eventually does this emotional reaction become incorporated into the participants' conscious understanding of the rules for playing the game. That is, even before the participant can consciously describe the rules, she has nonconscious "intuitions" about how things will turn out when she chooses from one or the other card decks. As we have seen, the development of these experience-based intuitions increasingly guides her decision making and eventually organizes the formation of conscious, cognitive rules for the game—in educational language, she has "learned"!

Just as the IGT participant needs a collection of both positive and negative experiences to help her learn the relevance of the different decks and the implications for the choices she should make, students must be offered adequate chances for the development and feeling of experience-based intuitions about how and when to use the academic material: "Is the use of this mathematical procedure warranted in this instance?" "Am I getting closer to the correct solution?" Students' private (or collective) reflections on questions such as these are critical to the development of useful, generalizable, memorable knowledge. And, at their base, answering these questions requires integrating emotional with cognitive knowledge to produce skilled intuitions—the kind of intuitions that will transfer to other academic and real-life situations.

While it is understandable that teachers feel pressured to help their students learn a lot of information as quickly as possible, and while it is true that, at least initially, students may be slower to build the full representation of the material, neuroscience suggests that in the long run it may be more effective for teachers to judiciously build into their curricula opportunities for the development of skilled intuition.Without the development of sound intuitions undergirding their representations, it is likely that the students will not remember the material in the long-term, and that even if they remember it in an abstract sense, they will have difficulty applying it to novel situations.

Strategy 3: Actively Manage the Social and Emotional Climate of the Classroom

In addition to the importance of the students' learning activities, the development of students' intuitions also depends on the social aspects of the classroom climate. While allowing for the development of skilled intuition is important, simply having the space to make mistakes will not be enough, since students will allow themselves to experience these failures only if they can do so in an atmosphere of trust and respect. It is here that the classroom climate and the social relationships between the teacher and students have crucial contributions to make.

Faced with the challenge of bringing positive emotions back into the classroom, teachers may feel tempted to take the easy route and stir up students' emotions in artificial and non-task-related ways, such as by telling jokes, showing cartoons, doling out prizes, or turning a blind eye to students acting out. And indeed, a carefully timed dose of humor or incentive can certainly help students to invest in the classroom culture as an enjoyable place to belong. Such activities can also go a long way in helping students to feel safe in expressing and learning from their mistakes, and in building social cohesion among the students and between the students and the teacher—necessary ingredients of engaged learning.

At the same time, the task-irrelevant emotions that activities such as contests and jokes are designed to generate may actually interfere with students' ability to feel the subtle emotional signals that steer the development and application of new conceptual knowledge. As we saw in the IGT, overanxious, overexcited, or distracted participants may have trouble learning the game. For emotion to be useful, it has to be an integral part of knowing when and how to use the skill being developed. Especially in young learners or in students whose engagement or connection to academic learning is tenuous, the emotional signals that undergird skilled intuition could easily be drowned out.

And so, effective teachers are faced with a balancing act. On the one hand, task-irrelevant emotions oftentimes serve an important initial role in establishing a safe and enjoyable social climate in the classroom. On the other hand, too much task-irrelevant emotion can undermine the development of students' ability to feel appropriately emotional about their academic learning. For teachers to effectively manage the social-emotional climate of their classroom, they must strike a balance between these two kinds of emotion by actively managing the emotions of their students, helping the learners to attend to, trust, and thrive on the subtle emotional signals they are slowly building as they accumulate meaningful academic experiences. As learners become more emotionally skilled, task-irrelevant emotional activities can fade, leaving actively engaging emotional learning experiences in their place.

A NEUROSCIENTIFIC PERSPECTIVE ON EMOTIONS, INTUITIONS, AND LEARNING

In conclusion, a rich body of recent neuroscience has demonstrated the interrelatedness of emotions and cognition and the importance of emotion in rational thought (Greene, Sommerville, Nystrom, Darley, & Cohen, 2001; Haidt, 2001; Immordino-Yang, 2008). Yet, much of contemporary educational practice considers emotion as ancillary or even as interfering with learning. In this chapter, we discussed the critical role of emotion in learning and showed that students' accumulation of subtle emotional signals guides their meaningful learning, helping them to build a set of academic "intuitions" about how, when, and why to use their new knowledge. Rather than trying to remove emotions from the learning context, teachers can use this neuroscientific perspective to actively orchestrate an emotional climate in the classroom that is conducive to feeling these subtle emotional signals. As students learn to notice and refine these signals, their learning will become more relevant and meaningful, and ultimately more generalizable and useful in their everyday lives.

REFERENCES

Ablin, J. L. (2008). Learning as problem design versus problem solving: Making the connection between cognitive neuroscience research and educational practice. *Mind, Brain, and Education, 2*(2), 52–54.

Bechara, A., & Damasio, H. (1997). Deciding advantageously before knowing the advantageous strategy. *Science, 275*(5304), 1293–1295.

Bechara, A., Damasio, H., Tranel, D., & Damasio, A. R. (2005). The Iowa Gambling Task and the somatic marker hypothesis: Some questions and answers. *Trends in Cognitive Sciences, 9*(4), 159–162.

Brackett, M. A., Rivers, S. E., Shiffman, S., Lerner, N., & Salovey, P. (2006). Relating emotional abilities to social functioning: A comparison of self-report and performance measures of emotional intelligence. *Journal of Personality and Social Psychology, 91*(4), 780–795.

Damasio, A. R. (2005). *Descartes' error: Emotion, reason and the human brain.* London: Penguin. (Original work published 1994)

Fischer, K. W., Daniel, D. B., Immordino-Yang, M. H., Stern, E., Battro, A., & Koizumi, H. (2007). Why *Mind, Brain, and Education?* Why now? *Mind, Brain and Education, 1*(1), 1–2.

Goswami, U. (2004). Neuroscience and education. *British Journal of Educational Psychology, 74*, 1–14.

Goswami, U. (2006). Neuroscience and education: From research to practice? *Nature Reviews Neuroscience, 7*(5), 406–411.

Greene, J. D., Sommerville, R. B., Nystrom, L. E., Darley, J. M., & Cohen, J. D. (2001). An fMRI investigation of emotional engagement in moral judgment. *Science, 293*(5537), 2105–2108.

Haidt, J. (2001). The emotional dog and its rational tail: A social intuitionist approach to moral judgment. *Psychological Review, 108*(4), 814–834.

Immordino-Yang, M. H. (2008). The smoke around mirror neurons: Goals as sociocultural and emotional organizers of perception and action in learning. *Mind, Brain, and Education, 2*(2), 67–73.

Immordino-Yang, M. H., & Damasio, A. R. (2007). We feel, therefore we learn: The relevance of affective and social neuroscience to education. *Mind, Brain and Education, 1*(1), 3–10.

Immordino-Yang, M. H., & Fischer, K. W. (2009). Neuroscience bases of learning. In V. G. Aukrust (Ed.), *International encyclopedia of education* (3rd ed.). Oxford, UK: Elsevier.

Pekrun, R., Goetz, T., Titz, W., & Perry, R. P. (2002). Academic emotions in students' self-regulated learning and achievement: A program of qualitative and quantitative research. *Educational Psychologist, 37*(2), 91–105.

vanGeert, P., & Steenbeek, H. (2008). Brains and the dynamics of "wants" and "cans" in learning. *Mind, Brain, and Education, 2*(2), 62–66.\

CHAPTER 6

Musings on the Neurobiological and Evolutionary Origins of Creativity via a Developmental Analysis of One Child's Poetry

Mary Helen Immordino-Yang
with poems by Nora Ming-Min Yang

Chapter description: This short essay was written to accompany a republication of Immordino-Yang and Damasio (2007 [see Chapter 1]). Working together with my daughter, I analyzed her poems to illustrate how emotions and relationships organize even young children's early disciplinary (here, scientific) learning. Creativity, I argue, is basically what happens when learners bring relational, emotional knowledge to bear as they make meaning of technical, academic information.

As Antonio Damasio and I discuss in the article "We feel, therefore we learn: The relevance of affective and social neuroscience to education" (see Chapter 1), all human thoughts and actions, and especially creative or innovative thoughts and actions, bear the shadow of the brain's original, evolutionary purpose—to keep one's body alive and functioning comfortably, efficiently, and appropriately in the world. Although neuroscience may simply confirm what experience has taught us, the evidence is plain: our brains sense the insides of our bodies not only to regulate their mechanics, for example, to adjust blood pressure and digestion appropriately to maintain our health, but also to play out the subjective, experiential dimensions of our social and emotional lives. We think something, consciously or not, and sometimes our brains adjust our physiology to reflect the emotional implications of that thought. Then, we may feel the results of those embodied changes, as a source of information about our own reaction. Neuroimaging experiments show us that we use the very same neural systems to feel our bodies as to feel our relationships, our moral judgments, and our creative inspiration. We really do live by "gut feelings," and of course these gut feelings are induced and felt by our brains in accordance with our beliefs, experience, and knowledge.

And yet, you might ask, what sense does it make to put creativity on an equal footing with survival? How, for example, could anyone find comfort and efficiency in crawling into a damp black cave in southern France to spit chewed pigments on entombed rock faces in patterns portraying wild beasts? Or how could a contemporary human find fulfillment in gazing at a gibbous moon on a clear night, wondering about the other side and what the view from there might be like, staring off into the blackness of space? And aside from *how* humans could do these things, *why* do we feel compelled to do them?

The short answer is that, as we became the most socially interdependent mammals known to exist, the mechanisms we evolved to survive in the physical world seem to have been co-opted to manage our well-being in the social world. Survival in the savanna depends on a brain that is wired to make sense of the environment and to play out the things it notices through patterns of bodily and mental reactions. Something catches our eye—we feel a jolt of adrenaline: is that a poisonous snake or a vine? This same brain, the same logic, helps us make sense of and survive in the social world of today. Does that look on my teacher's face suggest displeasure or approval? Will this poem I have written convey to others the essence of my experience? With all the interrelating, mind reading, and empathizing that we do with each other, and even with the moon when we so indulge ourselves, comes a drive to express ourselves, to understand and move others to live something from our own life, to assign meaning and purpose to the activities we engage in, the products we create, and the concepts we learn. The health of our social identity is every bit as important as our physical well-being because we *feel* them both on the same neural platforms. Why did that cave painter slither along that dank rock on his belly in the dark? Perhaps it had something to do with the satisfaction that comes from immortalizing one's own experiences, from affirming oneself by representing the feelings and thoughts witnessed by that self for someone, sometime, to see. After all, behind every painting or poem or essay or physics equation is a painter, a poet, a writer, a physicist—a real person, alive in both the biological and sociocultural senses, who is hoping to influence others' understanding by virtue of representing her own. What current neuroscience findings are showing us is that the feeling of creating, the satisfaction it provides, may get its inspirational power by virtue of its connections to the mechanisms that promote and feel our bodily survival and satisfaction, in the most basic, literal sense.

The poems included here provide an anecdotal but instructive example of how one child's developing understanding of the physical and social worlds are intertwined as she creates, just as they must have been for that mysterious cave painter from long ago. These poems were written on her own, just because she wanted to write them. You might even assert that she was *compelled* to write them, by virtue of the evolutionary origins of her modern, social mind, because just like all humans before this young author, and all who will come, what social and affective neuroscientific studies are revealing is that the legacy of our intelligent brain is our social mind. By virtue of its evolutionary connection to bodily feeling and survival, our social mind motivates us to create things that represent the meaning we have made by processes of noticing, feeling, and understanding, so that others can notice, feel, and understand what we have. While of course our bodies can no sooner live without food, water, and warmth than they ever could, these necessities alone are no longer sufficient for us. Our biological drives are co-opted over the course of cognitive development into a platform for making sense of the world in increasingly complex ways. We must *understand*, we must *know*, we must *share* our experiences. What follows is an analysis of one girl's maturing attempt to do these things.

Poem 1. Untitled, Age 6 Years 2 Months

Oh Teddy we love you mor then the whole rth sis as the rth spins evry day we love you as much as u shewell but sum timse evine mor as you mac us proud and happy tha chyr you!

[Oh Teddy we love you more than the whole earth size. As the earth spins every day we love you as much as usual, but sometimes even more, as you make us proud and happy that you're you!]

This poem was written as a song, with a melody, and was accompanied by a drawing of the author with a music stand singing to her brother, Teddy (Figure 6.1). What I love about this poem (song) is that it demonstrates so nicely the interdependence of emotion and even rudimentary disciplinary knowledge in learning. How does this little girl express the love and pride of her family for her little toddler brother—the love that she feels both biologically and socially? She references her newly acquired, simple knowledge

FIGURE 6.1. The poem in its original presentation.

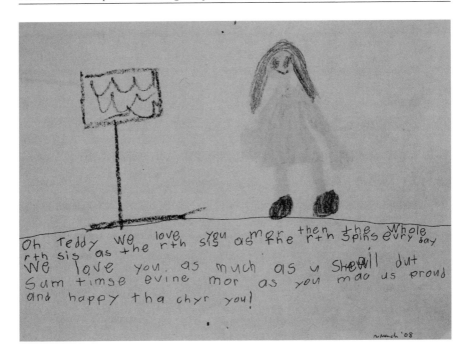

Oh Teddy we love you as mere then the Whole
rth sis as the rth sis as the rth spins evry day
We love you. as much as u She will dut
Sum timse evine mor as you mao us proud
and happy tha chyr you!

of planetary science. She likens the vastness of her feelings to the size of the biggest thing she can think of—the earth—and the endurance of the family's love over time to the constancy of the earth spinning to make days. In the end, this is both a poem about a family's love for their baby and one about the author's understanding of the planet she lives on.

Poem 2. Age 7 Years 3 Months

Universe

The stars are floating around the earth.
As the earth looks so peasfull,
there are no wars right now,
and rainbows are shining as the clowds are mooving.
What a butifull sight.

The end.

In this poem, the author treats us to a vision of the world, observed from the perspective of the stars. As in the first poem, her descriptions of the planet are imbued with social emotions, here about the value of peace. From a developmental perspective, though, the author has gained a more complex ability to represent multiple ideas at once, as well as a clearer literary structure for the poem (that is, she frames the poem between a title and a closing). She presents us with one "beautiful sight" but grounds her idea in several pieces of evidence, all simultaneously true: the lack of wars, the shining rainbows, and the moving clouds. She titles the poem using the grandest concept she can think of, and just as poets have for generations, she turns to her rudimentary knowledge of astronomy for inspiration.

Poem 3. Age 8 Years 10 Months

Let Love Flow Through You
(a poem for January)

There is a child
snuggled down for a good winter nap
Let him sleep peacefully
Let him blink silently
Let his mother's love flow through him
Don't wake him

This poem was written as part of a book that included one poem for each month of the year, given to the author's mother as a holiday present. In this poem, the first in the series, the author writes of a sleeping child. She takes the perspective of an omniscient onlooker, instructing the reader not to disturb the child's slumbers because even this simple action of sleeping is permeated with evidence of the child's close relationships—his mother's love flowing through him. Interestingly, the author titles the poem with a command to the reader, as if she can now mentally represent that her poems have a purpose—they can communicate her ideals to another person, the reader, and teach a lesson in the process. Her command of language is improving also, demonstrated by the alliterative repetition of the word "let" in the parallel structure of the middle lines.

Poem 4. Untitled, Age 9 Years 5 Months

Growing things are everywhere

and every day brings a new life
                    to Earth
          which grows
                    and grows
          until it reaches
                    its full height

it takes a last breath
and lies down
a new life
is born

In this final poem, the author connects her recurrent theme of the earth to her understanding of life and the life cycle. She returns to the idea she first presented earlier in poem 1, but with a new cognitive ability to represent systems of ideas, recurring in patterns. Whereas at age 6 she could relate one grand idea (strong and enduring love for her brother) to another grand idea (the earth spinning over time), here she can understand that many smaller processes come together to make a bigger cycle. This cycle also invokes more complex emotional consequences for the reader than the earlier poems do, starting with a celebration of growing things, passing through the process of dying, and returning to the hopefulness of new life. She accomplishes this increased emotional complexity also through her developing sense of structure, going beyond the conventional framing she used in poems 2 and 3 and instead chopping her phrases with line breaks and indents to mark new, impactful ideas.

In conclusion, to tie these poems together, we can see that they exemplify nicely the role of what Antonio Damasio and I termed "emotional thought" in Chapter 1. Even the driest and most concrete factual knowledge about the world, for example, facts about the workings of the physical planet on which we live, gains power when it is connected to this young author's social and emotional relationships and values. Her disciplinary knowledge of science becomes a source of metaphors for understanding and describing the social world, as well as the other way around—she uses the familiar feelings of social bonds to understand and appreciate the natural world. As she grows and builds more and more abstract disciplinary knowledge, knowledge that is separate from her social relationships, perhaps the childhood connections she once felt between her understanding of the physical world and the social experience of living on it will remain a source of inspiration.

ACKNOWLEDGMENTS

All poems are written by Nora Ming-Min Yang. Many thanks to Denny Blodget and Joanna Christodoulou for their comments on an earlier version of this essay.

CHAPTER 7

A Tale of Two Cases: Lessons for Education From the Study of Two Boys Living With Half Their Brains

Mary Helen Immordino-Yang

Chapter description: This chapter reports on the main findings from my dissertation study of two high-functioning hemispherectomized adolescent boys. Both of these boys came to us asking to be studied—they were very proud of their accomplishments. Nico came first, at age 10, traveling from Argentina with his parents and physician, Antonio Battro. Since Nico was missing the cerebral hemisphere that is thought to be central for producing and understanding emotional prosody (emotion conveyed through vocal pitch and tone), and since he had somehow managed to grow into a sweet, social, and engaging child whose speech was not at all unemotional or flat sounding, I became curious to understand how he was compensating. How could he learn to accomplish a skill that he was so neurologically predisposed against learning? And what could Nico's strategies teach us about how more typical learners may be able to strategically compensate for skills that they may not necessarily be neurologically inclined toward?

When the study of Nico's production and understanding of speech and emotion was already well under way, Brooke contacted us. Brooke was older, almost eighteen when I first met him, and he came into our lab with his beloved grandmother and father. Like Nico, Brooke was highly social, engaging, and outgoing. He was about to graduate from high school, and he told us of his future plans and of his love of art and drawing. He charmed us with his tendency to burst into song at the slightest provocation and amused us by imitating cartoon characters' voices. Though his plans were in some ways unrealistically ambitious, he impressed us with his good use of spoken language. This was quite unexpected from a young man missing the cerebral hemisphere that had been associated with spoken language for over a century! Juxtaposed with Nico's abilities, Brooke's strong emphasis on pitch fluctuation in his speech (sometimes with humorous effect) and effortful and strategic manipulation of emotion underscored what I came to believe are two basic tenets of successful learning: (a) learners need to find and capitalize on their strengths in order to overcome or work around their weaknesses, and (b) social-emotional profiles organize learning—not just what content kids are interested in but the processes by which they gather, interpret, and synthesize information and build skills.

These remarkable young men also taught us about the role of plasticity in learning—how individuals' neuropsychological skills change as a result of participation in tasks. The conventional view of plasticity mainly involves understanding how learners build new strengths to solve problems as they are put to them. Nico's and Brooke's profiles suggested an alternative: at least in some cases, plasticity could also be about how learners transform the problem itself into one which suits their existing processing strengths. This alternative underscores how brain development is an active, bidirectional dynamic process in which a learner's approach to problem solving may actually serve to organize his or her brain over time, and conversely, how a learner's particular neuropsychological strengths may shape his or her problem-solving approach. In the end, it turned out to be less interesting to know *where* functions are in the brain than to know *why* they are there, and less interesting to know *what* these learners could do than to know *how* they were doing it.

In recent years, educators have been looking increasingly to neuroscience to inform their understanding of how children's brain and cognitive development is shaped by their learning experiences (Diamond & Hopson, 1998; National Research Council, 1999). Brain development is coming to be viewed as an active, dynamic process, one in which a learner's approach to problem solving may actually serve to organize his or her brain over time and, conversely, one in which a learner's particular neuropsychological strengths may in turn shape his or her problem-solving approach. Because of the bidirectional nature of the relationship between learning and brain development, the fields of neuroscience and education are coming increasingly into a research partnership to investigate the ways that this developmental interaction plays out. However, while this new interdisciplinary approach presents an unprecedented opportunity to explore and debate the educational implications of neuropsychological research, relatively little is currently known about the basic principles governing the organization of children's brain and cognitive development in relation to experience.

Nico's and Brooke's Portraits

I include these portraits here because they are striking examples of how learners with different neuropsychological profiles can have very different approaches to the same task. Both young men produced highly competent likenesses. However, Nico's strategy was to reproduce brushstroke by brushstroke what he saw looking in a mirror placed to his side. Using this method, he used brushstrokes to create features of his face (e.g., eyebrow or ear), which could be recognized

BROOKE'S portrait

NICO'S portrait

even if the rest of the image were covered up. Brooke's method is strikingly different. The components of his image are (by his own description) meaningless shapes. Only when viewed together as a whole do they come to resemble a face.

Through his painting, Nico provides us a good example of a "left-hemisphere" strategy for creating, in which component pieces are hierarchically arranged to build bigger and bigger meaningful units. By contrast, Brooke provides a good example of a "right-hemisphere" strategy for creating, in which meaning emerges only when all the parts are considered together. A question I ask myself when I see these paintings is, if I were teaching painting (or, for that matter, any subject), how could I design the lesson so that both of these boys could thrive in my class?

One of the reasons for this lack of knowledge is that, although educators intuitively recognize the importance of emotional and social considerations in understanding children's development, there is currently very little research that effectively integrates social and emotional considerations into the study of brain development. The neurological research on emotions is unequivocal: the biological and cognitive processes that comprise emotion involve complex and dynamic feedback loops, at times under and at times out of our conscious control, between the physiology of the body and brain (Damasio, 1999). Imagine the automatic goose pimples you feel at hearing of another's misfortune, or the rush of memories you harbor of the moments just after the horrifying events of 9/11/2001. Contrary to a long philosophical tradition in which rational thought ruled (Damasio, 1994; Haidt, 2001), we now know that emotions involve the largely automatic and often nonconscious induction of behavioral and cognitive packages, which percolate into and out of our conscious minds, influencing our decision making, our thinking, our memory and learning (Immordino-Yang & Damasio, 2007; see Chapter 1). Add to this mix the concept of social emotions, that is, that we are influenced not only by our own but by others' emotions, behaviors, and mental states, and an amazingly complex landscape emerges. Very little is known about how all this plays out in educational contexts, in which people of different cultures, backgrounds, and neurological profiles are interacting, feeling, and learning. And so, while the few existing neurological studies of the development of emotion in children (e.g., Baird, Gruber, & Fein, 1999; Murray et al., 2006) have garnered much interest from the educational community and the general public, the application of these findings to educational contexts is difficult and often misguided because, unlike in psychological development (e.g., Case, 1997; Case & Okamoto, 1996; Fischer & Immordino-Yang, 2002), there is no good framework with which to understand the role of emotion in shaping the development of neuropsychological skills.

One window through which to investigate the developmental principles governing the brain-experience relationship and the organizing role of emotion is through case studies of atypical but highly functioning children. While their cases must be interpreted with caution, such children afford us a unique angle from which to explore these questions, as their active compensation for neuropsychological deficits can reveal subtle organizational principles that are better hidden in the more typical developmental trajectories of normal children. When a child is missing the brain areas that would normally be required to perform a particular task, and yet manages to successfully compensate, we are given a unique opportunity to learn about the emotional and motivational aspects of their recovery, as well as about cognitive compensation for basic neuropsychological skills. How are they learning what they should be "unable" to learn? Careful studies of such children's development can provide a good forum in which to debate the functional relationships between cognition and emotion in brain development, and from which to begin to establish a framework for understanding the hidden developmental processes acting in more typically developing children.

TRIANGULATING BETWEEN SOCIOEMOTIONAL, NEUROPSYCHOLOGICAL, AND DEVELOPMENTAL PERSPECTIVES: WHAT NICO AND BROOKE CAN TEACH US ABOUT THE NATURE OF LEARNING

Given these considerations, the purpose of this chapter is to illustrate the value of understanding the full range of variation in development by presenting comparative neuropsychological case analyses of the development of two exceptional adolescent boys, Nico and Brooke (both boys and their families asked that they be identified by their real first names), each of whom suffered severe localized brain seizures during childhood that resulted in the surgical removal of an entire hemisphere of his brain. In this comparative case method, each hemispherectomized boy was compared to normal matched peers on a series of educationally and socially relevant prosodic and emotional tasks, and the results of these comparisons were juxtaposed. This design was chosen for three main reasons. First, prosodic and emotional skills are thought to involve particular roles for each brain hemisphere, so studying these skills enabled rigorous assessments of how the boys had learned what they should not have been able to learn by traditional accounts. Second, this design revealed the possible organizing role of emotion in the boys' learning. Third, it allowed me to connect findings about these boys' functioning to issues of learning and development with broader educational relevance.

Amazingly, despite the poor cognitive prognosis generally associated with removal of a brain hemisphere, both Nico and Brooke have compensated to previously unexpected degrees. Nico lost his right hemisphere at age three yet grew into a charming and sociable teenager, attending a mainstream school in Spain. (His family is Argentine and moved to Spain after the testing described here.) His favorite activities were fencing, drawing cartoon characters, and singing in his school choir, and he rushed smiling to kiss my cheek whenever we met. Brooke lost his left hemisphere at age eleven but, despite predictions that he would never talk again, graduated from high school and began attending part-time college a few months after testing. He lives with family and continues to work to support himself. (For example, he worked for some time as a grocery bagger at a local supermarket, and later as a sorter at a recycling plant.) Both of these boys are hardworking young men, and while some effects of their neurological trauma endure, they are self-assured and proud of their accomplishments.

Such boys as these are extremely rare, and we will never know if their successful outcomes may have been possible in part because of individual differences in their presurgery neurological profiles. In addition, their families and teachers may have played a major role in their recoveries, through allowing these boys the freedom to actively engage in their own learning, without restricting them to preconceived notions about how they would function or recover after surgery. Their schools' help in overcoming the low-level mechanistic and motor skills that could have impaired their progress, such as providing a computer and typing instruction to Nico to circumvent his fine-motor difficulty with handwriting, may have also contributed. In short, we still have many questions about these boys, including why they have fared so much better than others with similar neurological histories, even many with strong educational and family support, and how their recoveries might have differed because of their different ages at the time of surgery.

Nonetheless, irrespective of the factors above, Nico's and Brooke's successful compensation for their extensive brain damage is extremely interesting from a developmental point of view and begs us to explore the broader principles governing the ways that they have adapted. How have these boys compensated, and what can we learn from them about how the developing brain makes sense of emotional and cognitive experience, given an extreme profile of strengths and weaknesses? In this chapter, I investigate these questions through analyzing these boys' emotional development and their use of emotional intonation (affective prosody) in speech, since these complex, socially relevant skills are thought to be carried out bilaterally in the brain, with each hemisphere having a particular role. Because each boy is missing half of the neural tissue normally recruited for these skills, understanding the boys' development in these areas could lead to important insights with implications for education, as well as for our understanding of prosodic and emotional processing in the brain.

Specifically, although we often assume that everyone perceives the same educational problems in the same ways, for example, a math problem is a math problem for everyone, Nico's and Brooke's cases suggest that we can in fact approach even relatively low-level, apparently automatic processing in very different ways, given extreme developmental circumstances. In particular, it appears that, perhaps in part due to highly supportive educational environments, both boys have compensated for lost abilities by transforming processing problems they should not be able to deal with, given their neurological profiles, into qualitatively different problems that better suit their remaining strengths.

Furthermore, it appears that for both boys their emotional profile plays a major role in shaping their brain development. In other words, both boys have distinctive emotional biases in approaching the social world, the signatures of which can be found in their solutions to cognitive problems, such as their approach to understanding and producing certain aspects of speech. Were this to hold true for other learners as well, it would imply that educators should think seriously about the problems they put to their students and about the various neuropsychological ways that these problems could actually be interpreted and processed. What we intend as a simple math exercise, for example, could in essence be a verbal problem to one child, a spatial problem to another, and even an affective or social problem to a third, who may be thinking of the emotional implications of, say, the solution to a mathematics word problem. As we could imagine, each of these children would be approaching the "math" problem from a very different angle that would have repercussions for their performance. While neuropsychology would have little to say about the most appropriate methods of support and teaching for each child, a neuropsychological approach could inform educators' understanding of the possible strategies each child could be using (Immordino-Yang, 2001a).

Working From a Neuropsychological Perspective

Before reading more about these cases, there are several background premises that would be useful to make explicit, since they are borrowed from standard neuropsychological approaches and may be unfamiliar to educators. First, in studying such cases we are comparing atypical to typical function to tell us about the component processes and developmental principles involved in normal functioning (Caramazza, 1992). That is, we seek to understand atypical function not simply for its own sake but also for what it can reveal about the ways all children learn and grow. When functions break down or fail to develop as expected, we are afforded a unique opportunity to learn about the ways in which the brain and mind organize themselves over time, in this case via the ways that children functionally compensate for their neurological deficits after hemispherectomy.

Second, to understand the principles that govern brain organization processes in Nico and Brooke requires a developmental analysis of their evolving skill profiles in a particular domain—in short, *how* they are doing what they are doing. It is this *how* that should be of most interest to educators, since it is presumably the aspect of neuropsychological development that is most influenced by developmental experience, as well as the most likely area in which to discover conclusions generalizable to other children. Too often in the past brain-based education has stymied itself with detailed accounts of neurological details that, quite simply, are not relevant to the majority of educational concerns (Bruer, 1997). Here, I take a more productive approach, in which educational and neuroscientific perspectives are brought together over specific cases to think about the interplay between learning experiences and biological predispositions and mechanisms, including emotional ones.

Third, and related, moving from the long, neuroscientific localizationist tradition in which cognitive functions were mapped onto specific locations in the brain (Harrington, 1991), in studying these cases our general interest is in the development of the relationship between brain and behavior and the role of experience in organizing the brain and mind (Immordino-Yang, 2001b). In other words, we are interested less in *where* functions are in the brain and more in *why* they are there (Bates, Thal, & Marchman, 1991; Deacon, 2000). This is a cutting-edge area that shapes the design and interpretation of experimental work in the neurosciences and is ripe for educational contributions, since educators and developmental psychologists see the behavioral manifestations of these hidden neuropsychological processes. In children, cognitive functions are more broadly distributed and less well localized to specific brain areas (Johnson, 2000; Snowling, 2001). This means that they are also less efficient and more plastic, usually able to shift their organization more readily than in adults (Bates et al., 2001). Over time and with experience, these cognitive functions become increasingly modularized and localized, as the brain networks on which they depend become more efficient and less susceptible to major reorganization through cognitive experience. It is this general trend through development from broadly distributed, relatively inefficient, but plastic processing to localized, efficient, but relatively fixed processing that makes neuroscientific concerns so relevant to education, as knowledge about this trend can inform the design of effective learning environments and experiences. It also forms my primary interest in the study of Nico and Brooke, as these boys' surprisingly successful outcomes probably depend heavily on this developmental canalization process. Through careful analysis of these boys' functioning, then, I aim to discover something about the compensatory logic underlying their developmental neuropsychological reorganization, and thereby to learn more about the interaction between brain development and cognitive and affective experience.

Bridging the Educational Gulf

After introducing these cases, we can see that they are especially appropriate for educational scrutiny for several reasons. First, too often neuropsychological work focuses overly on either the cognitive or the affective aspects of processing, a bias that is sometimes necessary for methodological reasons but that makes extrapolation to real-life learning contexts and educationally relevant learning principles infinitely more speculative. My study makes a compromise on this front, sufficiently narrowing the domain of processing studied to produce rigorous results but maintaining a sufficiently broad perspective to consider simultaneously both affective and cognitive contributions to the boys' compensatory strategies.

Second, rather than focusing in-depth on one kind of task and one level of analysis, this study moves from basic measures of neuropsychological processing through to more complex, naturalistic measures that more closely simulate skills relevant to real social contexts. In so doing, it provides entry points for both neuropsychologists and educators to debate the study's implications not just of *what* the boys are doing but of *how* they are doing it. For example, since prosody is a socially relevant cognitive skill, will there be differences in the ways the boys process prosody depending on whether the prosody is embedded in a social context or divorced from social concerns? And if so, will emotional considerations explain these differences? How will the two boys' processing differ, given that they are working with opposite hemispheres?

Third and related, to build more complete profiles of the boys than are typical in neuropsychology, the same data are analyzed on several dimensions: affective and cognitive, productive and receptive, and in individual and group analyses. Fourth, in making sense of neuroscientific work, educators are most concerned with understanding the interaction between the individual and the learning environment in building knowledge structures and shaping the brain. My study lends itself well to this concern, as it affords a unique window into developmental plasticity and the processes that govern neurological reorganization in response to experience.

Thus, this chapter is conceived as a narrative, an attempt to tell the story of two closely related domains of processing in Nico and Brooke, in order to engage neuroscientists and educators together in a discussion of the educational implications of data from these rare individuals. I first present nontechnical accounts of my work on the boys' emotion and use of emotional intonation in language, known as affective prosody. In these sections I describe my theoretical motivations, methods, and results with only the detail necessary to engage nonexperts in the topic and approach and to familiarize them with the findings. (Interested readers should refer to Immordino-Yang 2005 for full empirical reports on the prosody studies.) In interpreting the results, I use the emotional findings as a lens through which to more deeply understand the results of the neuropsychological prosodic assessments. The discussion explores the educational implications of bringing together these analyses and begins to build connections between these two boys and broader conceptual issues in education. Overall, this chapter is meant as a first foray

122   *Emotions, Learning, and the Brain*

into a new, smarter brand of brain-based education, one in which specific neuropsychological studies are presented, debated, and used to advance educational theory.

NICO'S AND BROOKE'S AFFECTIVE
PROSODY AND EMOTION: LEARNING
WHAT ONE IS "UNABLE TO LEARN"

In language, one way emotion is expressed is through prosody, which is the intonational contour, or melody, and stress pattern of speech (Crystal, 1997; Monrad-Krohn, 1947; Ross, 2000). Through manipulating the contour of an utterance, speakers can convey various emotional states and pragmatic intents, from the rising pitch of a question to the exaggerated emphasis of sarcasm:

PERSON A: "I'm going to Timbuktu next summer."
PERSON B: "YOU'RE going?"
PERSON C: "You're GOING?"

In this example, both B and C are incredulous about A's travel plans, but B thinks that someone else should go or that A in particular is not fit to go, while C had been under the impression that A had previously decided not to go. These nuances of meaning and affect are conveyed through linguistic intonation and accompanying paralinguistic cues, such as the facial expressions of B and C.

In normally developing children, emotion and prosody are likely integrated very early on, so that we do not think to examine the relationship between these two sets of skills (Bloom, 1997). However, in most adults, the syntactic and semantic aspects of language are mainly localized to the left hemisphere of the brain, while affective prosody and its associated skills are mainly handled by the right hemisphere (Kandel, Schwartz, & Jessell, 2000; Ross, 2000; Ross, Thompson, & Yenkowsky, 1997). This means that during normal development an integrative process between the two hemispheres must take place for appropriate affective intonation to be incorporated into the syntax and meaning of speech.

Further, while nonlinguistic emotional processing is not as clearly divided between the two hemispheres, the emotional profiles associated with left- and right-hemisphere damage are distinct (Lezak, 1995). Given this, extensive work over the past decades has attempted to divine the emotional profiles of the two hemispheres. This work has led to much controversy, but in general it is accepted that the right hemisphere is more strongly implicated in emotion (Adolphs, Damasio, Tranel, Cooper, & Damasio, 2000; Compton, Heller, Banich, Palmieri, & Miller, 2000; Perry et al., 2001), especially facial expression of affect (Borod, Koff, Yecker, Santschi, & Schmidt, 1998; Corina, Bellugi, & Reilly, 1999) and the ability to feel and perceive negative emotions (Campbell, 1982; Jansari, Tranel, & Adolphs, 2000).

As both Nico and Brooke have fully functional language despite missing a brain hemisphere, the question then arises as to how they have compensated, both prosodically and emotionally. In these boys, neurological damage has disassociated the skills associated with each hemisphere; each is missing half of the neural hardware normally relied upon for affectively appropriate language use.

One of the clues to understanding their good outcomes may well lie in concurrently examining not simply their cognitive ability to compensate for the basic-level perceptual mechanisms necessary to use and understand affective prosody but their emotional motivation and strategy for doing so. While there is a history of work on recovery of language in hemispherectomized children (e.g., Boatman et al., 1999; Piacentini & Hynd, 1988; Smith & Sugar, 1975), almost no work has been done on emotional or prosodic processing by these children, except to note that extensive brain injury usually results in behavioral and emotional problems (Hawley, 2003). Profiles of emotional (Trauner, Nass, & Ballantyne, 2001) and prosodic (Trauner, Ballantyne, Friedland, & Chase, 1996) deficit associated with less pervasive right-versus left-hemisphere lesions have yielded few differences between right- and left-hemisphere-damaged groups, although patients with right-hemisphere lesions may fare worse than those with left-hemisphere lesions on measures of recognition of facial affect (Voeller, Hanson, & Wendt, 1988).

These inconclusive results are related to the fact that brain processes seem to be less well organized in children than in adults. Processing in children is also more widely distributed around the brain and less focalized, and the localization of functions is more plastic (Kandel et al., 2000). Because of this, localized brain damage in children results in somewhat different patterns than does damage in adults, both of deficit and of recovery (Bates et al., 2001). Compared to adults, in children the location of damage corresponds less predictably to the resulting neuropsychological profile. And, while severely brain-damaged children usually do not catch up to their peers, they sometimes recover remarkably well, unlike adults with comparable brain damage (Reilly, Bates, & Marchman, 1998). In short, children benefit from increased plasticity, in which intact brain regions presumably compensate for damaged areas (Battro, 2000). Since there is significant variability in children's paths to recovery from brain damage, case studies can contribute important insights into these trends and the plasticity that created them.

In particular, a basic question has to do with the extent to which intact brain regions actually assume the processing characteristics of the damaged regions and the extent to which they adapt the cognitive problem to fit their characteristic mode of processing. In this study, Nico, with an intact left hemisphere, could be processing prosody in either of two ways, which would have distinct signatures in his data. He could be processing prosody much like his peers or younger children, which would suggest that his left hemisphere has, by necessity, taken on the kind of processing normally handled by the right hemisphere. Or, he could be processing prosody as if it were the kind of syntactic problem that the left hemisphere normally handles, in effect an aspect of grammar rather than a means to emotional expression, which would result in a qualitatively different data pattern than normal children show.

This distinction has implications for education. The first scenario suggests that plasticity mainly involves building new strengths to solve problems as they are put to you; the second scenario suggests that, at least in some cases, plasticity is about transforming the cognitive problem itself into a form that suits your processing strengths. While Nico and Brooke represent exceptional cases in which to study this distinction, their exceptionality offers unique viewpoints onto a normally hidden process. All children (and, in fact, adults) assimilate and adapt to new information and problems from their environments, and while we presume that this is an active process, the more we can learn about it, the better we can design learning environments and experiences to support it. In short, information about Nico's and Brooke's overall approach to compensating should be of interest to educators because it has potential implications for all children.

And thus we come back around to the *how* at the interface of education and neuroscience: taking a case study approach to studying these boys affords us a privileged view into a process that presumably all children are using in adapting their brains to the developmental challenges the world poses. To what extent are Nico and Brooke compensating by adapting their existing brain tissue to behave like the missing tissue would have, and to what extent are they transforming the processing problem to suit the original strengths of the tissue they have retained? To explore these questions, we move now to the methods and results of the study, starting with affective prosody and proceeding to nonlinguistic emotion.

DOING THE SCIENCE:
COMPARATIVE CASE ANALYSIS WITHIN A
DEVELOPMENTAL AND SOCIAL FRAMEWORK /

My study comprises a four-way design in which I compare production and reception of nonlinguistic emotion and affective prosody for Nico, Brooke, and comparison boys, to characterize the boys' functioning in these domains and investigate how functioning in emotion and prosody may covary after hemispherectomy (see Figure 7.1). I have included tests of both reception and production because, from a neuropsychological perspective, these may recruit different skills, strategies, or neuropsychological mechanisms, especially in two boys who are actively compensating both cognitively and neurologically for massive neurological trauma. For each hemispherectomized adolescent and each measure, a body of comparison data was collected, including cross-sectional longitudinal data from at least three eight-, ten-, and twelve-year-olds, in addition to data from at least ten age-matched comparison subjects and three adults. (Adult data were used only to verify the measures and were not included in the analysis.) Comparison boys were monolinguals of American English- or Argentine Spanish-speaking parents, with no diagnosed learning disabilities or neurological or hearing problems, matched to each hemispherectomized boy on linguistic dialect (either Buenos Aires Spanish or northeastern American English), approximate socioeconomic status, and approximate scholastic ability.

In all but Ekman's test of facial affect recognition, the boys' skills are characterized along a continuum of complexity as a means to describe a developmental trajectory. Here, I am extending an established microdevelopmental approach used for the study of emotion and cognition (Fischer & Bidell, 1998) into the domain of prosody. In this approach, single constructs, such as describing feelings of happiness or taking the first-order perspective of one other person, are presumed to be less developmentally advanced than an integrated description or display of a set of constructs, such as a joint description of happiness and feelings of reciprocated trust, or understanding one person's perspective on a second person's feelings. For prosody, I consider discriminating a single prosodic feature such as rising tone to be less complex and less developed than combining prosodic features to effect a subtler emotional message, such as sarcasm. In employing this complexity approach, I am bringing a developmental perspective to the established clinical neuropsychological dimensions of emotional and prosodic intensity and emotional valence.

FIGURE 7.1.   Overview of design, measures, research questions, and analyses.*

	Emotion	Prosody
Reception	**Ekman's Test of Facial Affect Recognition** (Ekman & Friesen, 1975) **RQ:** How can Nico's and Brooke's emotional receptive abilities be characterized, compared to established norms? • 110 close-up photos of actors' faces depicting anger, disgust, fear, happiness, surprise, sadness, and neutral affect • Data analyzed for emotion recognition ability as well as for any signs of bias towards emotions of a negative (-) or positive (+) valence (e.g. systematically mistaking fear (-) for surprise (+), or interpreting neutral affect as negative) • Has established norms; no need for comparison subjects	**Immordino-Yang's Test of Prosodic Discrimination and Comprehension** **RQ:** How can Nico's and Brooke's prosodic reception be characterized, both developmentally in terms of complexity and normatively in terms of strategy? • Designed audio-taped tests to measure basic discrimination of linguistic intonation and stress (e.g. rising vs. falling pitch), and comprehension of these features in story contexts (e.g. sarcastic vs. sincere tone of voice) • Data analyzed developmentally for ability to integrate increasingly complex cues (e.g. story context and speaker tone) and normatively for solution strategy used (e.g. perspective taking) • Comparison data collected from 10 age and language-matched boys for Nico and Brooke, from 3 adults in each language, and from three 8, 10 and 12-year-olds in each language
Production	**Self-In-Relationships Interview (SIR)** (Fischer & Kennedy, 1997; Kennedy, 1994) **RQ:** How can the complexity, valence and intensity of Nico and Brooke's emotional production be characterized, compared to typically developing boys? • Clinical-style emotional interview in which participants describe their feelings and thoughts about themselves and important personal relationships • Data analyzed by complexity (i.e. the ability to represent and integrate several emotions in one relationship) by, valence (e.g. a preference for describing mainly the negative or positive aspects of relationships), and by intensity • Typical performances well described; no need for comparison subjects	**Immordino-Yang's Analysis of Naturalistic Speech Production in the SIR** **RQ:** How can the intonation in Nico and Brooke's speech be characterized in relation to that of typically developing boys? • Using speech analysis software, analyzed sentence-level intonation fluctuation produced during prosodic receptive story conditions • Data analyzed for amount of pitch fluctuation and for distribution of pitch ranges across utterances • Audio-recorded data from prosodic reception story conditions from 3 age-and language-matched comparison boys for Nico and for Brooke

* All boys were tested in their native regional dialects. Comparison boys were monolinguals tested in Nico's and Brooke's home regions of Argentina and the United States, respectively. Test development, data analysis, and reliability coding were done with the help of native Argentine Spanish and American English speakers throughout the study.

Prosody

While I am drawing on established procedures to describe the boys' emotional functioning, the lack of appropriate developmental assessments for prosodic functioning required me to design my own measures. Basing my innovations on ideas and findings from the developmental and neuropsychological literatures, the prosodic receptive tests consist of a battery of tape-recorded items to which subjects respond and justify their answers. These items start with simple discrimination of the melodic patterns in speech and systematically increase in complexity to finally test inferences about speakers' affective intent in a naturalistic story (see Table 7.1 for a description of the test conditions). In my battery, story conditions systematically manipulate the presence of context information, tone-of-voice information, and a required integration of the two sources to predict the story outcome or infer a speaker's affect.

For example, a key distinction was between two story conditions: *context* and *tone*. Examine the following illustrative test items:

> John and Joe were playing soccer in the park. John kicked the ball towards the goal . . .
>> . . . The ball bounced off the goal post and hit John in the head. Joe told John it was a nice shot. (Story ending for the *context* condition)
>> OR
> . . . Joe said, "Nice Shot!" (Story ending for the *tone* condition)
>
>> Why did Joe say that it was a nice shot?
>> Was Joe being serious, being funny, or was he lying?
>> How do you know that?
>> Did John really make a nice shot?

In each case, the participant is asked to judge whether the final statement in the story had been sarcastic or sincere and to justify his answers via a series of follow-up questions. In the *context* condition, this judgment is based upon the congruence of the content in the utterance and story. That is, incongruence indicates that the speaker was joking (or lying), while congruence indicates sincerity. In contrast, in the *tone* condition, participants must judge a speaker's intent based on the intonation of their utterance alone, as the context of the story leaves ambiguous the speaker's intent.

I conducted two levels of analysis on the prosodic reception data. First, I scored the subjects' answers on each item as either correct or incorrect and calculated descriptive statistics for the comparison groups. Nico's and

Table 7.1.   Prosodic receptive test conditions, examples, and comments

- **Discriminate the rising intonation patterns of questions from the falling patterns of statements:** e.g., "You have a cat." vs. "You have a cat?" (This is relatively robust neuropsychologically and represents a very basic use of intonation to understand speaker's intent.)

- **Discriminate melodic patterns in speech ("pitch contour matching"):** Subjects listen to two phrases with the same number of syllables but different intonation, and then match an intonational pattern on "na na" to one of the original phrases. (Items were balanced for primarily rising vs. primarily falling pitch.)

- **Discriminate stress patterns that have differences for meaning:** Subjects differentiate by stress otherwise identical phrases (in English) or words (in Spanish), e.g., "hot dog" vs. "hotdog" or "papá" (daddy) vs. "papa" (potato).

- **Understand story context and use this to predict a speaker's intent to joke, deceive, or be sincere:** "John and Joe were playing soccer in the park. John kicked the ball towards the goal. The ball bounced off the goalpost and hit John in the head, and he slipped and fell in a mud puddle. Joe told John it was a nice shot."
  Why did Joe say that it was a nice shot?
  Was Joe being serious or funny when he said it was a nice shot?
  How do you know that?
  Did John really make a nice shot?

- **Identify sarcastic versus sincere tone of voice in the final statement of a sarcastically ambiguous story and associate these tones with a speaker's intent to either joke/disparage or be serious:** "John and Joe were playing soccer in the park. John kicked the ball towards the goal. Joe said, 'Nice shot!'" [Followed by similar questions to the context condition.]

- **Integrate story context with tone-of-voice information to infer the outcome of a story or to choose an appropriately intoned ending statement:** 13 items, e.g., "On her way home from school, Nina stopped at the candy store and asked for an orange lollipop. The woman at the store gave her an orange soda. Nina said, 'Excuse me, but I asked for an orange LOLLIPOP.'" Or, "Excuse me, but I asked for an ORANGE lollipop." (The stress and intonation in the first choice indicate that there was an error with the type, not flavor, of product. This is the correct choice, given the story context.)

Each test condition contained ten items plus a practice item, unless otherwise noted.

Brooke's scores were then compared, in standard deviations, to the mean scores of their same-language comparison groups and to the mean of their same-language age-mates. I next undertook a qualitative and quantitative analysis of the justifications that each subject used in the tests involving story scenarios and produced characterizations of the strategy profiles used by Nico and Brooke. Here, I analyzed how Nico, Brooke, and comparison boys explained correct and incorrect answers and investigated whether Nico and Brooke appeared to be developing normally, using strategies that are similar to those of their peers; whether they were delayed, using strategies similar to those of younger children; or whether they appeared to be following different developmental trajectories altogether. In particular, I was interested in Nico's and Brooke's use of tone of voice as a cue to sarcasm, as well as in the emotional and social aspects of their strategies. Dimensions on which the data were analyzed included subjects':

- judgments about the speaker's intent to joke, deceive, express sincerity, or some combination,
- perspective taking, which involved inferences about story characters' feelings or mental states,
- restating, inferring, or extrapolating factual information from the story,
- use of personal experience as a reference point in making judgments about story characters,
- explicit reliance on tone of voice information in making judgments,
- use of generalizable rules to justify judgments about story characters, and
- internal consistency and plausibility of their answers.

(See Immordino-Yang, 2005, for a detailed description of coding and analytic procedures. Here and below, comparisons were made on the basis of distributions, as this was the most sensible way to compare one boy to a group.)

In my prosodic production analyses, I investigated the boys' spontaneous speech during the prosodic receptive testing session, through acoustically analyzing the original recordings of their answers. Because the most important acoustic feature of affective prosody is the manipulation of pitch (Bolinger, 1989; Crystal, 1997; Ohala, 1984; Scherer, 1986), technically known as fundamental frequency, I measured the lowest and the highest pitches produced during each utterance for each boy and subtracted the low from the high value to produce a pitch range for each utterance. This enabled me to broadly characterize the boys' control of pitch in their expressive language, a neuropsychological skill that is heavily tied to emotion and, in most people, heavily recruits the right hemisphere but likely involves both brain hemispheres (Cancelliere & Kertesz, 1990; Kotz et al., 2003; Pell, 1998; Pell & Baum, 1997; Ross et al., 1997; Schlanger, Schlanger, & Gerstman, 1976; Starkstein, Federoff, Price, Leiguarda, & Robinson, 1994; Tompkins & Flowers, 1985; Van Lancker & Sidtis, 1992; Van Lancker-Sidtis, 2004).

Emotion

This study included two tests of emotion, one of production and one of reception. In order to describe the complexity, valence, and intensity of Nico's and

Brooke's emotional production, each boy participated in a standard cognitive and emotional "self-in-relationships" (SIR) interview (thanks to Catherine Ayoub, Harvard University Graduate School of Education, for providing these data for the purpose of this analysis). This clinical-style interview provides a supportive context in which participants are asked to describe their feelings and understandings about themselves in their important personal relationships. It has been shown to be an effective way to support adolescents in constructing complex understandings of themselves and their feelings and to assess the developmental level of these constructions (Fischer & Kennedy, 1997; Kennedy, 1994). In the interview, participants generate adjectives to describe their feelings in personal relationships, assign positive, negative, or neutral valence to these adjectives, and, with the help of a diagram, explain connections between different feelings. Normal adolescent boys can be expected to produce multifaceted positive and negative descriptions in this context and, when supported, to explain how different feelings go together. Boys of Brooke's age should also be able to integrate across emotions and relationships, to build abstract understandings of the ways that they feel, think, and act in their close relationships (Fischer & Bidell, 1998). Because typical performances for adolescents of different ages have been well described, no comparison data were collected for this phase.

In analyzing these data, I looked for evidence of emotional valence, from negative (e.g., sadness, anger) to positive (e.g., happiness, security), and of emotional intensity. To do this, I reviewed the list of adjectives that each boy produced and the valences that he assigned to these descriptors. For example, Nico had often been described as having very positive affect. Especially when specifically asked, did he talk about negative feelings, such as sadness or frustration, as well?

Next I assessed the complexity of the boys' understandings, looking for evidence of single emotions such as happiness being incorporated into richer descriptions of connections between emotions or between similar emotions within different personal relationships. For instance, in talking about the grandmother who raised him, did Brooke integrate his feelings in a complex way, to describe how his feelings of security, for example, related to his feelings of resentment at being disciplined? Alternatively, did he simply list several emotions, such as security and resentment, without forging connections? Assuming that he produced both positive and negative emotion terms, did he make equally complex connections between negative as between positive emotions?

To complement this assessment of emotional production, Nico's and Brooke's abilities to discriminate basic emotions on faces was also tested using Ekman's test of recognition of facial expression of emotion (Ekman & Friesen, 1975). This test consists of 110 close-up photos of actors' faces depicting anger, disgust, fear, happiness, surprise, and sadness, as well as photos depicting neutral affect. These photos were developed for basic and cross-cultural research on emotion and have been adapted for use in neuropsychological studies (Lezak, 1995). Nico and Brooke were asked to view each photo and to identify the emotion being produced by the person in the photo.

The boys' responses were analyzed in two ways. First, I calculated the percentage of correct answers and tabulated the patterns of errors that the boys made. Then, I conducted a secondary analysis of the boys' responses, looking for evidence of systematicity or bias in the boys' correct and incorrect answers. For instance, was there evidence that Nico tended to confuse negative emotions, such as fear and disgust, but accurately differentiate positive emotions, such as happiness and surprise? Alternatively, might he or Brooke have shown a tendency to misclassify negative emotions as positive, for example, confuse disgust with surprise? The results of this secondary analysis were then integrated with and understood in terms of the results of the SIR interview.

BUILDING CONNECTIONS BETWEEN THE BRAIN AND LEARNING: EMOTION SHAPES KEY LEARNING IN LANGUAGE

Overall, Nico and Brooke compensated remarkably well for prosodic capacities, accurately judging speakers' sarcastic and serious intents and producing adequate intonation in their spontaneous speech. However, further analysis revealed that they were using quite atypical strategies to make sense of the story characters' tones of voice and that their own prosodic production was generally exaggerated and unregulated. Specifically, while Nico made snap judgments about speakers' tone and showed little ability to reflect on the source of his judgments, Brooke mused extensively over the speakers' tones and their associated emotions, often bringing his own experiences to bear on the speakers' emotional situations. Both boys also showed distinctly atypical emotional profiles in the SIR interview, with Brooke explaining elaborate and effortful strategies for controlling his negative emotions and Nico seeming to avoid the discussion of emotion altogether. Both Nico and Brooke were moderately accurate at recognizing emotional expressions on faces, although Brooke's errors were less systematic than Nico's, which seemed to follow a predictable error pattern toward judging emotive faces as neutral. In general, these results suggest that while Nico was avoiding emotion and instead processing affective information in both modalities as something akin to "pseudo-grammatical," memorized categories, Brooke was attempting to solve these problems by reveling in the connections between emotion and tone of voice. In this way, both boys appear to be compensating by capitalizing on the neuropsychological strengths, including emotional strengths, associated with their remaining hemisphere, rather than by adapting their remaining hemisphere to act as the missing hemisphere would have.

Prosody

Understanding Others' Prosody. Figure 7.2 presents Nico's and Brooke's scores in relation to the scores of their same-age, same-language peers on the prosodic discrimination tasks. The first three measures involve tasks that are quite linguistic in nature, meaning that they rely on analyses of pitch but are not particularly emotional. As we can see, Nico was quite skilled at these tasks, while Brooke generally performed slightly below the mean. This is interesting in that, despite the right hemisphere's strong pitch-processing capabilities, Brooke was unable to effectively compensate for the loss of his left hemisphere in these tasks, likely because of their dissociation from emotion. Nico, on the other hand, was very competent on these tasks, despite the fact that they rely on pitch, normally associated more strongly with the right hemisphere. Together, Nico's and Brooke's results on these relatively straight-forward measures hint at a developmental connection between intonation and emotion in these boys, namely, that Brooke associates pitch with emotion, while Nico dissociates these two linguistic dimensions.

The second three tasks were story-based conditions, designed to assess the boys' abilities to use pitch information to make social and emotional inferences about a story character's intent. Here, quite an interesting pattern arose. Nico performed comparably to his peers on the context and tone conditions. Somehow, he had managed to recognize sarcasm based on tone alone, despite missing the hemisphere that would normally handle sentence-level tone and emotion. Brooke also performed comparably to his peers on the context condition. However, when given only tone-of-voice information and asked to make inferences about the characters' emotion or social intent, his performance rose to almost two standard deviations above that of his peers, who were themselves very competent. Also, Brooke loved using tone for such a purpose and greatly enjoyed this task. In the last story condition, in which context and tone information needed to be integrated to correctly answer, both Brooke and Nico showed impaired performance.

The results on the three story-based conditions present an intriguing scenario, in which both boys compensated remarkably well on the straight-forward context and tone tasks, but neither could handle the two sources of information together. What is more, while Nico performed adequately on the tone task, Brooke excelled at it. Clearly, to make sense of these patterns of performance requires moving beyond assessing the boys' abilities to complete

FIGURE 7.2. Nico's and Brooke's prosodic discrimination abilities, in standard deviations, compared to the means of their same-age, same-language peers. Tests are arranged in approximate order of difficulty from left to right. N10 and N12 represent Nico at ages 10 and 12, respectively. B represents Brooke at age 18. Note: Brooke's score on context-only stories is not included, as there was too little variation among scores for the standard deviation to be meaningful. (Scores ranged from 9 to 10 out of 10; Brooke received a 9.)

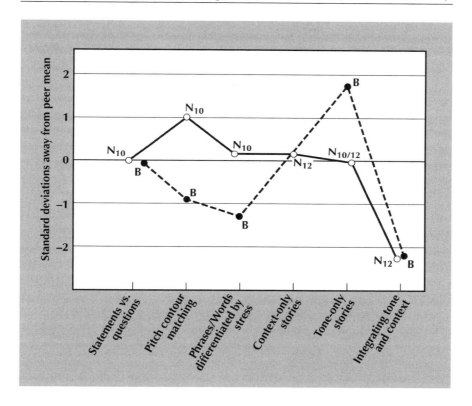

the task, instead examining in more depth their respective social, emotional, and cognitive strategies. That is, upon closer examination, it may be that these tasks present quite different cognitive and emotional problems to Nico and to Brooke and that these different problems may reflect the two boys' compensatory mechanisms.

Therefore, we move to comparing the boys' coded justifications for their answers in the context and tone conditions. Most striking in these results is that while Nico and Brooke performed somewhat atypically on the context condition stories, they performed very atypically on the tone condition stories. In the context condition, Brooke's strategy profile was different from the comparison boys' only in that he had a slight tendency to extrapolate beyond what was relevant. He also tended to maintain his own perspective more than the comparison boys, at times giving answers such as, "How do I know that? Because I read [*sic*] the story," or "because I'm psychic." In other ways, his strategies on the context condition stories were quite typical.

However, in the tone condition, a more complex pattern of differences emerged. He now overattributed speaker intentions and used more second-order perspectives than necessary to solve the items. He extrapolated beyond relevant information in eleven out of thirteen items and brought his own experiences to bear on the story more than nine times more often than his peers. Most important, he directly imitated the story characters' tone of voice in seven out of thirteen items, more than five times more often than his same-age peers. Overall, in the tone condition, while Brooke was highly accurate in judging speakers' intent, he tended to justify his answers by musing and empathizing more than his peers about story characters' motives, emotions, and tone of voice, often bringing his own experiences to bear on the problem. And, when Brooke worked from tone of voice, he would usually note the emotion that the tone seemed to portray and the implications of that emotion for the story. For instance, in a story in which an older sister sarcastically tells her younger sister, "Yeah, I'm sure you have *lots* of homework!" Brooke responded, "She was probably joking around. But I think she was serious at the same time. It's like two things at once . . . joking around is like, 'you don't have no homework' [said in a joking tone]. That's joking around. Serious is like, 'you have homework? That's a drag' [said in an exaggeratedly serious tone]. That's serious. So it's like a little mix." Here, Brooke justified his decision that the story character's intent was sarcastic by talking as the character would sound were she sarcastic or serious, and then explaining that the character's original statement was, in his opinion, a mix between these two tones.

For a further example, in describing how he knew that a speaker was lying when she said she had scored ten soccer goals when in fact she had scored only one in the story, Brooke said, "She didn't want to admit she only scored one point . . . And you can't even score 10 points. You can probably only score like 5, and that's the highest you can go. 'Cause I can only—out of a game—I can only score like 2 or 3 and that's if I really try." In this example, Brooke used his own experience with soccer to guide his judgment, even though the story had plainly stated how many goals the girl had scored.

Nico also made use of atypical answer strategies, especially in the tone condition, but showed a different pattern of answers than Brooke. In the context condition, Nico performed quite similarly to his peers, except for a strong tendency to maintain his own perspective rather than discuss the story characters' perspective. In the tone condition, however, Nico's differences became much more pervasive. He used the general strategy of restating information and talking about story characters' first-order perspectives or tone less often than his peers, failing to consider adequately the story characters' emotions. Rather than discuss a character's feelings, motives, and tone, his favored strategy was to produce accurate, snap judgments of a story character's tone and to avoid speculating about emotional or other implications. For example, he stated several times during the tone conditions, "How do I know that [she is joking]? Because I just heard it." Here, Nico shows no apparent awareness of the source of his judgment, although he was comparably accurate to his peers.

How Nico and Brooke Used Intonation.   Given that the neuropsychological substrate for prosodic production has been relatively understudied compared to that for comprehension (Schirmer, Alter, Kotz, & Friederici, 2001), and given the importance of pitch fluctuation to the expression of affective prosody (Pell, 1999; Ross et al., 1997), this portion of the study examined the pitch variation used by Nico and Brooke during the context and tone story conditions above. Each hemispherectomized boy's speech was compared to that from three matched peers.

In general, right-hemisphere damage in adults is associated with flattened intonational contours, or monotonic speech (Cohen, Riccio, & Flannery, 1994; Heilman, Leon, & Rosenbek, 2004; Pell, 1999), while left-hemisphere damage is associated only with minor affective prosodic difficulties, usually attributed to speech timing rather than to intonational problems (Danly & Shapiro, 1982; Gandour, Petty, & Dardarananda, 1989; Schirmer et al., 2001; Van Lancker & Sidtis, 1992). However, quite surprisingly, I found that both Nico, missing his right hemisphere, and Brooke, missing his left hemisphere, exhibited more intonational variation than their peers. While this was fairly subtle for Nico, Brooke's speech at times sounded hypermelodic, with quite exaggerated and almost humorous intonation, especially when he was enjoying himself. In statistical comparisons between each boys' distribution of utterances, both Nico's and Brooke's mean pitch ranges were significantly higher than those of their peers, and their pitch range distributions were visibly right-shifted, at times producing wildly fluctuating utterances unlike anything produced by their peers in this context.

In addition, both boys showed a flattening of their distribution of pitch ranges as compared to their peers, suggesting that they do not have a reliable "unmarked" prosodic state but, rather, assign pitch variations to utterances in a less organized or controlled fashion than their peers (see Figure 7.3). While this was dramatic for Brooke, whose intonation flared wildly at times on fairly ordinary utterances, it was more subtly apparent for Nico, who managed to produce a series of utterances that, as a group, approximated quite well those of his peers.

FIGURE 7.3.   (a) Distribution of utterance pitch range for Brooke and comparison boys. Note the consistent peak in distribution for the comparison boys at around 40 Hz, contrasted to the much flatter distribution for Brooke. Note also the long positive tail on Brooke's distribution.

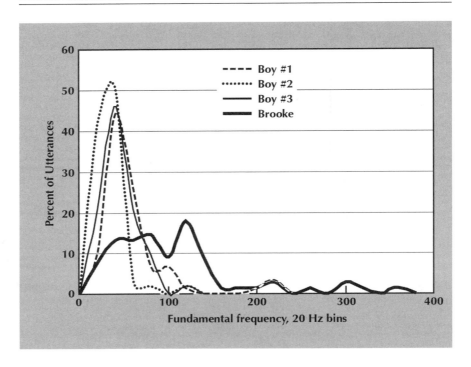

Nico's and Brooke's surprising prosodic production results are likely attributable to developmental compensatory mechanisms not available to brain-damaged adults and provide us with another set of clues as to the two boys' approaches to prosodic and emotional problem solving. In Brooke's case, his strong tendency toward heightened emotionality may be associated with his exaggerated use of intonation, especially because the speech context involved making inferences about others' intentions and emotions based on tone of voice. In Nico's case, tonal language speakers provide a precedent for left-hemisphere analysis of prosodic features (Gandour et al., 2000; Hughes, Chan, & Su, 1983; Moen & Sundet, 1996; Packard, 1986). In tonal languages, such as Mandarin Chinese, prosody is used to express both grammatical/lexical information and affective information. In tonal language speakers, while the right hemisphere is heavily recruited for affective prosodic processing, the left hemisphere specializes in processing prosodic grammatical information (Gandour, Ponglorpisit, & Dardarananda, 1992; Gandour, Wong, &

FIGURE 7.3 (b) Distribution of utterance pitch range for Nico and comparison boys. Note that, while all of the boys' distributions peak at around 60 Hz, Nico's distribution is visibly right-shifted. Note also the long positive tail on Nico's distribution.

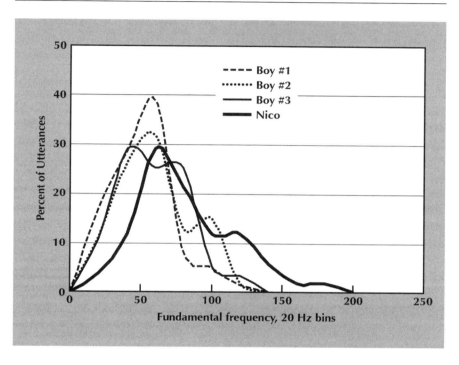

Hutchins, 1998), such as to distinguish between words. It is conceivable that Nico has approximated the intonation patterns of the language around him by learning and imitating through a nonaffective, "pseudo-grammatical" mechanism—in effect, that he has memorized particular pitch patterns with affective significance in the same way that a Mandarin speaker memorizes a list of differently intoned words. If this is the case, his hyperprosodic tendencies may be due to overcompensating for a left-hemisphere propensity for flatter intonation, possibly in order to be more socially engaging.

Emotion

Nico and Brooke participated in two complementary assessments of emotion: the SIR (Self in Relationships) interview, which is a clinical-style interview about the participant's thoughts and feelings about his personal relationships with close friends and family (Fischer & Kennedy, 1997; Kennedy, 1994), and a conventional assessment of emotion discrimination on faces (Ekman

& Friesen, 1975). On both tests, Nico's and Brooke's emotions were atypical: they were less accurate than normals on identifying emotions on faces, and they showed less complex representations of their feelings about close relationships. However, while the boys were atypical, their profiles were also quite distinct from each other. While Brooke showed a sophisticated strategy to actively dissociate negative and positive emotions, Nico seemed equally uncomfortable discussing positive as negative emotions.

The Self-in-Relationships Interview.   On the SIR interview, Brooke showed a distinct reluctance to think or talk about his personal relationships, despite the finding that, in general, adolescents greatly enjoy this interview protocol. He described himself as "gentle and open-hearted" but provided only concrete definitions of what these constructs meant, for example, "Open-hearted is like . . . you can talk to your friends whenever you want. If you have a problem or something they will understand." When asked to describe his feelings, the only adjectives he spontaneously produced were "happy" and, by way of something negative, "agitated." In talking about his surgery and hospitalization, he used words such as "psycho" (which he clarified as "angry" and produced in the context of explaining how he felt in the hospital after his surgery when he was physically restrained) and "out of control." His descriptions of personal relationships, such as with his best friend Pete, were given begrudgingly and mostly constituted an outright refusal to reflect on relationships. For example, when pushed to talk about what he and Pete enjoy doing together, he replied, "We're just friends. We're not like boyfriend/girlfriend . . . I don't know what Pete's real life is! I'm not like the mother of his family."

However, toward the end of the interview, Brooke revealed that he is in fact quite strategic about managing his thoughts and emotions and keeping them exclusively positive. As the conversation worked around again to negative feelings, Brooke explained, "I put those questions away in the back of my head . . . I really don't want to pull them out . . . It's like a locked door . . . All those things you are saying, that I don't want to do, 'cause I try to hide those things. I don't open it up. That's my theory. That's why I'm always happy."

Overall, Brooke's strategy with regard to emotion seemed to be to actively avoid negative emotions at all cost and to effortfully cultivate positive emotional states. He explained, "I just do things that make me happy . . . Just got to open up one of those boxes in your head to think about the fun thing you did. And when you are done with your happiness you close the box again to save." In describing how he "gets out of the dumps," he stated, "There's different kinds of methods I use to get out . . . I got to think of it, think of it hard, and sometimes it doesn't click 'til like two hours later."

As these statements reveal, Brooke seemed to modulate his emotions by consciously controlling the situations he allows himself to think about, cultivating positive emotions and refusing to think about negative emotions. It could be that Brooke's neurological condition has left him less able to modulate or control his own emotional states, a condition that he compensates for by strategically manipulating his thoughts.

While Brooke was quite calculated and reflective in his strategies during the SIR interview, Nico remained very concrete throughout. When asked to describe himself, he stated, "I like to swim" and "I like to travel." The only adjectives for emotional states that he produced were "calm (tranquilo)" in relation to how he feels with his family and "nervous (nervioso)" in school. He seemed to find the interview exceedingly tedious, and his descriptions of his friends and family were very concrete. In addition, he seemed to actively avoid discussing emotional aspects of personal relationships, saying that the task was "too hard." For example, when asked how he feels with his father, he replied, "I don't know, because the truth is that I don't like to go to the cinema and he does. I don't like to go to the cinema a lot." In this answer, rather than reflect even in a simple way on his feelings with his father (as a younger child might), Nico avoided thinking about this relationship and instead turned the discussion toward the concrete topic of the cinema.

Overall, Nico's understanding of emotional states was quite rudimentary and undifferentiated. Although he represented both positive and negative emotions in describing himself, he showed little willingness or ability to further differentiate his feelings.

The Ekman Test of Facial Affect Discrimination.   In the Ekman test, Nico and Brooke scored approximately equivalently, with Brooke correctly identifying 71 of 110 photos, or about 65 percent, while Nico correctly identified 75 photos out of 110, or about 68 percent. In analyzing responses, surprise and happiness were considered positive emotions, while fear, anger, disgust, and sadness were considered negative.

While Nico was comparatively accurate at recognizing positive emotions like happiness and surprise, he had two major trends in his pattern of errors. First, he tended not to notice the emotions portrayed on faces and to default toward neutrality, at times categorizing emotive faces as "neutral" or "thoughtful" (his word). Second, he tended to make errors distinguishing between negative emotions. In particular, he confused disgust and anger, a mistake common in patients with brain damage (Calder, Keane, Manes, Antoun, & Young, 2000), and had difficulties recognizing sadness. Notably, he never misattributed happiness to a face displaying a negative emotion, and his only error in identifying positive emotions was to mistake happiness for neutrality three times.

The most striking trend in Brooke's data was that he accurately attributed happiness; he labeled the eighteen happy photos and only those photos "happy." The majority of Brooke's errors were in distinguishing between negative emotions, especially miscategorizing disgust as other negative emotions, mainly anger. Overall, Brooke's errors were sprinkled throughout the exercise and occurred on both emotive and neutral items. Except for his complete failure to recognize disgust and his perfect record in recognizing happiness, Brooke seemed to be less systematic than Nico in his categorization of neutral and emotional faces.

FROM NEUROPSYCHOLOGICAL FINDINGS TO EDUCATIONAL IMPLICATIONS: NEUROPSYCHOLOGICAL STRENGTHS AS BASES FOR ACTIVE TRANSFORMATION IN LEARNING

In juxtaposing measures of affective prosody and emotion in Nico and Brooke, interesting complementary profiles emerge. These profiles provide tentative evidence for a strong developmental relationship between emotion and prosody, one in which the two neuropsychological skills seem to have remained closely associated in both boys through their cognitive and neurological compensation after brain damage. More important, though, these complementary profiles provide evidence for a broader trend that, arguably, holds implications for normal children as well. That is, rather than compensating for their extensive brain damage by painstakingly adapting their remaining hemisphere to take over functions normally associated with the missing hemisphere, both Nico and Brooke appear to have instead transformed the nature of the processing problem itself to suit the existing strengths of their remaining hemisphere. Simply put, both boys appear to be compensating so successfully because, instead of changing themselves to suit the problem, they have used their remaining strengths to reinterpret the processing problem itself into something they know how to do. Interestingly, their emotional skills appear to have played a major organizing role in this assimilation process.

The Organizing Role of Emotion

A review of the results demonstrates this trend. In Nico, we see a boy who is very skilled at categorizing affective prosodic information and differentiating statements from questions and sarcastic from sincere tone of voice but relatively poor at explaining what this information implies for the larger social context, such as the outcome of a story. In categorizing emotional faces in the Ekman test he was passably accurate but tended to regress toward neutrality and had a somewhat difficult time distinguishing between negative emotions. In the SIR interview he was similarly uninterested in emotional interpretations, saying that the questions were "hard" and attempting to change the topic of discussion, for instance, to the cinema. In each of these results, Nico was relatively efficient at categorizing based on tone or emotion but quite poor at making connections between his judgments and the broader social or emotional contexts that would normally inform them.

How was this possible? Nico, with his left hemisphere intact, seems to have recrafted the emotional and prosodic problems he should not have been able to accomplish into new, fundamentally different, unemotional problems. To do this, he appears to have memorized the relationships between certain tone patterns and their associated emotions, both in his own speech production and in understanding others' speech. This strategy recruits one of the strengths of the left hemisphere, namely, categorizing and labeling, such as associating words with meanings. However, it left him relatively impaired at discussing his own emotional relationships and at explaining what his judgments of tone would mean for a speaker's feelings.

Similarly, Brooke drew on the relative strengths of his intact right hemisphere, despite the fact that this left him with various unexpected vulnerabilities. The right hemisphere is generally strong in emotional and pitch processing, skills that Brooke recruited to solve all sorts of problems, whether or not they required it. He often spontaneously brought either emotional or intonational information explicitly to bear, even on basic discriminatory tasks requiring only categorical judgments. For example, in matching a pitch contour to the phrase "I'm happy to see her," he said, "hmm . . . she doesn't *sound* happy to see her." In the most complex test, requiring the integration of pitch and stress information with story context, Brooke's strategy was to explicitly describe the tone and pitch patterns in the two choices and then base his judgment on how emotionally or socially appropriate that pitch pattern sounded to him. For example, to one story Brooke responded, "Because [that choice] goes up and then down and then up again. Because it's the anger going on. It sounds meaner, but the other [choice] goes up at the last word, which is nicer." In the SIR interview, Brooke was quite direct about his cognitive strategies for modulating his all-consuming emotions. And in the Ekman facial affect test he was, if only moderately accurate, highly engaged, often talking as if he actually were expressing the emotion in the picture. For instance, he would use a humorously exaggerated angry voice to label an angry photo, or a depressed voice to label sadness. Overall, while Brooke's strategy enabled him to judge tone of voice more accurately than his peers, it also left him liable to serious errors on tasks where emotional interpretation of tone was not relevant, as in the task where utterance pitch contours are matched to contours on blank syllables. His heavy reliance on this strategy also means that he must spend significant effort controlling his emotions, as he described so well in the SIR interview.

Prosody as a Window Into Learning

While the interpretation of the prosodic production analyses is less straight-forward, circumstantial evidence suggests that a similar process is at play. Here, both Nico and Brooke flatly defied neuropsychological prediction. Despite the finding that right-hemisphere-damaged patients generally sound somewhat monotonic (Cohen et al., 1994; Heilman et al., 2004; Pell, 1999), Nico used slightly more intonation than he should have, and overall his utterances looked much like those of his peers. And, despite predictions that Brooke would speak with normal pitch variation, his intonation flared wildly, at times to humorous effect.

One possible interpretation of these findings is that an integration between the brain hemispheres is required in order to adequately modulate pitch and match it to the appropriate emotional intent. Without his right hemisphere, Nico could copy the intonation patterns he hears in his native language, but a careful listener notices that there is something stinted or unspontaneous about his speech. Without his left hemisphere, Brooke produces lots of emotional intonation but perhaps cannot regulate his production to suit the purpose of his utterance, such as to joke or express emphasis. While an intriguing possibility, this hypothesis could not be adequately addressed with these data, as the utterances in this sample are mainly simple declaratives and therefore do not contain the requisite broad range of affective intents or conversational purposes. However, the preliminary finding that the utterances Brooke and Nico produced with large pitch excursions seem unremarkable for their emotional and conversational intent, unlike the utterances with the widest pitch variations produced by the normal boys, supports this interpretation. For the normal boys, the widest pitch excursions seemed to be associated with either joking or quoting someone else, both of which are known to be accomplished by higher pitch fluctuation (Holt, 1996; Kreuz, 1996). However, Nico's and Brooke's most exaggerated utterances included many simple statements, such as Brooke's "to go to the park" and Nico's "because I just heard it."

Another suggestive piece of evidence comes from preliminary findings, not reported here, about Nico's and Brooke's understanding and production of emotion in their speech, including the ability to understand and express anger, sadness, surprise, happiness, and fear. While Nico could accurately label the emotions in others' speech, he was strikingly impaired at producing or copying emotion on cue, for instance, when asked to restate a simple sentence as if he were angry. Brooke, too, was moderately accurate at recognizing and categorizing emotional prosody. But, preliminary results suggest that listeners found his emotional speech, while intensely emotional, difficult to definitively categorize. In this way, Nico may be once again processing emotional speech as if it were categorical, listening for a memorized set of acoustic features and associating them with an emotional label, such as loudness associated with anger. Conversely, Brooke may be well attuned to the emotion in language but have trouble modulating his prosody to clearly express a particular emotion.

Overall, then, both Nico's and Brooke's profiles on the emotional and prosodic tests suggest a developmental dependency between prosodic and emotional processing and, in so doing, reveal what could be a basic principle of compensation after brain damage. Nico's rule-bound, categorical approach to prosodic processing leaves him largely unable to use the prosodic information for emotional ends. I would suggest that Nico's left hemisphere, rather than working to understand the affective information as affective, has instead modified the task to suit its relative strength, grammatical or lexical categorization. In effect, Nico may be interpreting different affective tones of voice as categorical rather than emotional information. Conversely, Brooke's apparent heavy reliance on prosody and emotion leaves him vulnerable to emotional regulation problems and to bringing emotional judgments to bear when they are not particularly relevant. Simply put, while both boys' profiles present them with liabilities, each boy seems to be building directly on his comparative neuropsychological strengths, even in the face of compensation for extreme neurological damage. Their approaches to processing reveal that they are bringing their relative strengths to bear, and perhaps modifying and specializing these strengths in the learning process, rather than grappling with the processing issue as it is generally perceived.

Insights for Education

Returning to educational considerations, studying Nico and Brooke gives us a glimpse into a possible neuropsychological principle governing learners' active accommodation to and assimilation of their cognitive and emotional environments. While effective educators generally assume that individual learners will approach new problems differently, this work suggests the possibility of an important complementary process as well. That is, in approaching problems from different angles, learners may not simply be bringing different strengths to bear on the same problem but may actually be transforming the intended problem into something new. This implies a need for careful attention to learners' perceptions of the educational problems put to them, as well as a need to design learning environments that capitalize on this process. Students from different cultural and social backgrounds may well interpret the same classroom exercises in very different ways.

For an anecdotal example, in a second grade math class I once observed a student confused over the correct answer to a problem about whether a six-foot-wide car could park in a seven-foot-wide garage. No, it could not, she explained, because the driver would not be able to open the car door. Clearly, although this student's initial response was labeled incorrect, she had indeed solved the math problem correctly but had gone beyond to consider the personal perspective of the driver. While a simple example and one that was quickly resolved, it nonetheless illustrates that this student was considering not simply numbers but practical, personal concerns in solving her math problems.

Another interesting implication of these findings is that, unlike what we might have expected, the hemispherectomized boys' abilities to compensate effectively were not entirely based on the apparent difficulty or complexity of the skill but instead also reflected the social nature of the task. We can see this especially when we compare two of the prosodic receptive conditions: matching the pitch contour of utterances to those on blank syllables and recognizing sarcastic pitch contour in the tone-of-voice stories. At first glance, and indeed when I designed these conditions, the pitch contour matching was meant to assess the basic-level melodic discrimination skills that underlie the sarcasm test. Imagine my surprise, then, when Brooke performed worse and Nico performed better than the comparison boys on this measure! And how could Brooke be so skilled at recognizing sarcasm despite his poor performance on pitch contour matching? The answer led to an interesting insight about the role of emotion and social context in learning, namely, that divorcing the skill from its social context changed its very nature and converted it into a problem that Brooke could no longer solve. Nico, of course, found this change made the task easier, since he was no longer confounded by social considerations. As educators, we generally assume that isolating a low-level skill will make it more accessible to students and easier, but this example highlights the fact that separating skills from their context can change them in unforeseen ways. To understand how skills function, then, we need to think carefully about how and why the skill is being used in that context, from the student's perspective, and to be mindful about the underlying purpose of the processing. Simpler skills may not necessarily be easier from a neuropsychological perspective. In some cases, students may be able to use complex, contextualized skills in ways that fall apart in stripped-down contexts, even when only the social or emotional context has changed.

Learning as an Active, Emotionally Mediated Process

To conclude, brain development must be viewed as an active process in which learners do not simply assimilate common experiences but instead interpret these experiences actively based on previous learning and innate neuropsychological strengths. Not only is the interpretation process subtle, but it engages social and affective considerations and may be influenced and supported by the particular environment to which a child is exposed. In the cases of Nico and Brooke, we cannot ignore that their successful compensations may be heavily attributable to the highly supportive and personalized educational environments their families and teachers created for them. Further, Nico's and Brooke's cases suggest that these adaptive interpretations are not limited to so-called cold cognition. Rather, affectively and non-affectively based strategies may at times be interchanged, just as Brooke interpreted all uses of pitch as emotional and Nico avoided emotion in analyzing pitch used for affective tone of voice.

Therefore, while the idea of active, individualized learning is far from new, the study of Nico and Brooke affords us a way to begin to flesh out and embody this principle in brain development and to test and debate its validity. I hope that educators will eventually be able to make use of my conclusions, in combination with those from other interesting examples, to inform their practice in some concrete way, such as helping to shape the design of a curricular intervention or learning environment. However, meeting this goal will require an iterative and difficult process, one that will first involve the integration of many such discussions and examples into a coherent conceptual framework incorporating neuropsychological, developmental, and educational principles. While Nico's and Brooke's results seem on the surface to contradict expectations based on neuropsychological findings with adults, they combine to reveal a compensatory logic that begins to elucidate the active role of the learner, as well as the organizing role of emotion in brain development, providing a jumping-off point for discussion between educators and neuroscientists.

ACKNOWLEDGMENT

I am deeply grateful to all those who made this work possible, especially Nico, Brooke, and their families, Kurt Fischer, Catherine Snow, Catherine Ayoub, Antonio Battro, Jane Holmes-Bernstein, Michael Connell, David Daniel, and numerous research assistants, particularly Lucia Maldonado. This work was supported by the Spencer Foundation, the American Association of University Women Educational Foundation, the Harvard University Mind Brain and Behavior Initiative, and an anonymous grant.

REFERENCES

Adolphs, R., Damasio, H., Tranel, D., Cooper, G., & Damasio, A. (2000). A role for somatosensory cortices in the visual recognition of emotion as revealed by three-dimensional lesion mapping. *Journal of Neuroscience, 20*(7), 2683–2690.

Baird, A. A., Gruber, S. A., & Fein, D. A. (1999). Functional magnetic resonance imaging of facial affect recognition in children and adolescents. *Journal of the American Academy of Child and Adolescent Psychiatry, 38*(2), 195–199.

Bates, E., Reilly, J., Wulfeck, B., Dronkers, N., Opie, M., Fenson, J., . . . Herbst, K. (2001). Differential effects of unilateral lesions on language production in children and adults. *Brain and Language, 79*(2), 223–265.

Bates, E., Thal, D., & Marchman, V. (1991). Symbols and syntax: A Darwinian approach to language development. In N. Krasnegor & D. Rumbaugh (Eds.), *Biological and behavioral determinants of language development* (pp. 29–65). Hillsdale, NJ: Erlbaum.

Battro, A. (2000). *Half a brain is enough: The story of Nico.* Cambridge, UK: Cambridge University Press.

Bloom, L. (1997). Language acquisition in its developmental context. In D. Kuhn & R. S. Siegler (Eds.), *Handbook of child psychology,* Vol. 2: *Cognition, perception and language* (5th ed., pp. 309–370). New York, NY: Wiley.

Boatman, D., Freeman, J., Vining, E., Pulsifer, M., Miglioretti, D., Minahan, R., . . . McKhann, G. (1999). Language recovery after left hemispherectomy in children with late-onset seizures. *Annals of Neurology, 46*(4), 579–586.

Bolinger, D. (1989). *Intonation and its uses: Melody and grammar in discourse.* Stanford, CA: Stanford University Press.

Borod, J. C., Koff, E., Yecker, S., Santschi, C., & Schmidt, J. M. (1998). Facial asymmetry during emotional expression: Gender, valence, and measurement technique. *Neuropsychologia, 36*(11), 1209–1215.

Bruer, J. (1997). Education and the brain: A bridge too far. *Educational Researcher, 26*(8), 4–16.

Calder, A. J., Keane, J., Manes, F., Antoun, N., & Young, A. W. (2000). Impaired recognition and experience of disgust following brain injury. *Nature Neuroscience, 3*(11), 1077–1078.

Campbell, R. (1982). The lateralization of emotion: A critical review. *International Journal of Psychology, 17*(2 Suppl. 3), 211–229.

Cancelliere, A. E. B., & Kertesz, A. (1990). Lesion localization in acquired deficits of emotional expression and comprehension. *Brain and Cognition, 13,* 133–147.

Caramazza, A. (1992). Is cognitive neuropsychology possible? *Journal of Cognitive Neuroscience, 4,* 80–95.

Case, R. (1997). The development of conceptual structures. In D. Kuhn & R. Seigler

(Eds.), *The handbook of child psychology*, Vol. 2: *Cognition, perception, and language.* (5th ed., pp. 745–800). New York, NY: Wiley.

Case, R., & Okamoto, Y. (1996). The role of central conceptual structures in the development of children's thought. *Monographs of the Society for Research in Child Development, 61*(1–2).

Cohen, M. J., Riccio, C. A., & Flannery, A. M. (1994). Expressive aprosodia following stroke to the right basal ganglia: A case report. *Neuropsychology, 8*(2), 242–245.

Compton, R. J., Heller, W., Banich, M. T., Palmieri, P. A., & Miller, G. A. (2000). Responding to threat: Hemispheric asymmetries and interhemispheric division of input. *Neuropsychology, 14*(2), 254–264.

Corina, D. P., Bellugi, U., & Reilly, J. (1999). Neuropsychological studies of linguistic and affective facial expressions in deaf signers. *Language and Speech, 42*(2–3), 307–331.

Crystal, D. (1997). *The Cambridge encyclopedia of language* (2nd ed.). Cambridge, UK: Cambridge University Press.

Damasio, A. R. (1994). *Descartes error: Emotion, reason and the human brain.* New York, NY: Avon Books.

Damasio, A. R. (1999). *The feeling of what happens: Body and emotion in the making of consciousness.* New York, NY: Harcourt Brace.

Danly, M., & Shapiro, B. (1982). Speech prosody in Broca's aphasia. *Brain and Language, 16*, 171–190.

Deacon, T. W. (2000). Evolutionary perspectives on language and brain plasticity. *Journal of Communication Disorders, 33*(4), 273–291.

Diamond, M., & Hopson, J. (1998). *Magic trees of the mind: How to nurture your child's intelligence, creativity, and healthy emotions.* New York, NY: Plume.

Ekman, P., & Friesen, W. V. (1975). *Pictures of facial affect.* Palo Alto, CA: Consulting Psychologists Press.

Fischer, K. W., & Bidell, T. R. (1998). Dynamic development of psychological structures in action and thought. In R. M. Lerner (Ed.), *Handbook of child psychology*, Vol. 1: *Theoretical models of human development* (5th ed., pp. 467–561). New York, NY: Wiley.

Fischer, K. W., & Immordino-Yang, M. H. (2002). Cognitive development and education: From dynamic general structure to specific learning and teaching. In E. Lagemann (Ed.), *Traditions of scholarship in education.* Chicago: Spencer Foundation

Fischer, K. W., & Kennedy, B. (1997). Tools for analyzing the many shapes of development: The case of self-in-relationships in Korea. In K. A. Renninger & E. Amsel (Eds.), *Processes of development* (pp. 117–152). Mahwah, NJ: Erlbaum.

Gandour, J., Petty, S. H., & Dardarananda, R. (1989). Dysprosody in Broca's aphasia: A case study. *Brain and Language, 37*, 232–257.

Gandour, J., Ponglorpisit, S., & Dardarananda, R. (1992). Tonal disturbances in Thai after brain damage. *Journal of Neurolinguistics, 7*(1–2), 133–145.

Gandour, J., Wong, D., Hsieh, L., Weinzapfel, B., Van Lancker, D., & Hutchins, G.

(2000). A crosslinguistic PET study of tone perception. *Journal of Cognitive Neuroscience, 12*(1), 207–222.

Gandour, J., Wong, D., & Hutchins, G. (1998). Pitch processing in the human brain is influenced by language experience. *Neuroreport, 9*(9), 2115–2119.

Haidt, J. (2001). The emotional dog and its rational tail: A social intuitionist approach to moral judgment. *Psychological Review, 108*(4), 814–834.

Harrington, A. (1991). Beyond phrenology: Localization theory in the modern era. In P. Corsi (Ed.), *Enchanted loom: Chapters in the history of neuroscience* (pp. 207–239). London: Oxford University Press.

Hawley, C. A. (2003). Reported problems and their resolution following mild, moderate and severe traumatic brain injury amongst children and adolescents in the UK. *Brain Injury, 17*(2), 105–129.

Heilman, K. M., Leon, S. A., & Rosenbek, J. C. (2004). Affective aprosodia from a medial frontal stroke. *Brain and Language, 89,* 411–416.

Holt, E. (1996). Reporting on talk: The use of direct reported speech in conversation. *Research on Language and Social Interaction, 29*(3), 219–245.

Hughes, C., Chan, J., & Su, M. (1983). Aprosodia in Chinese patients with right cerebral hemisphere lesions. *Archives of Neurology, 40,* 732–736.

Immordino-Yang, M. H. (2005). *A tale of two cases: Emotion and affective prosody after left and right hemispherectomy* (Unpublished doctoral dissertation). Harvard University Graduate School of Education, Cambridge, MA.

Immordino-Yang, M. H. (2001a). When 2 + 2 makes kids trip: Making sense of brain research in the classroom. *Basic Education, 45*(8), 16–19.

Immordino-Yang, M. H. (2001b). *Working memory for music and language: Do we develop analogous systems based on similar symbolic experience?* (Unpublished qualifying paper). Harvard University Graduate School of Education, Cambridge, MA.

Immordino-Yang, M. H., & Damasio, A. R. (2007). We feel, therefore we learn: The relevance of affective and social neuroscience to education. *Mind, Brain and Education, 1*(1), 3–10.

Jansari, A., Tranel, D., & Adolphs, R. (2000). A valence-specific lateral bias for discriminating emotional facial expressions in free field. *Cognition and Emotion, 14*(3), 341–353.

Johnson, M. H. (2000). Cortical specialization for higher cognitive functions: Beyond the maturational model. *Brain and Cognition, 42*(1), 124–127.

Kandel, E., Schwartz, S., & Jessell, T. (2000). *Principles of neural science* (4th ed.). New York, NY: McGraw-Hill.

Kennedy, B. (1994). *The development of self-understanding in adolescents in Korea* (Unpublished doctoral dissertation). Harvard University, Cambridge, MA.

Kotz, S. A., Meyer, M., Alter, K., Besson, M., von Cramon, D. Y., & Friederici, A. D. (2003). On the lateralization of emotional prosody: An event-related functional MR investigation. *Brain and Language, 86,* 366–376.

Kreuz, R. (1996). The use of verbal irony: Cues and constraints. In J. S. Mio & A. N. Katz (Eds.), *Metaphor: Implications and applications* (pp. 23–38). Mahwah, NJ: Erlbaum.

Lezak, M. D. (1995). *Neuropsychological assessment* (3rd ed.). New York, NY: Oxford University Press.

Moen, I., & Sundet, K. (1996). Production and perception of word tones (pitch accents) in patients with left and right hemisphere damage. *Brain and Language*, 53(2), 267–281.

Monrad-Krohn, G. H. (1947). Dysprosody or altered "melody of language." *Brain*, 70(4), 405–415.

Murray, J. P., Liotti, M., Ingmundson, P. T., Mayberg, H. S., Pu, Y., Zamarripa, F., . . . Fox, P. T. (2006). Children's brain activations while viewing televised violence revealed by fMRI. *Media Psychology*, 8(1), 25–37.

National Research Council. (1999). *How people learn: Brain, mind, experience, and school*. Washington, DC: National Academy Press.

Ohala, J. J. (1984). An ethological perspective on common cross-language utilization of F0 of voice. *Phonetica*, 41, 1–16.

Packard, J. (1986). Tone production deficits in nonfluent aphasic Chinese speech. *Brain and Language*, 29(2), 212–223.

Pell, M. D. (1998). Recognition of prosody following unilateral brain lesion: Influence of functional and structural attributes of prosodic contours. *Neuropsychologia*, 36(8), 710–715.

Pell, M. D. (1999). Fundamental frequency encoding of linguistic and emotional prosody by right hemisphere-damaged speakers. *Brain and Language*, 69, 161–192.

Pell, M. D., & Baum, S. (1997). The ability to perceive and comprehend intonation in linguistic and affective contexts by brain-damaged adults. *Brain and Language*, 57, 80–99.

Perry, R. J., Rosen, H. R., Kramer, J. H., Beer, J. S., Levenson, R. L., & Miller, B. L. (2001). Hemispheric dominance for emotions, empathy and social behaviour: Evidence from right and left handers with frontotemporal dementia. *Neurocase*, 7(2, pt. 2), 145–160.

Piacentini, J. C., & Hynd, G. W. (1988). Language after dominant hemispherectomy: Are plasticity of function and equipotentiality viable concepts? *Clinical Psychology Review*, 8(6), 595–609.

Reilly, J. S., Bates, E. A., & Marchman, V. A. (1998). Narrative discourse in children with early focal brain injury. *Brain and Language*, 61(3), 335–375.

Ross, E. D. (2000). Affective prosody and the aprosodias. In M. Mesulam (Ed.), *Principles of behavioral and cognitive neurology* (2nd ed., pp. 316–331). London: Oxford University Press.

Ross, E. D., Thompson, R. D., & Yenkowsky, J. (1997). Lateralization of affective prosody in the brain and the collosal integration of hemispheric language functions. *Brain and Language*, 56, 27–54.

Scherer, K. R. (1986). Vocal affect expression: A review and model for future research. *Psychological Bulletin*, 99, 143–165.

Schirmer, A., Alter, K., Kotz, S., & Friederici, A. D. (2001). Lateralization of prosody during language production: A lesion study. *Brain and Language*, 76, 1–17.

Schlanger, B. B., Schlanger, P., & Gerstman, L. J. (1976). The perception of emotionally toned sentences by right-hemisphere damaged and aphasic subjects. *Brain and Language, 3,* 396–403.

Smith, A., & Sugar, O. (1975). Development of above normal language and intelligence 21 years after left hemispherectomy. *Neurology, 25*(9), 813–818.

Snowling, M. (2001). What the brain learns and when: A contemporary view. In J. L. McClelland & R. S. Siegler (Eds.), *Mechanisms of cognitive development: Behavioral and neural perspectives.* Mahwah, NJ: Erlbaum.

Starkstein, S. E., Federoff, J. P., Price, T. R., Leiguarda, R. C., & Robinson, R. G. (1994). Neuropsychological and neuroradiologic correlates of emotional prosody comprehension. *Neurology, 44,* 515–522.

Tompkins, C. A., & Flowers, C. R. (1985). Perception of emotional intonation by brain-damaged adults: The influence of task-processing levels. *Journal of Speech and Hearing Research, 28,* 527–538.

Trauner, D. A., Ballantyne, A., Friedland, S., & Chase, C. (1996). Disorders of affective and linguistic prosody in children after early unilateral brain damage. *Annals of Neurology, 39*(3), 361–367.

Trauner, D. A., Nass, R., & Ballantyne, A. (2001). Behavioural profiles of children and adolescents after pre- or perinatal unilateral brain damage. *Brain, 124*(5), 995–1002.

Van Lancker, D., & Sidtis, J. J. (1992). The identification of affective prosodic stimuli by left- and right-hemisphere-damaged subjects: All errors are not created equal. *Journal of Speech and Hearing Research, 35,* 963–970.

Van Lancker-Sidtis, D. (2004). When only the right hemisphere is left: Studies in language and communication. *Brain and Language, 91,* 199–211.

Voeller, K. K., Hanson, J. A., & Wendt, R. N. (1988). Facial affect recognition in children: A comparison of the performance of children with right and left hemisphere lesions. *Neurology, 38*(11), 1744–1748.

CHAPTER 8

The Smoke Around Mirror Neurons: Goals as Sociocultural and Emotional Organizers of Perception and Action in Learning

Mary Helen Immordino-Yang

Chapter description: This article extends the work with Nico and Brooke presented in Chapter 7 in an attempt to integrate constructivist learning theories (starting with Piaget and Vygotsky) with new neuroscientific evidence about so-called mirror neurons. Combining these two very different approaches to understanding social learning leads to two basic insights for education: (a) Skills are, in essence, flexible repertoires of goal-directed, contextually relevant representations built from the convergence of actions (i.e., "what I did/what I thought") and perceptions (i.e., "what I noticed was the outcome, and how that made me feel/think"). (b) Artful and effective teaching involves modeling efficient, appropriate, and flexible skills in such a way that their implicit goals become apparent to the students. Neuroscientific evidence suggests that, if they do not recognize that the teacher's actions are goal-directed, the students will not simulate or internalize the teacher's thoughts and actions. To the students, the teacher's actions will appear random rather than meaningful and memorable.

From the pragmatists to the neo-Piagetians, development has been understood to involve cycles of perception and action—the internalization of interactions with the world, and the construction of skills for acting in the world. Chapter 7 showed that Nico, who was missing his right cerebral hemi-

sphere, and Brooke, who was missing his left, had compensated for basic neuropsychological skills to previously unexpected degrees, and it argued that the
ways they had compensated revealed general principles about the active role
of the learner and the organizing role of emotion and social interaction in
development. (As is described in Chapter 7, Nico and Brooke each underwent
hemispherectomy, a surgical procedure in which one cortical hemisphere
of the brain is removed or functionally disconnected to control severe and
intractable epileptic seizures.) In this chapter, I argue that the juxtaposition
of Nico's and Brooke's performances provides a powerful wedge into the problem of individual differences by providing an extraordinary example of the
relationship between perception and action in learning. This example leads
to a tentative scheme that brings together cognitive developmental theory
with recent neurobiological evidence on the functioning of mirror neuron
systems in the brain, to produce pedagogically relevant insights into the
nature of contextualized skill development.

In the sections that follow, I extend the argument from my original paper
to claim that Nico's and Brooke's patterns of skills for prosody (the affective
intonation or melody of speech) can be interpreted as complementary examples of the relationship between perception and action in development. I
argue that taking such an interpretation leads to a more differentiated view of
the relationship between perception and action that begins to account for the
role of neuropsychological strengths and weaknesses in creating variability
between learners. Taken together with recent evidence from cognitive and
affective neuroscience (Immordino-Yang & Damasio, 2007 [see Chapter 1]),
as well as with evidence from cognitive developmental theory and research,
this interpretation points us toward a more biologically grounded, testable
model of the relationship between perception and action in learning.

ACCOUNTING FOR VARIABILITY IN SKILL
DEVELOPMENT: UNDERSTANDING NICO'S AND
BROOKE'S BEHAVIOR IN TERMS OF PERCEPTION,
ACTION, AND THEIR CONVERGENCE

There is a long tradition in educational theory of analyzing development
in terms of dynamic feedback loops between action and perception, starting
with the pragmatists of the early twentieth century, including figures such as
John Dewey and Charles S. Peirce (see Hartshorne & Weiss, 1965; Hickman
& Alexander, 1998), and continuing into modern thinking in cognitive science and developmental psychology (e.g., Bruner, 1973; Case, 1998; Fischer
& Immordino-Yang, 2002). Piaget described this well with his concepts of

"assimilation," in which a learner acts in the world based on his or her current understanding, and "accommodation," in which feedback from these interactions is incorporated into the learner's understanding of how the world works (Piaget, 1937/1954). In these constructivist approaches, learning does not involve passively receiving information imparted by a teacher; instead, learning is an active, iterative process in which a student acts on and perceives the environment, in part through engaging in social interactions with other people.

Many modern views of development build on these ideas. For example, Fischer and his colleagues posit that the most basic elements of cognitive development, present at birth, are reflexes (Fischer & Bidell, 2006). Just as chemical elements are the smallest units of a substance that retain its properties, in Fischer's neo-Piagetian view, reflexes are the smallest coherent units of behavior and thought. Importantly, these reflexes function at the nexus of perception and action. When a reflex is triggered, a baby first perceives a stimulus that has the capability to produce a particular action, and the action automatically ensues. With development and experience, this cyclic process of moving between perception and action, in dynamic feedback loops with the world, becomes the substrate for increasingly complex behavior and thought. Actions and perceptions, and eventually thoughts about these actions and perceptions, are actively coordinated into functional skills for thinking, feeling, and acting in the social and physical world.

Moving back to the evidence described above, Nico's and Brooke's recoveries show us one example of how perception (instantiated in the brain as sensory processing) and action (instantiated in the brain as motor planning and representation) are grounded in neuropsychological strengths and weaknesses. That is, it could be argued that both boys are compensating for their neurological deficits by constructing skills that connect their perception of prosody as pitch contours with their motor plans for producing prosody. Because each boy is missing half of the neural hardware normally used for perception and motoric representation, the patterns of skills the boys create reflect the strengths of their perceptual and motoric origins, as well as the social and emotional goals of the skill. In this interpretation, each boy's motor plans for producing prosody are mapped onto his perceptions of others' prosody, with the goal of creating and understanding socially relevant speech cues. Together, these boys demonstrate that neuropsychological profiles of strengths and weaknesses in perception and action can vary quite a lot, yet if the social and emotional features of the context are well suited to the construction of meaningful, goal-directed skills, perception and action can come together, and the behavioral outcome can be surprisingly normative.

Brooke and Nico demonstrate this quite nicely in their discussions about prosody in sarcastic and sincere contexts. For example, Brooke talks extensively about how he would feel or talk in different social contexts, and with different prosodic intents; with each prosodic possibility he generates (via motor planning), he builds a connection to the sound of the speech he would create (via perceptual representations) and relates this to an associated social goal (e.g., how to talk appropriately to one's grandmother). Nico, on the other hand, maps his perception and motoric representation of prosody in the most efficient way possible to accomplish the goal of speaking normally and understanding social situations, skills that by conventional neurological wisdom he should not have. For him, perception and action come together to produce a set of features for categorizing pitch in the speech he hears and produces.

Interestingly, evidence from cognitive neuroscience suggests that the iterative, recursive process of bringing together perceptual and motoric representations in the brain forms a major component of learning and memory, as well as a basic mechanism for social interaction and learning. In the next section, I briefly outline this line of thinking and draw tentative connections to processes of skill development as they have been described in the developmental literature.

NEUROLOGICAL CONVERGENCE:
NETWORKS THAT SUPPORT SKILL DEVELOPMENT

As described above, dynamic cycles between perception and action have been understood for decades to be a major organizing force in development. Here, I will begin to integrate new information from cognitive neuroscience with this framework, with the aim of proposing a direction of thinking that may advance our understanding of the biological grounding of skill development, including in social contexts.

Specifically, the last decade marks the identification of a possibly new type of system in the brain, dubbed "mirror systems" by their discoverers (Arbib, 2012; di Pellegrino, Fadiga, Fogassi, Gallese, & Rizzolatti, 1992; Gallese, Fadiga, Fogassi, & Rizzolatti, 1996; Rizzolatti, Fogassi, & Gallese, 2001; Umiltà et al., 2001). The neural architecture that enables these systems was posited to exist by Antonio Damasio in his 1989 exposition of "convergence zones" (Damasio, 1989; Damasio & Damasio, 1993).[1] Damasio argued that

---

1. Antecedents of the idea that Damasio explicated more fully can be found in earlier writings, for example, in Donald Hebb's *Organization of Behavior* (1949). Importantly, though, while Damasio's convergence zones make use of Hebbian learning, they function in two directions. The con-

meaningful learning and memory for coherent, contextualized experiences would be physically impossible without a neurological mechanism for the interface of sensory and motor systems in the brain. He dubbed such systems "convergence zones"[2] and posited that association cortices in the brain were likely the neurological substrates for such processing. Deducing the functioning of particular association areas from the patterns of deficits associated with brain damage in different locations, Damasio and his colleagues (see Damasio, 1989, for a review) described selective deficits in various domains, for example, in language, social functioning, and visual processing, that when probed revealed a neurological system for learning and behaving in which perceptions (either from the environment or from recall) and actions (either in the environment or in the mind) are built into increasingly complex amodal representations, in effect memories of one's experiences. These memories, each the product of convergence between perception and action at increasingly complex levels, are embodied in recursive, looping networks that project both forward toward convergence zones and back again into perceptual and motor areas. These networks can be iteratively reactivated and modified as the situation requires, resulting in the construction of coherent, goal-directed thoughts, plans, and behaviors. Notably, a person need not directly experience in the environment every action or perception; instead, he can mentally conjure these experiences based on memory or imagination. Of necessity, these internally derived activations in the form of memories or imaginings will reflect the biological predispositions and previous subjective experiences of the learner.

Although not described as such at the time, I would argue that this iterative reconstruction of perceptual and motoric experiences is, in essence, the basic process that allows the development and calling up of contextually relevant skills. As a learner interacts with the social and physical environment, either

---

nectivity of these networks brings together neural signals about simpler pieces of information to create the neural substrates of more complex mental representations. Once bound together, the activity in convergence zones also feeds back, retroactivating simpler perceptual and motoric units upstream and thereby reconstituting the original separate set of perceptual and motoric activations. It is this looping, recursive quality that allows these networks to support skill development as I am describing it.

2. Note that Damasio laid out a hierarchical neural architecture with early, modal cortices feeding into and receiving projections from "local" convergence zones, which in turn reciprocally connect to "nonlocal" convergence zones, located in higher-order association cortices. The mirror systems I am describing correspond to "nonlocal" convergence zones, which are amodal and carry out the lowest level of processing in which sensory and motor representations are brought together. While not all convergence at this level involves both sensory and motor components, I would argue that the goal-directed processing that is relevant to my argument about skill development does involve both of these aspects.

by mentally conjuring it or directly experiencing it, she engages dynamic feedback loops between what she perceives and how she acts, thinks, and feels. As she moves through dynamic cycles of perception and action, whether actual, recalled, or imagined, she creates skills that reflect three general dimensions: one that is perceptual, one that is motoric, and one that is goal-directed and results from the convergence of the other two. Because she is acting and perceiving in a social and physical world, the goals she constructs will reflect the social, cultural, and physical constraints of the environment.

One important feature of skill development is that children and adults construct their own skills, but they do so in part by learning from other people. Intriguingly, as alluded to above, the last decade marks major discoveries about the biological mechanisms by which this may happen. In particular, this work collectively suggests that the same association areas that are active when one's own perceptual and motoric representations converge are active, albeit to a lesser degree, when we witness this convergence process for another person, providing that we implicitly understand the context and goals of the other person's actions. It has been hypothesized that this "mirror" property may form the most basic biological mechanism by which we internalize and learn from another person's thoughts and actions (for a discussion, see Oberman & Ramachandran, 2007).[3]

While the functioning of mirror systems in the brain continues to be actively investigated, this research is revealing some of the mechanisms that permit people to learn from social contexts (Wood, Glynn, Phillips, & Hauser, 2007; Oberman, Pineda, & Ramachandran, 2007). While in no way do mirror neuron systems tell the whole story of the neurological processing of social interaction, they do provide a necessary mechanism for the translation of another person's perceived, goal-directed action into the neurological motor plans that would produce it in one's own body. In this way, mirror systems enable at the most basic level the internalization of the goals of another's actions, including actions that reflect emotion states, onto the substrate of one's own self. As Frith and others have described (Frith & Frith, 2006), this process is critical for imitation or other social learning to take place, as well as for empathy, in essence the vicarious experience of another's emotional state. In this way, convergence zones form a basic neurological mechanism

---

3. It is important to note that convergence zones with mirror properties have been discovered in characteristic anterior (frontal) and posterior (mainly inferior parietal) locations in the brain. The mirror systems that I am describing as sensitive to the goals of actions are generally the frontal systems. While the parietal systems are mainly perceptual, the frontal systems are mainly motoric and are therefore engaged when perception and action converge to make goal-directed motor plans and representations.

for learning, by enabling the convergence of action and perception in context, either directly or vicariously experienced. Because convergence zones are connected bidirectionally to perceptual and motoric networks, I propose that the recursive looping of activations between these three types of networks ultimately gives rise to the development of goal-directed skills.

One important aspect of motor planning in the brain that is critical to understanding perceptuomotor convergence lies in the assumption that behavior is goal-directed. Motor plans are not randomly generated; instead, they reflect the cognitive and emotional goals, knowledge, and context of the person creating them. Because of this, mirror systems seem likely to be recruited only when we understand the implicit goal of another's actions. For a simple example from nonhuman primates, Kohler et al. (2002) showed that when monkeys allowed to play with and rip pieces of paper listen to the sound of paper being ripped, their brains show an increase in activity in mirror areas. This is presumed to be because the monkeys understand the meaning or goal of the sound they have perceived and have translated this goal into its accompanying motor plan. By contrast, monkeys who have never played with paper show no increase in mirror neuron activity when they perceive evidence of that particular action, for example, the sound of paper being ripped, presumably because there is no convergence happening. These monkeys do not know about the relationship between the action of ripping paper and the perception of this process; to them, the sound of paper ripping is akin to white noise.

For a complementary example, Umiltà et al. (2001) showed that monkeys show increases in mirror activity when watching experimenters undertake goal-directed actions. Whether the culminating goal-directed action is completed in or out of view, if the monkey inferred the goal-directed nature of the movement, the appropriate mirror systems responded and convergence between perceptual and motoric representations took place. However, when the action was pantomimed such that there was no apparent goal, the monkeys showed no increase in mirror neuron activity. Interestingly, this result differs between monkeys and people—because people do appreciate the implicit goal in pantomimed actions, human subjects have been shown to activate mirror areas when observing pantomimes of goal-directed actions, for example, opening a bottle, but not when observing non-goal-directed actions (Grèzes, Costes, & Decety, 1998). While the research with people is not yet conclusive, there is increasing evidence that if people do not recognize that another's actions are goal-directed, mirror systems will not be activated and convergence will not take place.

Overall, I am proposing an integrative model in which the cognitive constructs of perception and action are operationalized neurologically in sensory and motor processing, respectively. Sensory and motor processing then converges in the brain, a process that involves networks of association areas referred to by Damasio (1989) as "convergence zones." The iterative and dynamic process of convergence results in the formation of goal-directed actions and thoughts, by connecting actions and perceptions, including mental actions and simulated perceptions, to memory for the social and physical context. This process leads to the development of skills, in essence flexible repertoires of goal-directed, contextually relevant representations built from the convergence of actions and perceptions. These skills can be experienced directly or vicariously, thanks to the "mirror" properties of some convergence zones, enabling us to learn from another person's goal-directed action, provided this action makes sense within our developmental and cultural frame of knowledge.

THE SMOKE AROUND THE MIRRORS: ACTION AND PERCEPTION IN SOCIOCULTURAL CONTEXT, AND IMPLICATIONS FOR PEDAGOGY

In the original papers outlining the discovery and functioning of brain mechanisms for comprehension of other's actions, Rizzolatti and his colleagues (di Pellegrino et al., 1992; Gallese et al., 1996; Rizzolatti et al., 2001; Umiltà et al., 2001) dubbed their discovery *mirror neuron systems*. While this term captures one essential feature of the functionality of some neurological association areas, I would argue that the term *mirroring* could be misleading for educators and neuroscientists alike, as it suggests a direct and largely passive internal transposition of another person's goals and actions into one's own brain. The job of mirrors is to reflect what is before them, and mirror systems in the brain, as they have been described, reflect the actions and goals of another person. In this sense, *mirroring* suggests a direct internalization of another's actions, emotions, and goals, which are then automatically experienced in parallel in the onlooker. But, while this internalization of another's situation can be automatic, the representation of another's situation is constructed and experienced on one's own self in accordance with cognitive and emotional preferences, memory, cultural knowledge, and neuropsychological predispositions—the "smoke" around the mirrors.

Returning to my original argument, analyzing Nico's and Brooke's recoveries in light of neurobiological evidence for the convergence of perception and action with socioculturally relevant goals gives us new, testable insights into the development of skills and into the role of neuropsychological strengths and weaknesses in constraining development. In interpreting the evidence in this way, we come closer to accomplishing the goals I set out in my original article (Immordino-Yang, 2007 [see Chapter 7]), including shedding some light on the relationship between brain and experience in development, the organizing role of emotion in this process, and new insights into how students' unique profiles of strengths and weaknesses may play out in learning contexts.

In particular, analyzing these boys' development in this way helps us to understand that the convergence between perception and action in the brain is a socially and emotionally organized process that involves what van Geert and Steenbeek described as "interacting creative minds" (2008, p. 65). For minds to creatively interact, some mechanism for the dynamic transference of goals between people must exist. Further, for the goals to be recognized by both people involved in an interaction, they must be understood as sensible in the sociocultural context of the interaction. I refer to this as the "smoke around the mirrors"—knowledge about the sociocultural context, and its role in organizing the convergence of perception and action to produce goal-directed skills. Commensurate with van Geert and Steenbeek's model, artful and effective teaching and learning depend on the efficient, appropriate, and flexible modeling of skills and their implicit goals, to maximize the efficacy with which skills are shared within classroom contexts. Of course, effective education is also dependent on the productive nature of the goals—for example, students whose main goal is to avoid learning math will not build competent math skills.

Further, this approach sheds light on the neuropsychological sources of variability in students' learning. It suggests that, to learn from a teacher, each student must perceive the lesson and, via neurological convergence, represent what they perceive in terms of motor plans and goals. Therefore, just as we saw for Nico and Brooke, sources of variability will include each student's unique profile of strengths and weaknesses in mechanisms of perception as well as action (motor planning). In addition, because these goals are conceived in a sociocultural context that brings to bear a student's previous experiences and preferences, a third source of variability will be in the construction and interpretation of the goals themselves. For example, the common goal of Nico's and Brooke's compensatory processing is to use and understand affective prosody as a window into participation in social interactions. However, the skills that subserved this goal for each boy were different and reflected each boy's neurological profile of strengths and weaknesses in perception and motor planning for speech.

In terms of implications for mainstream classrooms, Ablin (2008) related this process to principles of lesson design and student-teacher interaction with his description of skill development as one of individualized problem construction. That is, rather than encouraging students to try to directly internalize a teacher's goals, he suggests we provide students with opportunities to engage with the teacher's goals indirectly through a process of active problem construction. As he describes, incorporating this pedagogical method into lessons may facilitate each student in developing skills that will best capitalize on his or her own abilities and preferences.

Thinking about skill development in this way, we see that a student's profile of neurological strengths and weaknesses, while constraining the particulars of what Snow (2008) called "procedures" of learning, does not independently determine the behavioral outcome. Neural strengths and weaknesses cannot be the only factors that predict a student's outcome because, as we have seen, the outcome is influenced as well by the sociocultural knowledge context in which convergence happens and the (often) implicit goals of the skill development. Borrowing from van Geert and Steenbeek's view, the outcomes of learning are the product of a dynamic interaction between perceptual and motoric representations, either directly or empathically experienced or simulated, organized by a person's socioculturally relevant goals and history. For example, it could be said that Nico and Brooke achieved their good prosodic skills in part because they *wanted* to and in part because their supportive social environments encouraged them to.

As Snow (2008) noted, this has important implications for pedagogy and assessment, as educators and policy makers often focus too heavily on standardizing the means to achieving a particular skill, be it long division in math or phonological processing in reading, without providing adequate support for learners to achieve similar skills by different means—what Christoff (2008) referred to in a neuropsychological context as "solution-oriented" learning. As Nico and Brooke demonstrate, the interplay between each student's perceptual and motoric representations could lead to outcomes in behaviors and skills via convergence that are quite similar across students, while the nature of each student's underlying representations and skills could be quite different. As Snow describes, it is therefore important that pedagogical and assessment tools are designed to test students' functional abilities, without penalizing them for constructing knowledge in disparate ways. Further, building from Snow's and Christoff's commentaries, I suggest that designs for lessons and learning experiences should be mindful of each aspect of the process of constructing goal-directed skills, perhaps specifically addressing the range of ways that students may be perceiving, acting upon, and socioculturally understanding a domain of knowledge. Indeed, the most successful educational tools and assessments already incorporate these considerations into their design, allowing many different pathways to similar ends. Some examples include Universal Design for Learning (Rose & Meyer, 2006) and Singer's (2007) model of math teaching. However, I suggest a further refinement to the understanding of the alternate pathways students could follow as they pursue the development of skills: consider explicitly the perceptual, motoric, and socioemotional aspects of the skill to be constructed and examine each in light of the learner's own goals.

In conclusion, in this chapter I bring together the insights of my colleagues with neurobiological evidence and the interpretations I suggested in Chapter 7 to propose a more biologically grounded approach to skill development. In this approach, processing for perception and action converge in the brain, in a way that is socially and emotionally organized and that involves a dynamic interplay between minds. Social and emotional reactions and desires, as well as cultural knowledge, modulate this convergence, resulting in the development of skills that are goal-directed and influenced by the social context, and that reflect the perceptual and motoric strengths and weaknesses of the learner. This approach suggests pedagogically relevant insights into the sources of variability between learners, as well as implications for more effective teaching and assessment of varied learners.

ACKNOWLEDGMENT

This chapter was originally published as a response to my colleagues' commentaries on my empirical work with Nico and Brooke (see Chapter 7). For engaging me in this dialogue, warm thanks go to Jason Ablin, Kalina Christoff, Catherine Snow, Henderien Steenbeek, and Paul van Geert. This work was supported by the Spencer Foundation, the American Association of University Women Educational Foundation, the Harvard University Mind Brain and Behavior Initiative, and an anonymous grant.

REFERENCES

Ablin, J. L. (2008). Learning as problem design versus problem solving: Making the connection between cognitive neuroscience research and educational practice. *Mind, Brain, and Education*, 2(2), 52–54.

Arbib, M. (2012). *How the brain got language: The mirror system hypothesis*. New York, NY: Oxford University Press.

Bruner, J. S. (1973). Organization of early skilled action. *Child Development* (44), 1–11.

Case, R. (1998). The development of conceptual structures. In D. Kuhn & R. Seigler (Eds.), *The handbook of child psychology*, Vol. 2: *Cognition, perception, and language* (5th ed., pp. 745–800). New York, NY: Wiley.

Christoff, K. (2008). Applying neuroscientific findings to education: The good, the tough and the hopeful. *Mind, Brain, and Education*, 2(2), 55–58.

Damasio, A. R. (1989). Time-locked multiregional retroactivation: A systems-level proposal for the neural substrates of recall and recognition. *Cognition*, 33(1–2), 25–62.

Damasio, A. R., & Damasio, H. (1993). Cortical systems underlying knowledge retrieval: Evidence from human lesion studies. In T. A. Poggio & D. A. Glaser (Eds.), *Exploring brain functions: Models in neuroscience* (pp. 233–248). New York, NY: Wiley.

di Pellegrino, G., Fadiga, L., Fogassi, L., Gallese, V., & Rizzolatti, G. (1992). Understanding motor events: A neurophysiological study. *Experimental Brain Research*, 91(1), 176–180.

Fischer, K. W., & Bidell, T. (2006). Dynamic development of action and thought. In W. Damon & R. Lerner (Eds.), *Handbook of child psychology*, Vol. 1: *Theoretical models of human development* (6th ed., pp. 313–399). Hoboken, NJ: Wiley.

Fischer, K. W., & Immordino-Yang, M. H. (2002). Cognitive development and education: From dynamic general structure to specific learning and teaching. In E. Lagemann (Ed.), *Traditions of scholarship in education*. Chicago: Spencer Foundation.

Frith, C. D., & Frith, U. (2006). The neural basis of mentalizing. *Neuron*, 50(4), 531–534.

Gallese, V., Fadiga, L., Fogassi, L., & Rizzolatti, G. (1996). Action recognition in the premotor cortex. *Brain*, 119, 593–609.

Grèzes, J., Costes, N., & Decety, J. (1998). Top down effect of strategy on the perception of human biological motion: A PET investigation. *Cognitive Neuropsychology*, 15(6), 553–582.

Hartshorne, C., & Weiss, P. (Eds.). (1965). *Collected papers of Charles Sanders Peirce*, Vols. 1 and 2: *Principles of philosophy and elements of logic*. Cambridge, MA: Harvard University Press.

Hebb, D. O. (1949). *The organization of behavior: A neuropsychological theory*. New York, NY: Wiley.

Hickman, L., & Alexander, T. (Eds.). (1998). *The essential Dewey* (Vols. 1 and 2). Bloomington, IN: Indiana University Press.

Immordino-Yang, M. H. (2007). A tale of two cases: Lessons for education from the study of two boys living with half their brains. *Mind, Brain and Education*, 1(2), 66–83.

Immordino-Yang, M. H., & Damasio, A. R. (2007). We feel, therefore we learn: The relevance of affective and social neuroscience to education. *Mind, Brain and Education*, 1(1), 3–10.

Kohler, E., Keysers, C., Umiltà, M. A., Fogassi, L., Gallese, V., & Rizzolatti, G.

(2002). Hearing sounds, understanding actions: Action representation in mirror neurons. *Science, 297*(5582), 848–848.

Oberman, L. M., Pineda, J. A., & Ramachandran, V. S. (2007). The human mirror neuron system: A link between action observation and social skills. *Social, Cognitive and Affective Neuroscience, 2*(1), 62–66.

Oberman, L. M., & Ramachandran, V. S. (2007). The simulating social mind: The role of the mirror neuron system and simulation in the social and communicative deficits of autism spectrum disorders. *Psychological Bulletin, 133*(2), 310–327.

Piaget, J. (1954). *The construction of reality in the child* (M. Cook, Trans.). New York, NY: Basic Books. (Original work published 1937)

Rizzolatti, G., Fogassi, L., & Gallese, V. (2001). Neurophysiological mechanisms underlying the understanding and imitation of action. *Nature Reviews Neuroscience, 2*(9), 661–670.

Rose, D. H., & Meyer, A. (Eds.). (2006). *A practical reader in universal design for learning.* Cambridge, MA: Harvard Education Press.

Singer, F. M. (2007). Beyond conceptual change: Using representations to integrate domain-specific structural models in learning mathematics. *Mind, Brain, and Education, 1*(2), 84–97.

Snow, C. (2008). Varied developmental trajectories: Lessons for educators. *Mind, Brain, and Education, 2*(2), 59–61.

Umiltà, M. A., Kohler, E., Gallese, V., Fogassi, L., Fadiga, L., Keysers, C., & Rizzolatti, G. (2001). I know what you are doing: A neurophysiological study. *Neuron, 31*(1), 155–165.

van Geert, P., & Steenbeek, H. (2008). Brains and the dynamics of "wants" and "cans" in learning. *Mind, Brain, and Education, 2*(2), 62–66.

Wood, J. N., Glynn, D. D., Phillips, B. C., & Hauser, M. D. (2007). The perception of rational, goal-directed action in nonhuman primates. *Science, 317*(5843), 1402–1405.

CHAPTER 9

Admiration for Virtue: Neuroscientific Perspectives on a Motivating Emotion

Mary Helen Immordino-Yang and Lesley Sylvan

Chapter description: When people learn of another's incredible accomplishments, moral fortitude, and determination in the face of difficulties and obstacles, often they become inspired to do meaningful work themselves. Despite the power of such motivation, though, these emotions have rarely been examined in the context of education. This article centers on findings we originally reported in Immordino-Yang, McColl, Damasio, and Damasio (2009). In that study, we found that social emotions such as admiration for another's virtue resulted in subcortical neural activations in brain stem regions responsible for regulation of survival-relevant mechanisms, including consciousness, cardiac functioning, and respiration. The most notable implication for education is that meaningful, socially relevant thinking *moves* us—inspiration changes our physiology, heightens our conscious awareness, and impels us to act purposefully toward our goals.

Social emotions, such as admiration for another person's virtue, play a critical role in interpersonal relationships and moral behavior and often lead to a sense of heightened self-awareness that is profoundly motivating (i.e., the desire to be virtuous and to accomplish meaningful actions despite difficult obstacles; Haidt & Seder, 2009). Our recent study of the brain and psychophysiological correlates of experiencing admiration revealed that the feeling of this complex, culturally constructed, motivating emotion involves not only high-level "cognitive" systems but also the neural systems for the feeling of one's own body, especially the gut and viscera (Immordino-Yang, McColl, Damasio, & Damasio, 2009). The experience of this emotion was also associated with increased heart rate and increased blood flow to brain systems that operate outside of conscious control to regulate consciousness and basic biological survival, such as blood pressure and hormone regulation. These findings contribute an interesting jumping-off point for reexamining the educational study of motivation states, in that they suggest that, contrary to dominant conceptions in educational research, nonconscious, low-level physiological processes related to survival, consciousness, and their modulation by emotion may be critical contributors to motivation. In contrast, most current educational research on motivation examines only high-level processing of cognitive conceptions as contributors to motivation, for example, self-report of perceived self-competence. In the end, it may be that considering processing associated with non-consciously controlled physiological processes in relation to processing of conscious, cognitive self-knowledge would afford educational researchers a new vantage point from which to investigate and understand the nature of motivation. Consistent with recent discoveries from neuroscience, this new vantage point would consider motivation as simultaneously cognitive and emotional, inherently embodied, and possessing both conscious and nonconscious dimensions.

NEURAL BASES OF EMOTION, SOCIAL EMOTION, AND SELF

Basic emotions, such as anger, fear, happiness, and sadness, are cognitive and physiological processes that involve an interplay of body and mind (Barrett, 2009; Damasio, 1994/2005). As such, they utilize brain systems for body regulation (e.g., for blood pressure, heart rate, respiration, digestion), including for the maintenance of consciousness (e.g., in the brain stem) and body sensation (e.g., for physical pain or pleasure, for a racing heart or stomachache). They also influence brain systems for cognition, changing thought in characteristic ways—from the search for escape strategies in fear, to the wish to seek revenge in anger, to acceptance and openness to others in happiness, to dwelling on something or someone lost in sadness. In each case, the emotion is played out in the mind and can also be displayed through characteristic changes on the face and in the body. (Notably, these bodily and facial changes can be real, resulting in actual modulation of the body state or face, or simulated, wherein a person does not show the emotion outwardly in behavior but uses an "as if" mental process that recruits body-related brain systems [Damasio, 1999].) These changes are in turn felt via neural systems for sensing and regulating the body, and the resulting feelings interact again with current thoughts, helping people to regulate and learn from their experiences. In other words, what affective neuroscience is revealing is that the mind is influenced by an interdependency of the body and brain through processes that can be organized into complex and variable but coherent constructions we call emotions, and that the relationship between the body and brain likely plays a critical role in motivating our individual thoughts and learning, at both conscious and nonconscious levels (Immordino-Yang & Damasio, 2007).

However, while there is extensive evidence that the body and brain are interdependent during basic emotion states, the extent to which the feeling of complex social emotions relies upon this codependence is less well understood. In designing our experiment, we set out to investigate whether the feeling of this motivated emotion state—not merely recognizing this state in another person but actually subjectively *experiencing* it oneself—would recruit low-level brain systems that regulate and feel the body. For example, the neural correlates of a highly motivating social emotion like admiration for virtue would likely be extremely complex because they ought to involve high-level systems that support other aspects of cognition, such as regions involved in episodic memory retrieval, empathy, and perspective taking in relation to the self (Zaki, Ochsner, Hanellin, Wager, & Mackey, 2007; Gray, 1999). And yet, would calling up complex, conscious knowledge about memories, plans, and their meaning be sufficient to sustain such a strongly motivated state? Or, would the feeling and regulation of such basic survival-related processes as respiration and heart rate modulation also become involved at a later stage of processing, in the phase of the emotion that corresponds to a desire for meaningful action? If these lower-level processes were especially activated late in the time course of the emotion experience, it would suggest that the motivating power of an emotion like admiration comes not simply from the conscious calling up of relevant knowledge in relation to one's own situation, but also from nonconscious processes related to the interdependence of the body and mind. It would lend support to the idea that our intense desire to *socially* survive and flourish by accomplishing meaningful actions in the social world derives its power by co-opting systems whose original purpose is to maintain *basic* survival through the maintenance of the body.

INDUCING ADMIRATION FOR VIRTUE: A COMBINED NEUROSCIENTIFIC AND PSYCHOLOGICAL APPROACH

In our experiment, we tested hypotheses related to the idea that complex social emotions like admiration for virtue would engage not only neural systems related to representing cognitive knowledge but also systems in the brain related to the regulation of consciousness and the feeling of the body. That is, we hypothesized that despite the complexity of the culturally relevant knowledge required to fully induce the emotion of admiration for virtue, once this complex knowledge was called up, we would see also the activation of systems in the brain and brain stem that maintain basic survival and prepare the body for action. These would include such systems as those that modulate heart rate, blood pressure, and hormone regulation and those that feel the gut and viscera. Importantly for the discussion here, while we knew that the calling up of complex knowledge described above may be done consciously, the secondary (i.e., later and longer-lasting) modulation of low-level systems related to the body could not be under conscious control or awareness.

To test our hypotheses, we involved thirteen participants in a combined fMRI (functional magnetic resonance imaging), psychophysiological recording, and psychological experiment with three phases. In the experiment, six women and seven men participated individually in a one-on-one, two-hour videotaped interview in which they discussed with an experimenter true narratives about real people's lives, some of which involved recounting highly virtuous acts that are highly admirable. (Participants' mean age was 30.3 years, range was 19–57 years; for methodological details, see supplementary information for Immordino-Yang et al., 2009). For example, in one true story, a young blind German woman, despite all odds, learns fluent Tibetan language by ear, invents a computerized Tibetan Braille system to translate texts, and travels into the mountains of Tibet to open a school for blind children, to which she dedicates her life. For methodological reasons relating to fMRI analyses, other "control" narratives involved recounting stories that involved interesting but fairly commonplace social circumstances or achievements, such as the story of a high school student who organizes a drama production at her school and donates the proceeds to the school library. Participants were not told the specific emotion categories in the experiment and were asked to be as honest and reflective as possible in their discussions of their feelings and thoughts about the stories.

After learning about stories such as these, experiment participants were scanned using fMRI while they viewed five-second reminder versions presenting the crux of each of the stories, followed by a thirteen-second period of gray screen. Participants were asked to try to become as emotional as possible about each story and to rate the strength of their real-time emotional response by pressing buttons. Psychophysiological data on heart rate change and respiration rate were also collected as corroborating measures of the participants' bodily changes in the scanner, and in order to identify the timing of the emotional response. After participants completed the scanning phase, which lasted approximately one hour, they were again individually interviewed about the experiences and thoughts they had had while in the scanning phase of the experiment.

Analysis of the data proceeded in several steps. First, videotaped pre- and postscan interviews were examined by two independent raters, with the aim of identifying and removing from the fMRI analysis any trial corresponding to a narrative to which a participant did not react with the emotion established by prior piloting, for example, when a participant did not feel admiration for the virtue of the Tibetan woman described above or felt some strong emotion for the high school drama student. (Interrater reliability calculations on the whole data set revealed 96 percent agreement, with Cohen's kappa = 0.8.) Next, participants' button press data were examined, so that fMRI results from admiration-inducing trials in which the participant reported feeling strong emotion could be contrasted with control trials in which the participant reported no strong reaction. (This is necessary in order to identify regions of the brain whose increased activity is associated with the emotion state, above what is necessary for basic social and body-regulatory processing.) Finally, the psychophysiological data were examined in order to determine the time course of participants' emotional responses to the narratives while in the scanner; once identified, the fMRI data corresponding to this time window were built into a general linear model that enabled us to contrast the patterns of brain response during the feeling of admiration for virtue with the patterns associated with reflecting on the nonemotional control stories. As is standard in fMRI research, we tested our hypotheses by examining whether there was significantly different blood flow in regions of the brain and brain stem associated with our hypotheses during the feeling of admiration for virtue compared to the processing of interesting but not strongly emotion-inducing stories. We also conducted secondary analyses of the time course of the activation in a brain region important for the feeling of gut and viscera (the anterior insular cortex) and of the direction of "effective connectivity" or so-called causal influence between key homeostatic regions of the brain stem and the anterior insula. This final analysis allowed us to probe relationships between the time courses of activation in the two regions, to investigate whether the activation one region could be "driving" or "influencing" the other. (The anterior insula is a somatosensory region that feels the inside of the body, for example, allowing a person to feel a stomachache or a racing heart beat. This region has also been associated with the process of feeling emotion-related changes in the body, such as the "punched in the gut feeling" associated with learning bad news or sense of disgust associated with unfair decisions. The middle portion of the brain stem contains densely packed and tightly arranged nuclei important for regulating bodily survival and consciousness; damage to the sectors of interest here leads to coma and/ or persistent vegetative state.)

In examining the neural data, we found that our hypotheses were confirmed. Not only was a strong feeling of admiration for virtue associated with significantly greater activation in regions of the brain related to memory retrieval and other conscious processes, it was also associated with activation of non-consciously controlled regions that regulate the body and consciousness, including regions extending all the way into the brain stem (survival-relevant nuclei found far below the high-level cortices associated with conscious thought). What is more, activation in the anterior insular cortex, involved in feeling these bodily changes and relating them to learned behavioral choices, began on average four to six seconds later in the emotion process and was subsequently sustained. In contrast, activation in this area during less complex emotions unrelated to meaningful motivation, such as empathy for another person's injured leg, happened almost immediately and died down relatively quickly, on average after a few seconds. (Note that the extent to which these changes in body-related neural processing pertain to real versus simulated bodily changes is the focus of current investigations.) Lastly, during less complex and less motivating emotions, such as compassion for pain and admiration for skill, we found that activations in key regions of the brain stem systematically preceded (i.e., were "driving") activations in the anterior insula (responsible for emotion-related feeling states). However, these same nuclei in the brain stem were being driven *by* the anterior insula during the intensely motivating feeling of admiration for virtue. (That is, the average direction of statistical "causal influence" between certain brain stem nuclei and the anterior insula was reversed in admiration for virtue compared to in other social emotions.) Together, these findings suggest that the feeling and representation of non-consciously induced bodily and emotional changes happens mainly after the cognitive processing necessary to induce admiration for virtue, and that this cognitive processing leads to a state of visceral self-awareness that prepares the body and mind for meaningful, motivated action.

ADMIRATION FOR VIRTUE:
A MOTIVATING SOCIAL EMOTION

Emotions such as admiration for virtue are intrinsically motivating—they incite people to act in ways that are meaningful for themselves and beneficial for society (Haidt, 2003). While the study of positive, social, elevating emotions of the sort that lead to some kinds of motivation has been largely neglected relative to the study of basic (mainly negative) emotions such as fear and disgust, there is a building movement investigating the functioning of positive, elevating emotions such as admiration and gratitude, from both a psychological and a neuropsychological perspective (Algoe, Haidt, & Gable, 2008; Bartlett & DeSteno, 2006; Zahn et al., 2009).

In our experiment, participants who felt a strong emotion of admiration for another person's virtuous accomplishments often spontaneously described in their discussions a strong desire to lead better lives themselves and to accomplish noble deeds. Intriguingly, in addition to the neural signatures of episodic memory, social perspective taking, and various other high-level cognitive processes, the feeling of this motivational emotion state was associated with the recruitment of neural systems related to basic maintenance and sensation of the body, especially of the internal, visceral body (i.e., the "gut"), and systems related to maintenance of consciousness and self-awareness in the cortex and brain stem. Furthermore, analyses of the time courses of activation in these regions suggested that the motivated state associated with feeling admiration for virtue may be due in part to high-level cortical processing influencing the neural machinery in the brain stem that is associated with biological regulation and drives.

What was demonstrated, from a neuropsychological perspective, is that this motivated state, despite its complex cognitive origins, appears not to play out as a purely "rational" process engaged only at the level of the conscious mind. Instead, the feeling of this motivational emotion is deeply rooted in the very systems that keep us alive, that make us act, that organize and regulate the functioning of our body. This finding supports the notion that the body and mind are dynamically interrelated to motivate meaningful thought and action. From a psychological perspective, this finding, if replicated and extended to other emotions and situations, may hint at why strong social emotions, both positive emotions like admiration and negative emotions like hatred, have the power to motivate our decisions and actions, including our educational decisions and actions, so powerfully.

Relating this to educational research on motivation, what these data reveal is that experiencing this motivating emotion involves two kinds of processing:

(a) high-level neural systems for consideration of the current circumstances in light of past learning, which leads to cognitive understanding and emotion induction, and (b) low-level systems that play out the readiness for action on the body and mind and give the cognitive process its motivating power. This distinction and the contribution of each system are essential. (Think of this as the difference between knowing that engaging in a certain action would be beneficial but not feeling any impetus to begin, versus the motivated behavior that ensues when a person knows what to do, feels the desire to do it, and satisfies this desire by continuing to persist in pursuit of the desired goal.) Without the cognitive appraisal, no emotion induction ensues; without the induction of low-level processes related to biological regulation and feeling of the body, especially the "gut," the cognitive appraisal has no motivating power, no "punch."

EDUCATIONAL RESEARCH ON INTRINSIC MOTIVATION: INCORPORATING NONCONSCIOUS AND BIOLOGICAL PROCESSES INTO COGNITIVE MODELS

Intrinsic motivation (at least the variety that is of greatest interest to educators) is a positive and socially contextualized process, and a process that is highly prized in educational environments. That is, educators are largely concerned with promoting learning behaviors that lead to successful academic outcomes, beneficial life choices, and ultimately the production of socially responsible, engaged, life-long learners. Intrinsic motivation is known to be affected by a person's autonomy in relation to others, by a person's perception that he or she is likely to succeed at a task that is valued by others or by society (e.g., going to college), and by other equivalently emotional and social measures of relative self-efficacy (e.g., Forgas, Bower, & Moylan, 1990; Pintrich & Schunk, 2002). Although intrinsic motivation is by definition conjured within an individual person, educationally relevant motivated states are nonetheless, in this sense, both socioemotional and personal (Dweck, 2000; Haidt & Morris, 2009; Pekrun, Goetz, Titz, & Perry, 2002). As such, data on social emotions like admiration can contribute to the study of intrinsic motivation by suggesting that intrinsically motivated states involve both high-level cognitive and affective processing that can be available to the conscious mind, and low-level homeostatic processing for the regulation and sensation of basic bodily survival mechanisms and drives.

However, nearly all of the current theories of intrinsic motivation in the field of education focus on cognitive processes, and in part because many of the critical components of these existing theories are generated from self-report and behavioral choice measures (Karabenick et al., 2007), the issue of conscious versus nonconscious processing has generally not been addressed. It is not that educational theories deny the existence of nonconscious contributors to motivation; rather, the lack of methods for systematically investigating these nonconscious contributors has led to a strong bias in the field toward accounting for motivation in terms of conscious processes exclusively. While these theories are useful in predicting many aspects of student learning and performance in academic and other settings, they may be unable to provide a thorough explanation of the underlying processes that give rise to motivated behavior.

Take, for one of the best-known examples, self-determination theory (e.g., Ryan & Deci, 2000). This theory and its components, in particular basic needs theory, predict that when students feel autonomous and competent, they will be more intrinsically motivated, and that when students are extrinsically rewarded for activities that they previously found engaging, intrinsic motivation and overall interest in the activity will decrease. The authors account for this relationship in part by explaining students' behavioral choices in terms of the satisfaction of basic psychological needs, an account that has been remarkably productive and successful. At the same time, it leaves implicit and unexplored the possible connection of psychological needs to the fulfillment of biological and bodily needs, and unanswered the potential contribution of nonconscious physiological processing and biological drives to the creation of an intrinsically motivated psychological state. The fundamental questions of *why* psychological drives and needs exist and *how* they motivate our behavior and conscious choices remain. (See Izard [2001] for a related discussion about the adaptive functions of emotions, but without a specific connection to education or intrinsic motivation.)

While Pintrich (2003) presciently suggested that future research on intrinsic motivation should build models that integrate nonconscious with conscious processes, the lack of interdisciplinary methods for studying relations among these processes has prevented the field from moving in this direction. One promising way to address these questions, we would argue, may be to develop novel methods to align conscious reports and measurements of behavioral choices with indexes of nonconscious psychological and biological mechanisms. We hope that our study of admiration for virtue takes one small step in this direction by incorporating qualitative interviews and neuroscientific data to induce and study one type of intrinsically motivated state. An expansion of theories of motivation to include a focus on nonconscious and emotion-related processes could yield new insights into student behavior, leading to testable, educationally relevant hypotheses. For example, incorporating a nonconscious emotional focus may help to explain why a student may "know" at the conscious level that he should engage in a particular learning behavior but still not "feel" the impetus to begin or to persist. Conversely, the finding that emotions like admiration for virtue may recruit systems responsible for managing life regulation may give some insight into the power of psychological needs and drives by suggesting that they harness machinery meant to incite, enact, and feel the biological drives that keep us physically alive.

To sum up, in light of new evidence from psychology and neuroscience, including the evidence on admiration that we present here, we argue that current educational theories of motivation might gain predictive and explanatory power were they expanded to account for the role of nonconscious processing related to regulation of biological drives and the feeling of the body—in essence, by considering the biological substrates of emotion and feeling as they motivate behavior and thought. This renewed focus on nonconscious processing in the domain of motivation would mark a departure from current approaches but would not be unprecedented in the history of thought on this topic, as briefly discussed below. Further, the combined focus on nonconscious and biological processes would be consistent with current trends in cognitive psychology and neuroscience, for example, in the study of emotional processing (Phelps & Sharot, 2008), of certain aspects of social processing (Stanley, Phelps, & Banaji, 2008), or of automated and implicit knowledge (Clark, 2008; Eitam, Hassin, & Schul, 2008).

A HISTORICAL PERSPECTIVE ON THE STUDY OF NONCONSCIOUS MOTIVATIONAL PROCESSES

While current educational theories of motivation do not focus on nonconscious processes, nonconscious processes have been part of some past theories of motivation. For example, early thinkers in the field of motivation such as Clark Leonard Hull (1884–1952) and Sigmund Freud (1856–1939) placed great emphasis on biological drives and nonconscious processes (originally referred to as unconscious processes). In fact, Freud built an extensive theory of psychotherapy around this concept (e.g., Freud, 1915; Solms, 2004). Some of Freud's contemporaries were also interested in nonconscious processes, such as Hermann von Helmholtz (1821–1894), who noted that nonconscious processes are central to visual perception, and Friedrich Nietzsche (1844–1900), who focused on the power of nonconscious driving forces. However, Freud was the first to separate philosophical from scientific approaches to consciousness and to use data from clinical work to support his theories.

Freud's basic proposition was that human motivation is largely hidden from conscious reflection and that conscious thought is not the main source of motivation.

Freud's and other's theories on the role of nonconscious processes in motivation were largely rejected as behaviorism became the dominant school of thought in the 1930s and 1940s. Behaviorism, with its strong focus on observable behaviors, did not place weight on either conscious or nonconscious processes, because it focused on behavior rather than on understanding the mind. Although the cognitive revolution did lift the taboo on the discussion of consciousness in cognitive psychology, psychodynamic psychologists remained alone in arguing for the importance of nonconscious processes in guiding human motivation (see Westen, 1998, for a review).

In providing this brief historical overview, we are in no way advocating for a wholesale return to early approaches in which all human behavior and motivation could be explained in terms of nonconscious drives (e.g., Hull, 1943). Neither is our position that intrinsically motivated states relevant to education are the result of, an extension of, or a conscious interpretation of biological drives for survival-related behaviors. Instead, we are suggesting that intrinsically motivated states may get their psychological power by co-opting the machinery for biological drives and survival-related physiological processes. Because of this, further work is needed on the relations among (a) non-consciously controlled physiological processes responsible for regulating basic survival-related functions of the body and brain (e.g., heart rate, consciousness), (b) nonconscious cognitive processes directly related to the induction and experience of motivating emotions, and (c) conscious experiences of motivating emotions. There is now accumulating evidence that nonconscious processes play an important role in behavior and thought and that cognition is embodied (e.g., Borghi & Cimatti, 2010). A movement in the field of educational motivation research to accommodate this information would parallel similar trends in cognitive psychology and neuroscience. In our view, it is through considering interactions between conscious and non-conscious processing in relation to physiological substrates that real progress will be made in the future study of motivation.

IMPLICATIONS FOR EDUCATIONAL RESEARCH ON MOTIVATION: USING NEUROSCIENCE TO ITS BEST ADVANTAGE

The time is ripe to build a connection between educational and cognitive neuroscientific research for the purpose of studying motivation. This is because the neuroscientific study of social and affective functioning is gain-ing unprecedented momentum, and there is now a substantial body of evidence about the neural processes supporting social and emotional systems in the brain (Immordino-Yang & Damasio, 2007 [see Chapter 1]; Mitchell, 2008). Recent discoveries in social and affective neuroscience reveal intriguing relationships in the brain between the physiological systems that support social interaction, those that support emotion, and those that support the feeling of the body, especially the gut (Hooker, Verosky, Germine, Knight, & D'Esposito, 2008; Lamm, Batson, & Decety, 2007; Singer, 2006). These relationships suggest that emotion and cognition, feeling and thinking, are fundamentally interrelated and that motivated thought emerges as a function of the interaction between the body and the mind in social and cultural contexts (Immordino-Yang, 2008 [see Chapter 8]).

While this work remains as yet mainly unconnected to educational constructs such as motivation and self-efficacy, some of the processes that are being described in this body of research, such as the neural correlates of feeling admiration for virtue in our study, have unexplored but potentially interesting and novel implications for educational constructs like these. For example, returning to Ryan and Deci's model (see, e.g., Ryan & Deci 2000) in which autonomy is associated with intrinsic motivation, could it be that, because autonomy is related to psychological self-awareness, and because self-awareness is associated with increased activity in neural systems related to the regulation and high-level representation of the visceral body (i.e., the inferior/posterior posteromedial cortices; see Immordino-Yang et al., 2009; see also Chapter 2), autonomy and intrinsic motivation are associated by way of their shared connection to neural processes that regulate and feel the body's internal condition (just as we hypothesize is the case during the feeling of admiration for virtue)? By contrast, it is notable that these neural processes are suppressed during contingency learning and other cognitive functions in which attention is directed into the environment, of the sorts that would be invoked during situations involving extrinsic reward. Taken together, this account could provide new hypotheses as to why intrinsic motivation is undermined by extrinsic reward and new, testable implications for education.

Although detailing further specific implications would be premature, it is possible that an interdisciplinary neuroscientific approach to motivation could lead to a better understanding of, for instance, why there is often a disconnect between students' stated intentions and their actual behavior, why social processing seems so critical to the cultivation of the most profoundly motivating states (see Haidt & Morris, 2009, for a discussion of this in relation to the research presented here on admiration for virtue), how cultural biases in social interaction may alter the conscious interpretation and attribution of nonconscious processes and therefore the ensuing motivation, why individual differences in motivation may exist, and how those differences may relate to relationships between biological tendencies and personal history. Alternatively, such an approach may lead to new insights into how motivation relates to other affective and cognitive states relevant to achievement, such as engagement and interest. (See Hidi [2006] for a related discussion pertaining to "interest" as a biologically grounded motivational variable.) This list is entirely speculative, of course, but because each of these motivation-relevant questions pertains to an interaction between nonconscious and conscious processing in accordance with biological predispositions and mechanisms, it aims to provide a sense of the possibilities.

To conclude, relating these findings back to the argument about the importance of considering nonconscious processing in the study of motivation, it is apparent that most current motivation research in education uses self-report measures and other measures of conscious processing, without a way to measure the contributions of more basic, non-consciously controlled body-related systems. In our experiment on the neural correlates of admiration, we have found a way to measure the contribution of these systems using neuroimaging, and the data suggest that their contribution is fundamental. Motivation is a state that appears to involve the body and the mind in a dynamic interaction that produces alertness, arousal, and a profound readiness to engage in meaningful action. As more is learned about the neural bases of these processes, fruitful connections to educational research may become increasingly apparent—provided that educational researchers and cognitive neuroscientists are in productive dialogue.

ACKNOWLEDGMENTS

We thank Reinhard Pekrun, Robert Rueda, and Richard Clark for their insightful discussions about the manuscript. Partial support for this work was provided by the Brain and Creativity Institute Fund, by the Rossier School of Education, and by grants to Antonio Damasio and Hanna Damasio from the National Institutes of Health (Grant P01 NS19632) and the Mathers Foundation.

REFERENCES

Algoe, S. B., Haidt, J., & Gable, S. L. (2008). Beyond reciprocity: Gratitude and relationships in everyday life. *Emotion*, 8(3), 425–429.

Barrett, L. F. (2009). Variety is the spice of life: A psychological construction approach to understanding variability in emotion. *Cognition and Emotion*, 23(7), 1284–1306.

Bartlett, M. Y., & DeSteno, D. (2006). Gratitude and prosocial behavior: Helping when it costs you. *Psychological Science, 17*(4), 319–325.

Borghi, A. M., & Cimatti, F. (2010). Embodied cognition and beyond: Acting and sensing the body. *Neuropsychologia, 48*(3), 763–773.

Clark, R. E. (2008). Resistance to change: Unconscious knowledge and the challenge of unlearning. In D. C. Berliner & H. Kupermintz (Eds.), *Changing institutions, environments and people* (pp. 75–94). New York, NY: Rutledge.

Damasio, A. R. (1999). *The feeling of what happens: Body and emotion in the making of consciousness.* New York, NY: Harcourt Brace.

Damasio, A. R. (2005). *Descartes' error: Emotion, reason and the human brain.* London: Penguin. (Original work published 1994)

Dweck, C. (2000). *Self theories: Their role in motivation, personality and development.* Philadelphia, PA: Psychology Press.

Eitam, B., Hassin, R. R., & Schul, Y. (2008). Nonconscious goal pursuit in novel environments—the case of implicit learning. *Psychological Science, 19*(3), 261–267.

Forgas, J. P., Bower, G. H., & Moylan, S. J. (1990). Praise or blame: Affective influences on attributions for achievement. *Journal of Personality and Social Psychology, 59*(4), 808–819.

Freud, S. (1915). *The unconscious.* London: Hogarth Press.

Gray, J. A. (1999). Cognition, emotion, conscious experience and the brain. In T. Dalgleish & M. J. Power (Eds.), *Handbook of cognition and emotion* (pp. 83–102). New York, NY: Wiley.

Haidt, J. (2003). Elevation and the positive psychology of morality. In C. L. M. Keyes & J. Haidt (Eds.), *Flourishing: Positive psychology and the life well-lived* (pp. 275–289). Washington, DC: American Psychological Association.

Haidt, J., & Morris, J. P. (2009). Finding the self in self-transcendent emotions. *Proceedings of the National Academy of Sciences, USA, 106*(19), 7687–7688.

Haidt, J., & Seder, P. (2009). Admiration/awe. In D. Sander & K. R. Scherer (Eds.), *The Oxford companion to emotion and the affective sciences* (pp. 4–5). New York, NY: Oxford University Press.

Hidi, S. (2006). Interest: A unique motivational variable. *Educational Research Review, 1*(2), 69–82.

Hooker, C. I., Verosky, S. C., Germine, L. T., Knight, R. T., & D'Esposito, M. (2008). Mentalizing about emotion and its relationship to empathy. *Social Cognitive and Affective Neuroscience, 3*(3), 204–217.

Hull, C. (1943). *Principles of behavior.* New York, NY: Appleton-Century-Crofts.

Immordino-Yang, M. H. (2008). The smoke around mirror neurons: Goals as sociocultural and emotional organizers of perception and action in learning. *Mind, Brain, and Education, 2*(2), 67–73.

Immordino-Yang, M. H., & Damasio, A. R. (2007). We feel, therefore we learn: The relevance of affective and social neuroscience to education. *Mind, Brain and Education, 1*(1), 3–10.

Immordino-Yang, M. H., McColl, A., Damasio, H., & Damasio, A. (2009). Neural correlates of admiration and compassion. *Proceedings of the National Academy of Sciences, USA, 106*(19), 8021–8026.

Izard, C. E. (2001). Emotional intelligence or adaptive emotions? *Emotion, 1*(3), 249–257.

Karabenick, S. A., Woolley, M. E., Friedel, J. M., Ammon, B. V., Blazevski, J., Bonney, C. . . . Musu, L. (2007). Cognitive processing of self-report items in educational research: Do they think what we mean? *Educational Psychologist, 42,* 1–17.

Lamm, C., Batson, C. D., & Decety, J. (2007). The neural substrate of human empathy: Effects of perspective-taking and cognitive appraisal. *Journal of Cognitive Neuroscience, 19*(1), 42–58.

Mitchell, J. P. (2008). Contributions of functional neuroimaging to the study of social cognition. *Current Directions in Psychological Science, 17*(2), 142–146.

Pekrun, R., Goetz, T., Titz, W., & Perry, R. P. (2002). Academic emotions in students' self-regulated learning and achievement: A program of qualitative and quantitative research. *Educational Psychologist, 37*(2), 91–105.

Phelps, E. A., & Sharot, T. (2008). How (and why) emotion enhances the subjective sense of recollection. *Current Directions in Psychological Science, 17*(2), 147–152.

Pintrich, P. R. (2003). A motivational science perspective on the role of student motivation in learning and teaching contexts. *Journal of Educational Psychology, 95*(4), 667–686.

Pintrich, P. R., & Schunk, D. H. (2002). *Motivation in education: Theory, research, and applications* (2nd ed.). Upper Saddle River, NJ: Merrill.

Ryan, R. M., & Deci, E. L. (2000). Self-determination theory and the facilitation of intrinsic motivation, social development, and well-being. *American Psychologist, 55*(1), 68–78.

Singer, T. (2006). The neuronal basis and ontogeny of empathy and mind reading: Review of literature and implications for future research. *Neuroscience and Biobehavioral Reviews, 30*(6), 855–863.

Solms, M. (2004). Freud returns. *Scientific American, 290*(5), 82–88.

Stanley, D., Phelps, E., & Banaji, M. (2008). The neural basis of implicit attitudes. *Current Directions in Psychological Science, 17*(2), 164–170.

Westen, D. (1998). The scientific legacy of Sigmund Freud: Toward a psychodynamically informed psychological science. *Psychological Bulletin, 124*(3), 333–371.

Zahn, R., Moll, J., Paiva, M., Garrido, G., Krueger, F., Huey, E. D., & Grafman J. (2009). The neural basis of human social values: Evidence from functional MRI. *Cerebral Cortex, 19*(2), 276–283.

Zaki, J., Ochsner, K. N., Hanellin, J., Wager, T. D., & Mackey, S. C. (2007). Different circuits for different pain: Patterns of functional connectivity reveal distinct networks for processing pain in self and others. *Social Neuroscience, 2*(3–4), 276–291.

CHAPTER 10

Perspectives from Social and Affective Neuroscience on the Design of Digital Learning Technologies

Mary Helen Immordino-Yang and Vanessa Singh

Chapter description: Many people think of digital learning experiences as nonsocial, as long as the student is interacting with the media on his or her own. Here we turn the tables and suggest that many people may interact with their digital tools as if they were social partners, even when no other humans are involved. Thinking of digital learning as happening through dynamic, supported social interactions between learners and computers changes the way we design and use digital technologies for learning—and could help shed light on why we become so attached to our devices.

HUMANS AND COMPUTERS INTERACTING: REFRAMING THE DIGITAL LEARNING EXPERIENCE AS A SOCIAL ENCOUNTER

We begin with a familiar scenario: A group of high school students are sitting in a computer classroom. Some are slumped over their desks or staring aimlessly out of the window. Others, though, appear to be highly engaged in the task, working in pairs or alone and obviously absorbed in the digital environment. What accounts for the differences between these groups? How is it that some students may find a digital learning environment engaging and useful, while others may wonder, "Why am I doing this?"

Both social-affective neuroscientists and learning technology designers are interested in scenarios such as this one and in explaining the motivation and learning differences between the two groups of students. However, while the neuroscientists would focus on the question of how neural systems enable some students to experience the digital classroom as a motivating environment and how both perception and learning are altered as a result, learning technology designers would focus on the tools and setup that characterize the digital environment as their starting point, asking, "What technology designs promote more efficient and effective learning?"

In this chapter, we argue for a different, complementary approach—one that advocates that social affective neuroscientists and digital learning designers meet in the middle. In this productive middle ground, we suggest, a new question emerges: "How could digital learning environments be designed more effectively if we were to consider digital learning as happening through a dynamic brain-computer interaction?" In this view, the use of a computer learning technology by a person would be akin to a social encounter between a mind and a machine. While there is a long tradition of studying mind-machine interfaces, our hope is that framing the problem in terms of the neurobiology of human social emotion may give technology designers a new perspective into their craft, by paving the way for a dialogue with affective and social neuroscientists about what we can expect from social humans when they interact with each other or, by extension, when they interact with silicon.

EMBODIED BRAINS, SOCIAL MINDS: THE NEUROBIOLOGY OF BEING HUMAN

Think back to the atrocities committed on 9/11/2001. How do we know these actions were wrong? And why do most Americans have such a difficult time understanding how the terrorists were able to carry out these plans? To decide these things, we automatically, albeit many times nonconsciously, imagine how the passengers on those planes must have felt, empathically experiencing both what they were thinking about and their emotions around these thoughts by imagining ourselves in the fateful plane. For many, just thinking of the images of planes hitting buildings induces a fearful mindset with all its physiological manifestations, such as a racing heart and anxious thoughts. Similarly, we have difficulty empathizing with the terrorists who brought down the planes, because the values, morals, and emotions that motivated these men are so different from our own.

Recent advances in methodologies such as brain imaging have led to unprecedented explorations into the neuroscientific bases of such social processing, affective responding, and their relation to learning and shed new light on their workings. These new discoveries link body and mind, self and other, in ways that call into question the traditional dissection of the mind and the brain into modality and domain-specific modules, underlain by unique and nonoverlapping physiological and brain responses. In demonstrating the functional overlap between low-level systems for physiological regulation and somatosensation and systems involved in the most complex of mental states (Immordino-Yang, McColl, Damasio, & Damasio, 2009; see also Chapter 9), they dissolve traditional boundaries between nature and nurture in development (Immordino-Yang & Fischer, 2009 [see Chapter 4]) and suggest instead that complex social and emotional processing co-opts and specializes regions originally evolved for more primitive functions, such as homeostatic regulation, consciousness regulation, and the feeling of the body (Immordino-Yang, Chiao, & Fiske, 2010). Further, these findings underscore the importance of emotion in "rational" learning and decision making in both social and nonsocial contexts (Damasio, 2005; Haidt, 2001; Immordino-Yang & Damasio, 2007 [see Chapter 1]), demonstrating the primacy of evaluative, reward-based and pain-based processing to learning and our human propensity toward subjective, social thinking.

These new discoveries stand in contrast to traditional Western views of the mind and body, such as that of Descartes, that divorced high-level, rational thought from what were thought of as the basal, emotional, instinctual processes of the body (Damasio, 1994/2005). Far from divorcing emotions from thinking, the new research collectively suggests that emotions, such as anger, fear, happiness, and sadness, are cognitive and physiological processes that involve both the body and mind (Barrett, 2009; Damasio, 1994/2005; Damasio et al., 2000). As such, they utilize brain systems for body regulation (e.g., for blood pressure, heart rate, respiration, digestion) and sensation (e.g., for physical pain or pleasure). They also influence brain systems for cognition, changing thought in characteristic ways—from the desire to seek revenge in anger, to the search for escape in fear, to the receptive openness to others in happiness, to the ruminating on lost people or objects in sadness. In each case, the emotion can be played out on the face and body, a process that is felt via neural systems for sensing and regulating the body. And in each case, these feelings interact with other thoughts to change the mind in characteristic ways and to help people learn from their experiences.

Further, educators have long known that thinking and learning, as simultaneously cognitive and emotional processes, are carried out not in a vacuum but in social and cultural contexts (Fischer & Bidell, 2006). A major part of how people make decisions has to do with their past social experiences, reputation, and cultural history. Now, social neuroscience is revealing some of the basic biological mechanisms by which social learning takes place (Frith & Frith, 2007; Mitchell, 2008). According to current evidence, social processing and learning generally involve internalizing one's own subjective interpretations of other people's feelings and actions (Uddin, Iacoboni, Lange, & Keenan, 2007). We perceive and understand other people's feelings and actions in relation to our own beliefs and goals, and we vicariously experience these feelings and actions using some of the same brain systems that would be invoked if the feelings and actions were our own (Immordino-Yang, 2008). Just as affective neuroscientific evidence links our bodies and minds in processes of emotion, social neuroscientific evidence links our own selves to the understanding of other people.

For example, it is now known that the key brain systems involved in the direct sensation of physical pain, especially systems for the sensation of the gut and viscera (e.g., during stomachache or cigarette craving), are also involved in the feeling of one's own social or psychological pain (Decety & Chaminade, 2003; Eisenberger & Lieberman, 2004; Panksepp, 2005; see also Chapter 6), as well as in the feeling of social emotions about another person's psychologically or physically painful, or admirable, circumstances (Immordino-Yang et al., 2009). Put simply, the poets had it right all along: feeling emotions about other people, including in moral contexts such as for judgments of fairness, virtue, and reciprocity, involve the brain systems responsible for "gut feelings" like stomachache (Greene, Sommerville, Nystrom, Darley, & Cohen, 2001; Lieberman & Eisenberger, 2009) and systems that are responsible for the construction and awareness of one's own consciousness (i.e., the experience of "self"; Damasio, 2005; Moll, de Oliveira-Souza, & Zahn, 2008; see also Chapter 2). Overall, affective neuroscience, together with psychology, is documenting the myriad ways in which the body and mind are interdependent during emotion, and therefore the myriad ways in which emotions organize (and bias) reasoning, judgments of self and others, and retrieval of memories during learning (Immordino-Yang & Damasio, 2007 [see Chapter 1]).

Related to this, the physiology of the social emotions that govern our interpersonal relationships and moral sense appears to involve dynamic interactions between neural systems for bodily sensation and awareness—the same systems that are known to be involved in the feeling of basic emotions, such as anger, fear, and disgust—and systems that support other aspects of cognition and emotion regulation, including regions involved in episodic memory retrieval and perspective taking in relation to the self (Harrison, Gray, Gianaros, & Critchley, 2010; Zaki, Ochsner, Hanellin, Wager, & Mackey, 2007). During such complex social emotions as admiration and compassion, for example, neural regions associated with memory and social cognitive functions appear to be functionally interconnected, or "talking," with neural systems involved in somatosensation for the internal, visceral body and systems involved in consciousness regulation, in patterns that reflect not only involvement in the induction or onset of the emotion but also its maintenance and experiential aspects. The cross talk between these neural systems suggests that social emotions endure, guiding our decisions, ongoing engagement, and learning. Moreover, the data suggest that these emotions may get their motivational power through coordinating neural mechanisms responsible for complex computations and knowledge with mechanisms that facilitate retrieval of our own personal history, all the while colored by reactions played out on homeostatic regulatory systems that, in the most basic sense, keep our bodies alive and our minds attentive.

INFORMATION PROCESSING IN HUMANS AND COMPUTERS: TOP-DOWN, BOTTOM-UP, AND THE FUNDAMENTAL IMPORTANCE OF HUMAN SUBJECTIVITY

Let us begin this section with a simple question: why are you, the reader, interested in neuroscientific perspectives on the design of digital learning environments? Of the range of all the possible of intelligent behaviors available to you, from planting a garden to playing a piano sonata to drinking a coffee with friends, you chose to spend energy on thinking about ideas and evidence pertinent to this topic at this moment. Why?

We suspect that, although this obvious question may initially puzzle you, it would then compel you to respond to the effect that you feel this topic is useful and engaging and warrants attention, that designing better digital learning technologies will help learners and may gain you recognition and notoriety in the process, that you take pleasure in working on this problem, or a myriad of other possible answers in the same vein. And your answers would reveal a central and common misconception in understanding learning: that rational, logical intelligence is somehow separable or independent from emotion and from subjective, self-relevant goals.

Human cognition, or the faculties for processing information, applying knowledge, and making decisions, differs in important ways from information implementation and computation by computers. Most important, human information processing is driven by subjective and culturally founded values. Building from what we saw in the previous section, these values are instantiated—they come to organize our behavior—through dynamic interplays between complex thought and knowledge and generally nonconscious, low-level physiological reactions that shape our feelings and behavior and motivate us toward particular forms of engagement (see also Chapters 8 and 10). Put another way, we humans are capable of both top-down and bottom-up strategies of attending and information processing; our cognition involves decomposing or breaking information into its composite parts, as well as piecing together and integrating information into more complex representations (Immordino-Yang & Fischer, 2009 [see Chapter 4]). What is more, because these processes happen in accordance with prior learning and expectations, both top-down and bottom-up processing is organized by our desires, needs, and goals, sometimes conscious and sometimes not. As biological beings, a central part of explaining *how* we do things lies in explaining *why* we do them.

To see what we mean, let us return to the neurobiological evidence presented above, concerning the relationship between the body and the mind. If the feeling of the body (or simulated body) during emotion can shape the way we think, which ample evidence suggests that it can, this shaping would happen via the sensing of the body, or via perception. However, such sensations are not merely recorded in a value-neutral or objective way. All sensations are not of equal importance. Rather, sensations are assigned valence, starting with pleasure and pain and growing from there in complexity. Even the simple visual perception of objects or situations in the environment is understood in terms of its propensity to cause harm or good in relation to the current situation and context. In turn, we respond accordingly to maximize good and avoid harm, as we subjectively perceive and understand the consequences. Depending on the context, these responses can relate to our well-being in a basic survival sense, or in a more evolutionarily evolved, sociocultural sense.

Taken together, these appraisals, values, and sensations lead to emotion, which supports and drives what we traditionally call cognition. Quite literally, and as the term *emotion* suggests, we are "moved by" the valences we assign to perceptions (or simulated perceptions), and in this way our perceptions and simulated perceptions "motivate" us to behave in meaningful ways (Immordino-Yang & Sylvan, 2010 [see Chapter 9]). Although a purely cognitive account of information processing describes perfectly the computations that govern artificial intelligence and embodiment (in the form of mobile robots' behavior), this from our perspective represents a fundamental rift between artificial and biological intelligence that must be dealt with in the design of interfaces that facilitate useful interactions between the two.

FROM ME TO IT AND IT TO ME: APPLYING PRINCIPLES FROM AFFECTIVE AND SOCIAL NEUROSCIENCE TO DESIGN BETTER LEARNING TECHNOLOGIES

Humans are born with the propensity to impose order, to classify and organize our environment in accordance with our individual ways of theorizing about and acting in the world. The content and order of these theories and actions are the result of interaction among biological, social, and cultural life experiences.

As children develop, they encounter new experiences that shape and reshape existing neural networks and schemas and impact their cognitive, social, and emotional development. Because of this, the hardwired patterns of neural connectivity that underlie innate functional modules, such as those that facilitate social evaluation, are dynamically sculpted by social and cultural experiences as they are subjectively perceived and emotionally "felt." In short, our personal experiences through development provide a platform on which to understand and relate to the thoughts and actions of other people.

But what if our social companion is not an acculturated, sentient, subjectively evaluating biological being, but instead a computer? How, then, can our past experiences and cultural knowledge help us to predict our companion's actions, to understand its purpose, to collaborate on problem solving? Although it is not usual to conceive of the human-computer interface this way, new advances in social and affective neuroscience are making increasingly clear that humans use subjective, emotional processing to think and to learn. Given the various forms of evidence that humans naturally anthropomorphize computers, how can social emotions be accommodated in the design of digital learning environments?

In a learning environment such as a traditional classroom, each student brings her unique goals, knowledge, and decisions that have been shaped by her social and cognitive experiences and that she must learn to use empathically to understand the teacher's actions, whether the teacher is a person or a computer. For example, to learn how to build a model using a computer, the student must first understand the goal of the exercise, be able to relate this goal to her own skills and memories, and be able to translate her skills into commands that describe the procedures of the computer. Using computers and other technologies to learn and perform tasks presents the student with the challenge of mentally discerning and reconstructing actions with often times invisible goals and procedures. Not only do these processes depend upon knowledge of how computers work, but they also vary with the student's subjective, emotional, and personal history and with her present interests and goals.

Here we suggest that perhaps one of the main difficulties that humans (and especially computer novices) have with computer interfaces is that the humans have trouble anticipating and understanding what the computer will do and why—in effect, because we have never lived as a computer, we have trouble "empathizing" with them and sharing their processing state, the way we would naturally strive to do with another person. If this is the case, perhaps rather than striving to build computer interfaces that seem as human-like and emotionally competent as possible, we should aim instead to make the programs and interfaces as transparent as possible. This does not mean that the technical information that makes the computer run would necessarily be available, but that the *goals* and the *motivations* of the digital environment would be readily apparent. A learner using the digital environment would understand what the program is good for, what the learning goal is, and therefore how best to engage with the computer without frustration or boredom.

Related to this, because computers do not have emotion, why not find ways that the human user can supply the emotion-relevant features to the human-computer interaction by giving the person some control over the critical aspects of how the interface and environment look, feel, and behave? A vast body of literature in education implicates "locus of control" as an important consideration when helping students in higher education environments to perform better (Dweck, 1999). That is, when students perceive that they have intrinsic control over the content, context, and pace of their learning, they begin to believe that they can be successful, and they invest more personal effort toward the academic task. Drawing from this, it seems crucial for learning technologies to be designed such that they do not give the students using them a sense of reliance or dependence on the machine, but instead foster a sense of agency that empowers the student to master skills that he could not have managed without computerized assistance. Engaging the student in an interaction rather than in a unidirectional manipulation by one conversational partner or the other (where either the person or the machine drives), students may be more likely to productively interact with the digital learning environment and to use it to facilitate performance.

FROM SOCIAL INTERACTIONS
TO DIGITAL MEDIA FOR LEARNING

We began our chapter with a scenario involving students interacting with digital media and asked why some students may be engaged with the activity, while others may be bored and listless. How can this question be informed by the above discussions on the embodiment of emotion, the interdependence of the body and mind, and the involvement of self-related processing in social emotions and motivation?

Affective and social neuroscience findings are suggesting that emotion and cognition, body and mind, work together in students of all ages. People behave in accordance with subjective goals and interests, built up over a lifetime of living and acting in a social and emotional world. By contrast, the values, judgments, and calculations made by computers follow from the data, algorithms, and system constraints that their programmers choose to give them. Because the parameters governing these calculations are decided beforehand and are mainly invisible to the novice human user, many people may have trouble understanding and predicting the computer's actions. In effect, they may have trouble "empathizing"—and therefore become frustrated and disengaged. For the actions and responses of the digital interface to be perceived as useful and productive, and for novice learners to effectively engage the digital learning environment as a collaborative partner, digital media designers might consider ways to make human-computer exchanges more akin to good social encounters: the goals should be transparent, the computer partner's actions should be predictable and related to the subjective needs of the human learner, and each partner in the exchange should have an appropriate share of the control.

REFERENCES

Barrett, L. F. (2009). Variety is the spice of life: A psychological construction approach to understanding variability in emotion. *Cognition and Emotion, 23*(7), 1284–1306.

Damasio, A. R. (2005). *Descartes' error: Emotion, reason and the human brain.* London: Penguin. (Original work published 1994)

Damasio, A. R. (2005). The neurobiological grounding of human values. In J. P. Changeux, A. R. Damasio, W. Singer, & Y. Christen (Eds.), *Neurobiology of human values* (pp. 47–56). London: Springer.

Damasio, A. R., Grabowski, T. J., Bechara, A., Damasio, H., Ponto, L. L., Parvizi, J., & Hichwa, R. D. (2000). Subcortical and cortical brain activity during the feeling of self-generated emotions. *Nature Neuroscience, 3*(10), 1049–1056.

Damasio, H. (2005). Disorders of social conduct following damage to prefrontal cortices. In *Neurobiology of human values* (pp. 37–46). Springer Berlin Heidelberg.

Decety, J., & Chaminade, T. (2003). Neural correlates of feeling sympathy. *Neuropsychologia, 41*(2), 127–138.

Dweck, C. S. (1999). *Notes to guided reading self-theories.* Philadelphia, PA: Psychology Press.

Eisenberger, N. I., & Lieberman, M. D. (2004). Why rejection hurts: A common neural alarm system for physical and social pain. *Trends in Cognitive Sciences, 8*(7), 294–300.

Fischer, K. W., & Bidell, T. (2006). Dynamic development of action and thought. In W. Damon & R. Lerner (Eds.), *Handbook of child psychology*, Vol. 1: *Theoretical models of human development* (6th ed., pp. 313–399). Hoboken, NJ: Wiley.

Frith, C. D., & Frith, U. (2007). Social cognition in humans. *Current Biology, 17*(16), R724–R732.

Greene, J. D., Sommerville, R. B., Nystrom, L. E., Darley, J. M., & Cohen, J. D. (2001). An fMRI investigation of emotional engagement in moral judgment. *Science, 293*(5537), 2105–2108.

Haidt, J. (2001). The emotional dog and its rational tail: A social intuitionist approach to moral judgment. *Psychological Review, 108*(4), 814–834.

Harrison, N. A., Gray, M. A., Gianaros, P. J., & Critchley, H. D. (2010). The embodiment of emotional feelings in the brain. *Journal of Neuroscience, 30*(38), 12878–12884.

Immordino-Yang, M. H. (2008). The smoke around mirror neurons: Goals as sociocultural and emotional organizers of perception and action in learning. *Mind, Brain, and Education, 2*(2), 67–73.

Immordino-Yang, M. H., Chiao, J. Y., & Fiske, A. P. (2010). Neural reuse in the social and emotional brain [Commentary]. *Behavioural and Brain Sciences, 33*(4), 275–276.

Immordino-Yang, M. H., & Damasio, A. R. (2007). We feel, therefore we learn: The relevance of affective and social neuroscience to education. *Mind, Brain and Education, 1*(1), 3–10.

Immordino-Yang, M. H., & Fischer, K. W. (2009). Neuroscience bases of learning. In V. G. Aukrust (Ed.), *International encyclopedia of education* (3rd ed., pp. 310–316) Oxford, UK: Elsevier.

Immordino-Yang, M. H., McColl, A., Damasio, H., & Damasio, A. (2009). Neural correlates of admiration and compassion. *Proceedings of the National Academy of Sciences, USA, 106*(19), 8021–8026.

Immordino-Yang, M. H., & Sylvan, L. (2010). Admiration for virtue: Neuroscientific perspectives on a motivating emotion. *Contemporary Educational Psychology, 35*(2), 110–115.

Lieberman, M. D., & Eisenberger, N. I. (2009). Pains and pleasures of social life. *Science, 323*(5916), 890–891.

Mitchell, J. P. (2008). Contributions of functional neuroimaging to the study of social cognition. *Current Directions in Psychological Science, 17*(2), 142–146.

Moll, J., de Oliveira-Souza, R., & Zahn, R. (2008). The neural basis of moral cognition: Sentiments, concepts, and values. *Annals of the New York Academy of Sciences, 1124*, 161–180.

Panksepp, J. (2005). Why does separation distress hurt? Comment on MacDonald and Leary (2005). *Psychological Bulletin, 131*(2), 224–230.

Uddin, L. Q., Iacoboni, M., Lange, C., & Keenan, J. P. (2007). The self and social cognition: The role of cortical midline structures and mirror neurons. *Trends in Cognitive Sciences, 11*(4), 153–157.

Zaki, J., Ochsner, K. N., Hanellin, J., Wager, T. D., & Mackey, S. C. (2007). Different circuits for different pain: Patterns of functional connectivity reveal distinct networks for processing pain in self and others. *Social Neuroscience, 2*(3–4), 276–291.

Afterword

By Antonio Damasio

It is not possible to imagine a good and just society that does not care for the education of its young. It is also not possible to imagine current attempts at educating the future citizens of good and just societies without considering the recent and extraordinary advances of psychology and biology, as well as the rapidly changing circumstances of humanity in terms of cultural and physical environments. When one considers the knowledge accumulated by the sciences and reflects on the current predicaments of humans, two conclusions follow naturally. First, education must become a social and political priority. Second, for education to succeed, it is essential that new knowledge gathered about the human condition be placed at the service of education.

Mary Helen Immordino-Yang, who is a neuroscientist, an educator, and also an intelligent and caring mother, is in a unique position to contribute to this challenging undertaking. The current collection of studies she has published in this area demonstrates that it is possible to link neuroscience to the practice of education. The collection also gives the reader a preliminary taste of the possibilities the new perspective holds.

The organization and contents of this volume clearly show why the time has come to bring biology, psychology, and the social sciences to bear on the complicated machinery of education. One reason behind the apparent timeliness and the compelling inevitability of the enterprise has to do, I believe, with the particularly exuberant scientific moment through which we are living. We appear to have reached a tipping point, one in which the traditional compartments of the sciences and of the arts and humanities are breaking down, and cross-disciplinary interchanges are recognized as valuable and actively sought. Still, not every conceivable cross-disciplinary transfer is possible or advisable, let alone productive, and not every cross-disciplinary bridge is worth crossing. Immordino-Yang's focus, which joins education and affective neuroscience, is most felicitous. Education especially needs the facts and the wisdom that affective neuroscience can provide, because meaningful learning and thinking are inherently emotional endeavors.

Immordino-Yang is engaging and convincing, perhaps because of her encompassing view of the developing human mind, which is itself drawn from a mature view of both cognitive science and neuroscience. She does not fall into the reductive trap, a practice that has been rampant in cognitive neuroscience and that often plagues the presentation of potentially important scientific findings and limits their impact and significance. An understanding of how the brain generates feelings and supports intellectual and social achievement must be accomplished without reducing the status of minds or societies, and without diminishing the dignity of the individual. Immordino-Yang cultivates interdisciplinary respect quite naturally. This is good news for her audience of educators, who can welcome the information she brings to the table and the suggestions she makes precisely because they honor both the neuroscientific and the human developmental traditions she builds from. Of course, this should also be good news for anyone interested in the destiny of humankind, which is, after all, the quietly unstated topic of this volume.

Credits

PART I: WHAT ARE EMOTIONAL FEELINGS, AND HOW ARE THEY SUPPORTED BY THE BRAIN?

Chapter 1. Immordino-Yang, M. H., & Damasio, A. R. (2007). We feel, therefore we learn: The relevance of affective and social neuroscience to education. *Mind, Brain and Education, 1*(1), 3–10.

Chapter 2. Immordino-Yang, M. H., Christodoulou, J., & Singh, V. (2012). "Rest is not idleness": Implications of the brain's default mode for human development and education. *Perspectives on Psychological Science, 7*(4), 352–364.

Chapter 3. Immordino-Yang, M. H. (2011). Implications of affective and social neuroscience for educational theory. *Educational Philosophy and Theory, 43*(1), 98–103.

PART II: WHAT INSIGHTS CAN AFFECTIVE NEUROSCIENCE OFFER ABOUT LEARNING AND TEACHING?

Chapter 4. Immordino-Yang, M. H., & Fischer, K. W. (2010). Neuroscience bases of learning. In P. Peterson, E. Baker, & B. McGaw (Eds.), *International encyclopedia of education* (3rd ed., pp. 310–316) Oxford, UK: Elsevier.

Chapter 5. Immordino-Yang, M. H., & Faeth, M. (2010). The role of emotion and skilled intuition in learning. In D. A. Sousa (Ed.), *Mind, brain and education: Neuroscience implications for the classroom* (pp. 66–81). Bloomington, IN: Solution Tree Press.

Chapter 6. Immordino-Yang, M. H. (2011). Musings on the neurobiological and evolutionary origins of creativity via a developmental analysis of one child's poetry. *Learning Landscapes, 5*(1), 133–139.

Chapter 7. Immordino-Yang, M. H. (2007). A tale of two cases: Lessons for education from the study of two boys living with half their brains. *Mind, Brain and Education, 1*(2), 67–83.

Chapter 8. Immordino-Yang, M. H. (2008). The smoke around mirror neurons: Goals as sociocultural and emotional organizers of perception and action in learning. *Mind, Brain, and Education, 2*(2), 67–73.

Chapter 9. Immordino-Yang, M. H., & Sylvan, L. (2010). Admiration for virtue: Neuroscientific perspectives on a motivating emotion. *Contemporary Educational Psychology, 35*(2), 110–115.

Chapter 10. Immordino-Yang, M. H., & Singh, V. (2011). Perspectives from social and affective neuroscience on the design of learning technologies. In R. Calvo and S. DiMello (Eds.), *Affective prospecting: New perspectives on affect and learning technologies* (pp. 233–242). Sydney: Springer.

Index

Ablin, J.L., 159–60
Abraham, A., 57
academic skills
    teaching skills for productive internal,
        self-directed processing in schools
        and, 55–56
ACC. *see* anterior middle cingulate cor-
        tex (ACC)
accommodation
    described, 153
action(s)
    in learning, 151–63
    perception with, 154–58, 156*n*
    in sociocultural context and implica-
        tions for pedagogy, 158–61
    understanding behavior in terms of,
        152–54
action(s) of others
    social processing and learning related
        to, 183–84
admiration for virtue
    fMRI in study of, 168–69
    as motivating social emotion, 171–72
    neuroscientific perspectives on, 165–
        79. *see also* social emotions
adolescent(s)
    need for quiet reflection and day-
        dreaming, 45
adolescent boys living with half their
        brains, 113–50. *see also* brain and
        learning; high-functioning hemi-
        spherectomized adolescent boys
        living with half their brains
adult-onset prefrontal brain damage
    childhood-onset brain damage *vs.*, 33
affective neuroscience
    advances in, 69–72
    in education, 27–42

future directions in, 73–74
implications for educational theory,
        69–75
insights about learning and teaching,
        77–192
perspectives on design of digital learn-
        ing technologies, 181–90
affective neuroscience principles
    in designing better learning technolo-
        gies, 186–88
affective prosody
    in case study of two boys living with
        half their brains, 122–31, 126*f*,
        128*t*
American Association of University
        Women, 12
Annenberg Learner Foundation, 12
anterior middle cingulate cortex (ACC),
        47, 47*f*
assimilation
    described, 153
attention
    memory and, 87–88
autobiographical self
    when brain is "at rest," 51–52
awareness
    bodily sensation and, 184–85

basic emotions
    described, 166–67
    types of, 166
Battro, A., 7, 113
BCI. *see* Brain and Creativity Institute
        (BCI)
Bechara, A., 93
behavior(s)
    emotion in shaping future, 98
    moral, 165

About the Author

Mary Helen Immordino-Yang is an Associate Professor of Education, Psychology and Neuroscience at the University of Southern California (USC). A former public junior high school teacher, she earned her BA at Cornell University and her doctorate at Harvard University. She has received numerous national awards, including from The American Educational Research Association (AERA), The American Association for the Advancement of Science (AAAS), The Association for Psychological Science (APS), The Federation of Associations in Behavioral and Brain Sciences (FABBS) Foundation, and the U.S. Army. She shared the 2009 Cozzarelli Prize with Antonio and Hanna Damasio. In 2008 she was the inaugural recipient of the International Mind, Brain and Education Society (IMBES) award for Transforming Education through Neuroscience, and in 2015 was elected IMBES president by the society's membership. She has an NSF CAREER award, and her work has also been supported by the AAUW, the NIH, DARPA, the Templeton Foundation, the Spencer Foundation, the Foundation for Psychocultural Research, the USC Provost, and other sources. Since 2012 she has consistently been named among the most influential scholars in education by Education Week's RHSU Edu-Scholar Public Presence Rankings. Currently she conducts research at the USC Brain and Creativity Institute and teaches at the USC Rossier School of Education. She lives with her husband and two children in Manhattan Beach, California.

Also available from

The Norton Series on the
Social Neuroscience of Education